Save Our Reservoirs

Jean,
Enjoy the read!
Love,
Philip
—x—

Save Our Reservoirs

The Story of Llanishen and Lisvane
Reservoirs and the
Reservoir Action Group

Richard Cowie

First published in 2023

Copyright © 2023 Richard Cowie

All rights reserved. No part of this book may be reproduced or used in any manner without the prior written permission of the copyright owner.

ISBN: 978-1-3999-5911-7

Printed by Gomer Press, Llandysul, Ceredigion

Published by the Reservoir Action Group
32 West Rise, Llanishen, Cardiff, CF14 0RE
Email: info@LlanishenRAG.com Tel: 02920 752673
Web: www.LlanishenRAG.com

This book is dedicated to the late
Ted Thurgood and to Andrew Hill, both of
whom did so much to save our reservoirs.

Table of Contents

Preface	i
1. The History of the Reservoirs in the 19th Century	1
2. The History of the Reservoirs in the 20th Century	17
3. Recreational Use	25
4. Wildlife at the Reservoirs	36
5. The Formation of the Reservoir Action Group	53
6. The First Planning Application	70
7. Waxcap Fungi (Part 1)	74
8. Wildlife Organisations	80
9. The Campaign Ramps Up (2003 - 2005)	91
10. Waxcap Fungi (Part 2)	103
11. The Third and Fourth Planning Applications	111
12. The First Planning Inquiry	115
13. The Village Green Application	125
14. The Run-Up to the Second Public Inquiry	134
15. The Second Planning Inquiry	136
16. The Second Listing Application to Cadw	146
17. The Draining of Llanishen Reservoir	151
18. The Nant Fawr Local Nature Reserve	165
19. The Second Planning Inquiry Resumes	172
20. The Minister's Decision	188
21. RAG Finances	195
22. Celsa Purchases the Reservoirs	199
23. Celsa Engages with RAG	210
24. Welsh Water Returns	218

Appendices

1. Sources of Information — A-1
2. Scientific Names of Species — A-9
3. Grassland Fungi List — A-14
4. Members of the RAG Committee — A-19
5. Timeline of Key Events — A-21
   Index — A-29

Preface

Had I known in 2001, when I became involved in the campaign to save Llanishen reservoir from a housing development, that I was taking on a 22-year commitment, I would probably have had second thoughts. Many times during that period, I thought that, ultimately, we would lose, as it seemed inconceivable that a group of local residents could take on a well-financed, American-owned company and win. But thanks to the experience and resourcefulness of my colleagues in RAG and the steadfast support of many local people, we eventually prevailed in what must be one of the longest-running battles in UK planning history between a local community group and a multi-national corporation. After so many people devoted so much time, effort and financial resources to the campaign, it seemed wrong, as it draws to its conclusion, to let the whole episode sink slowly into the oblivion of time. This book attempts to provide a history of Llanishen and Lisvane reservoirs and to record the story of the Reservoir Action Group (RAG) and its eventual success.

Much of this success was down to the efforts of RAG's first two Chairmen: the late Ted Thurgood and Andrew Hill, both of whom worked tirelessly on the campaign and each of whom brought a unique set of skills that were just what was needed at the time. This book is dedicated to them both. They were assisted by many other colleagues on the RAG Committee who brought additional experience over various periods of time (See Appendix 4). These committee members also made a great contribution, and whilst I hesitate to single out individuals, I must record my thanks to the current vice-Chair, Ceri Davies, and Treasurer, Bernard Adshead. Since I took over as Chair in 2013, they have provided invaluable advice and played an important part in the negotiations with Celsa and Welsh Water. Ceri has also been involved with RAG since its outset and, throughout this period, has taken the lead on planning issues. His annual planning reports at the RAG AGMs were a highlight of the meetings.

Although not on the Committee, I would also like to record my thanks to both the late Ewart Parkinson and to Mike Sant. Ewart gave tremendous support and encouragement to the campaign and provided much useful advice on planning issues. Mike was RAG's lead in the 2006 and 2008 planning inquiries, which involved much time and effort.

The unsung heroes of RAG are the many people who gave their time to organising newsletter deliveries in their local patch and those who trudged the streets in all weathers delivering newsletters. They are too many to list, and I'm sure I would inadvertently miss someone out, but they know who they were, and I would like them to know how much their time and efforts were appreciated. Finally, I would like to thank all the RAG members (there were over 2,000 at one time) who underpinned the campaign with generous donations, letter writing, attending meetings and steadfast support. It was a community effort that showed how effective it can be when everyone pulls together.

The other group of people I need to mention are our local politicians. RAG must be almost unique in that all the main political parties supported our campaign. Despite being a dyed-in-the-wool Conservative, Ted Thurgood insisted from the outset that RAG should stay apolitical and not associate itself with any particular party. By definition, in a democracy, politicians tend to come and go with elections, and over the years, many local Members of Parliament, Members of the Senedd and Councillors helped our campaign. But two long-standing politicians stand out because of the enormous contribution they made over many years. They are Julie Morgan, MS for Cardiff North, and Baroness Jenny Randerson, formerly the Cardiff Central Assembly Member. It is only since I have been going through the RAG files collating material for this book that I have realised fully all they did for the RAG campaign in terms of contacting people, writing letters, making speeches and helping in many other ways. RAG owes both of them a great debt of gratitude. Others who made significant

Preface

contributions include Cllr Phil Bale, Sue Essex AM, Jonathan Evans MP, Cllr Anne Gee, Cllr Garry Hunt, Cllr Kate Lloyd, Cllr Julia Magill, Eluned Parrott AM, Cllr Owen Pryce, and Craig Williams MP. Thank you all.

Writing this book provided me with a good distraction during the Covid-19 lockdown, and inevitably, numerous people played a part in its successful completion.

The staff in Cathays Heritage Library tolerated my many requests for Cardiff Corporation Minutes and other documents as I researched the history of the reservoirs. This library is a wonderful resource. Andrew Hill also made available his research into the history of the reservoirs and passed on several other historical documents, all of which were immensely helpful. John and Diana Pierce provided computer files from the late Ted Thurgood, for which I am very grateful.

The late Richard Bosworth, Cathays Branch and Heritage Library, Andrew Crowder, Denise Dalley, Sally Cotterell, the Industrial Locomotive Society, Diana Pierce, Reach plc, Bill Symondson and Craig Williams MP all gave permission to use photographs. They are acknowledged in the figure legends where appropriate. Where not specified, all other photos and figures are by the author.

My daughter, Liz Mosley, a graphic designer, provided advice about the layout and design of the book, as well as helping me negotiate the printing process.

Draft chapters were read by Bernard Adshead, Anne Barrett, John Cowie, Ceri Davies, Mike Dean, Andrew Hill, Rob Pickford, Bill Symondson, Dulcie Wilks and Ray Woods. Their comments were all extremely helpful, and any remaining errors are down to me.

Finally, I would like to say a special thank you to my family, who have had to share me with the reservoir campaign for the last 22 years. In particular, my wife Elsa has put up with a houseful of documents for the last ten years, helped me sort out papers that were spread all over our living room floor on numerous occasions and read through a final draft of the whole book. She has been a brick. (As English is not her first language, I hope she now understands this is meant as a compliment!)

I should stress from the outset that this book is a personal account. I'm sure many of my RAG colleagues could have written alternative versions, emphasising different issues, which would be equally valid. My particular interest is in the wildlife and ecology of the reservoirs, and that's the area on which I have focused. Some of the chapters are also quite detailed, especially those dealing with the formation of RAG. This is quite deliberate, as I hope they may prove helpful to others organising similar community campaigns.

I have tried to present the RAG campaign in more or less chronological order, but this has sometimes been difficult as there were often separate aspects occurring simultaneously. To help understand the overall sequence of events, I have included a 'timeline' in Appendix 5 at the back of the book.

Most of the action in the book takes place in committee meetings, public inquiries and the courts. Our opponent, Western Power Distribution, proved to be a highly litigious company. Over the course of the campaign, it took Cardiff Council, the Welsh Government, the Countryside Council for Wales, and Cadw, the Welsh heritage organisation, to the High Court. Some private individuals were also threatened with legal action. In addition, there were effectively four public planning inquiries at which a high-powered legal team from London represented Western Power. Much of the book deals with these legal cases and planning inquiries. I have tried to summarise the arguments put by each side, some of which were somewhat arcane and others which were downright absurd. Nevertheless, I hope you find it interesting and will learn more about Llanishen and Lisvane reservoirs and how our local community eventually 'Saved Our Reservoirs'.

Richard Cowie
July 2023

Part One

The History and the Natural History of the Reservoirs

Chapter 1

The History of the Reservoirs in the 19th Century

The story of the Cardiff reservoirs is intimately linked to the story of Cardiff itself, especially its development as a major port for exporting iron, steel and coal in the nineteenth century. The reservoirs form an important part of our cultural heritage and are a great example of the foresight and engineering skills of the Victorian era. Lisvane reservoir was built in one year, and Llanishen reservoir in two years. For all our heavy machinery and computer-aided design, it is almost impossible to imagine such a rate of progress today.

The Growth of Cardiff and Public Health

At the start of the 19th century, Cardiff was a small coastal town. The population was recorded as just 1,870 in the 1801 census. The Glamorgan Canal had recently been completed and was designed to bring iron products from Merthyr Tydfil down to the coast, where they could be shipped out from Cardiff. At the time, Merthyr was the largest town in Wales, with a population of 7,700. This was due to the abundant local supply of iron ore, coal and limestone, which resulted in the establishment of four large ironworks: Dowlais, Cyfartha, Plymouth and Penydarren. However, with the establishment of the docks, Cardiff began to grow rapidly. By 1821, the population was 3,250; by 1851, it was 18,350; and by 1861, it had risen to almost 49,000. By the end of the 19th Century, Cardiff had switched from exporting iron and steel to become one of the world's major coal-exporting ports, and its population was over 163,000.

Unfortunately, as Cardiff grew rapidly in the middle of the century, its infrastructure did not keep pace with the population. There was enormous overcrowding and poverty. This was exacerbated by Irish immigrants escaping the Potato Famine and seeking work in the expanding docks. The drainage system was pretty much non-existent, and untreated drinking water was drawn from the River Taff, the Glamorgan Canal, and a few shallow wells scattered around the city.

Such insanitary conditions led to outbreaks of infectious diseases, both in Cardiff and in many other towns and cities throughout the UK. In 1830, a virulent new form of Asiatic cholera spread westward from India and arrived in northeast England during October 1831. It quickly spread throughout the UK. Accurate figures are not available for the number of people who died in Cardiff, as there was no official registration of births and deaths at the time. However, during 1832, there were particularly bad outbreaks in South Wales. The disease burned itself out in Wales early in 1933, but overall, about 52,000 people are thought to have died in the UK.

Other infectious diseases were also prevalent in the overcrowded conditions, including typhoid, typhus, tuberculosis, scarlet fever, diphtheria, smallpox and scarlet fever. Yet cholera was one of the most feared diseases because of its rapid onset and unpleasant symptoms, which included severe diarrhoea and vomiting, followed by dehydration, leading to low blood pressure and asphyxiation. It was nicknamed the 'blue death' because, in the final stages, the skin often turned bluish-grey from lack of oxygen.

In 1848, another cholera epidemic was sweeping westwards across Europe, and, in response, the UK Government passed the Public Health Act 1848. Although the exact cause of cholera had not been established at the time, it was widely suspected that it was linked to the insanitary conditions in many towns and cities. The Public Health Act allowed the establishment of Local Boards of Health and the appointment of Medical Officers of Health. However, this was not compulsory and was left to the discretion of local communities.

In Cardiff, there was considerable opposition to the formation of a Local Board of Health as it was seen as interference from central government. However, after intense lobbying by the medical establishment and a petition signed by over 10% of ratepayers, the Council decided to appoint an inspector to produce a report on the desirability of applying the Act to the town. Thomas Webster Rammell was appointed to lead this inquiry, which began on 4th July 1849.

Unfortunately, shortly before he started work, the first case of cholera appeared in Cardiff on 13th May 1849, and in subsequent months the disease spread throughout the Welsh Valleys. The epidemic was particularly bad in Cardiff at the end of May and early June. It finally disappeared by mid-November, by which time it had killed 396 people. In Merthyr, a larger town with similar overcrowding, it was even more devastating and over 1,660 died.

Rammell published his report in June 1850. It provided a grim account of Cardiff's insanitary conditions. He found that there were no proper drains but just a succession of pits joined by covered channels in which excrement accumulated until removed by hand. He reported that many of the houses did not have toilets and cited the slums at Landore Court, located in what is now the Brewery Quarter just off St. Mary's Street. Here, there were 21 houses occupied by nearly 500 individuals, with just four public 'privies', which were 'open and without covering'. As to the water supply, he found that the domestic supply came from the canal, the River Taff and a few wells in different parts of the town. However, there was only one public pump providing tolerable drinking water; the rest were contaminated by leaking cesspools and filthy surface drainage.

Rammell recommended that all the provisions of the 1848 Health Act be applied to Cardiff and that a Local Health Board should be established along with a Medical Officer of Health. He suggested that a thorough system be installed for surface and refuse drainage, as well as the provision of an abundant supply of fresh water.

The combination of Rammell's report and the recent cholera epidemic led the Council to act. The Town Council took on the role of the Local Health Board, and one of their first priorities was to establish a wholesome supply of drinking water.

Construction of Lisvane Reservoir 1864

Initially, the provision of new supplies of freshwater was outsourced to a group of businessmen from Bristol who set up the 'Cardiff Waterworks Company'.

The company's first project was a pumping station near the village of Ely, which was commissioned in 1852, and pumped water from the river Ely. Sometime after this, a collecting culvert was constructed on the south side of the river, and water was pumped up to a service reservoir constructed at Penhill in Llandaff, at the top of Thompson's Park. This had a capacity of two million gallons, and from there, the water flowed down into the town by gravity.

However, it soon became apparent that this would not suffice for the ever-growing population, and in 1860, an Act of Parliament was obtained to construct a storage reservoir at Lisvane. This would be fed by the surrounding streams, which included the Llanishen Brook, the Nant Fawr, Nant-ty-draw, Nant-y-felin and Nant Glandulas. The water catchment covered an area of 2,200 acres, with channels and pipes conveying the water to the reservoir. Construction started in 1864 and was finished in 1865. The new reservoir had a surface area of 20 acres and could hold 60 million gallons. Filter beds were also constructed near the reservoir, on the bed of what would later become the adjacent Llanishen reservoir. A new trunk main, 15 inches in diameter, was laid from these filter beds into the town, connecting with the existing mains from Ely.

Lisvane proved a great success, and after its construction, pumping from the river Ely was discontinued for a while. However, the demand for water continued to increase, and by the end of the 1870s, there was again a shortfall in supply. In 1878, the Waterworks Company went to Parliament with a proposal to build a new storage reservoir next to the Lisvane reservoir and further smaller reservoirs to supply Llandaff and Whitchurch. However, Cardiff Corporation's Borough Engineer, Mr J.A.B. Williams, did not consider that these proposals were radical enough and would not solve Cardiff's water supply demands in the longer term. The Corporation, therefore, ended up opposing the Parliamentary Bill to construct the reservoirs that the Waterworks Company were promoting. On the eve of the bill going forward, Cardiff Corporation reached an agreement to purchase the company's entire water supply infrastructure for £300,000. The price agreed was arrived at on the basis of 25 years of the company's net annual revenue, which was shown by their accounts to average £12,000 per year. The total sum paid, taking inflation into account, would represent about £30 million in today's terms.

On 29th September 1879, the Waterworks Company's undertaking came into the possession of Cardiff Corporation, and the final deed for the transfer was executed on 24th December 1879. Interestingly, the solicitors for the company refused to accept a cheque for the purchase price, so the Corporation's bankers arranged for the Bank of England to print two special bank notes for the purchase: one for £165,000 and the other for £135,000!

The Corporation carried out certain extensions to the works at Ely, which increased the yield from that source, and also raised the height of the embankments at Lisvane reservoir to increase the capacity to 80 million gallons. However, these were both 'stop-gap' measures. In March 1881, it instructed Mr Williams, the Borough Engineer, "to prepare a report forthwith of every source yielding an abundant supply of water available for Cardiff and within a reasonable distance thereof".

The Taf Fawr Scheme

Just over two months later, in May 1881, Mr Williams came back with his report, and he considered three main sources of water.

Save our Reservoirs

The first was extending the present sources of supply in the catchment area of Lisvane reservoir and the river Ely Pumping Station. However, he calculated that given the continuing growth of Cardiff and increasing demand for water, this would not be sufficient for the city in ten years' time, let alone further into the future.

The second source he considered was called the Aber Valley Scheme. This involved either building a new reservoir near Abertridwr, northwest of Caerphilly or piping the water down from the Aber Valley to a new holding reservoir alongside Lisvane reservoir at Llanishen. As the Aber Valley was situated in the South Wales Coalfield, and the strata of the coal measures were generally unstable, the construction of an impounding reservoir there would be unusually complicated and expensive. Mr Williams thought that piping water from the streams above Abertridwr to a new holding reservoir at Llanishen was a better option. His calculations showed that this was likely to provide an adequate water supply to Cardiff for the next ten or fifteen years, but not beyond this.

Figure 1.1. Mr John Avery Brandon Williams the architect of the Taf Fawr scheme. Photo from Cardiff City Council (1930), accessed at Cathays Branch and Heritage Library.

The third scheme was by far the most radical. It involved building a number of reservoirs in the Taf Fawr Valley in the Brecon Beacons and then constructing a 32-mile pipeline back to Cardiff, where the water could be stored in a new holding reservoir at Llanishen, adjacent to Lisvane reservoir. If this holding reservoir were built first, it had the added advantage that any surplus water from the existing Lisvane watershed could be stored there while the reservoirs in the Beacons were constructed. He anticipated that this scheme would provide four million gallons of water per day to Cardiff, along with a backup of the 300 million gallons in the Llanishen holding reservoir. Mr Williams concluded that the proposed Taf Fawr scheme would provide very high-quality water to Cardiff for at least twenty years and probably much longer.

At first, this proposal met with considerable opposition due to the costs involved, and in December 1881, a well-known independent engineer, Mr John Frederick Bateman, President of the Institution of Civil Engineers, was called in to assess the various proposals. His report, published in June 1882, came down strongly in favour of the Taf Fawr scheme as being the most effective way to meet present and future water demands at the least cost.

The Cardiff Corporation Waterworks Committee met on 6th April 1883 to consider five different options for the Taf Fawr scheme and agreed to option 'B' proposed by Mr Williams. This included a detailed specification and tender for constructing the new reservoir at Llanishen. It also involved abandoning the current filter beds for Lisvane, which were on the site of the proposed new reservoir, and building new filter beds off Allensbank Road in the Heath area of Cardiff. The wider scheme consisted of three storage reservoirs in the Taf Fawr Valley with a total capacity of 1,220 million gallons, three small balancing reservoirs on the pipeline, and a high-level service reservoir at Rhiwbina. The water was to be brought down the Taf Valley in a 24 to 29-inch pipe, more or less following the route of the current A470 all the way to Rhiwbina. From there, the bulk of the water would go on to be stored in Llanishen, but the high-level reservoir at Rhiwbina could also supply some of the higher areas of Cardiff directly by gravitational feed. Under this plan, up to ten million gallons of Taf Fawr water could be supplied every day.

On 11th June 1883, the Waterworks Committee met again and appointed Mr J.A.B. Williams as the Water Engineer in charge of the scheme. He retained his annual salary of £150 but, in addition, was to be paid a commission of 4% upon the total outlay, though this commission would only be paid when the certificates of completion were issued on the work done by the various contractors. By the time of his retirement in 1901, Mr Williams was estimated to have earned a commission of between £25,000 and £30,000, equivalent to almost

Save our Reservoirs

Figure 1.2. The ceremony to mark the start of construction at Llanishen reservoir on 18th March 1884. The Lord Mayor, Cllr Robert Bird, is holding the spade; Mr W. Hill, the contractor, is in the foreground holding a top hat; and J.A.B. Williams, the Waterworks engineer, is in the front row just to the right of Mr Hill, wearing a top hat. Photo from Cardiff City Council (1930), accessed at Cathays Branch and Heritage Library.

£3 million in today's money. One can only assume he had a comfortable retirement!

Construction of Llanishen Reservoir

Mr Williams produced a detailed specification for the construction of Llanishen Reservoir, and contractors were asked to submit tenders by 31st December 1883. A tender from Hill Bros. of High Wycombe for £52,554 13s 3d was accepted with an agreed completion date of the summer of 1886, and work began early in 1884. However, some weeks later, there was a ceremonial start to the project, and on 18th March 1884, the Mayor of Cardiff, Mr R. Bird, cut the 'first' sod with a silver spade. The Western Mail, which covered the event, goes on to report that the party then returned to town and lunched with the Mayor at the Town Hall. It mentions that the luncheon was of a sumptuous character, followed by a number of toasts being drunk and that a very pleasant afternoon was passed by all!

Unfortunately, the project quickly ran into trouble, and by June 1884, it was seriously behind schedule. The Cardiff Waterworks Committee reminded Hill Bros. of its contractual obligations but to no avail. One month later, a formal breach of contract notice was served on the company. The Waterworks Engineer was instructed to 'take the necessary precautions for ensuring that none of the plant provided by Messrs Hill Bros. is removed from the land of the Corporation'. The Hill Bros. failed contract caused the Corporation a loss of £1,387 and instructions were given for the recovery of the money from the company's estate. On 18th July 1884, Hill Bros. filed for bankruptcy.

A valuation of plant and materials on the site was undertaken, and on 29th July 1884, the contract was re-advertised in the South Wales Daily News with a closing date of 22nd August 1884. On the closing date, a tender from T.A. Walker of Westminster was accepted, and Mr Walker was asked to make an immediate start.

The South Wales Daily News of 4th December 1884 reported that Mr Walker was sparing no effort in hastening the completion of the

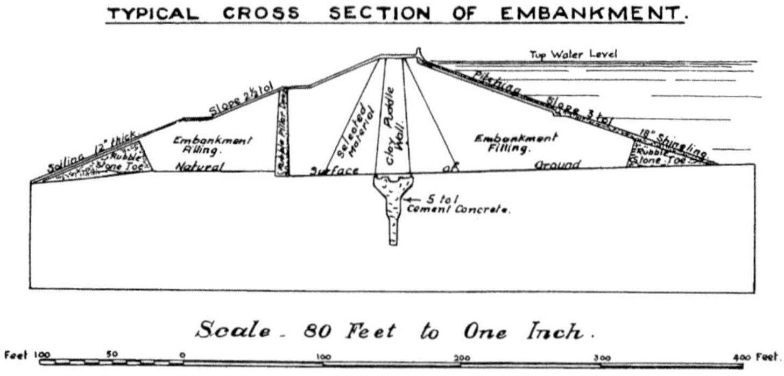

Save our Reservoirs

Figure 1.3 Cross-section of a typical 'Pennine' embankment with puddled clay core. (Source unknown).

undertaking. He had arranged for the construction of a short branch line from a point about half a mile north of Llanishen station on the Rhymney railway, which led directly to the reservoir. This meant that stones coming from the Penyrheol Quarry, near Caerphilly, could be brought by train and deposited directly at the construction site. The article concluded that 'The works are proving very beneficial for the district [of Llanishen], but much difficulty is being experienced by the men in procuring shelter for the night, although the contractor is doing all in his power for their comfort.'

Early in 1885, it was reported that work was progressing well and that Mr Walker had at least 150 men on site each day. By March 1885, the daily workforce had increased to an average of 428 men, and by May, to 540. The reservoir embankments were being built at this time, following a construction method called a 'Pennine embankment' (see Figure 1.3), which was widely used for dam construction between 1840 and 1960. These dams have a slender upright puddle clay core, which provides the waterproofing, supported on both sides by earthen 'shoulders'. To prevent seepage under the clay, there is a concrete 'cut-off' trench immediately below the clay core.

At Llanishen, Mr Williams gave detailed instructions for the construction of the clay core. The puddle clay was to be laid down in layers no more than 6in thick, and each layer had to be trodden and well 'punned' or tamped down to make sure it formed a 'perfect union' with the layer below. Throughout, the moisture content of the clay also had to be carefully controlled. With almost a mile of embankments to construct, it was very labour-intensive work.

At roughly the same time as Llanishen reservoir was being built, new filter beds were also being constructed off Allensbank Road (see Figure 1.4). They were sited between the road and the railway line and sandwiched between Cathays Cemetery and Highfields Road. The contractor was Mr John Mackay, and his men began work in December 1884. There were three sand-filled filter beds and a small covered service reservoir capable of holding 1.3 million gallons of treated water. Each filter bed measured 200ft x 75ft x 7ft deep and was capable of treating one million gallons of water per day. The filter material was shingle, gravel, and sand, most of it coming from Bideford in North Devon. The original filter beds were completed in 1886, and in 1898 three additional filter beds were added, along with another covered storage reservoir in 1904 for an additional 1.75 million gallons of treated water.

Figure 1.4. The Heath Filter beds located between Allensbank Road and the Rhymney railway line. Photo from Cardiff City Council (1930), accessed at Cathays Branch and Heritage Library.

Llanishen reservoir was finally completed in the autumn of 1886, although construction of the Cantref reservoir in the Brecon Beacons had only been started six months earlier, and the pipeline connecting the two reservoirs was still being laid down. However, this was all part of Mr Williams' grand scheme. The reason for building Llanishen first was so that it could, in the meantime, be used as an 'overflow' for any excess water collected from the Lisvane reservoir catchment.

This turned out to be inspired, as the reservoir was finished in time to store water from the winter rains in 1886 and the following summer, there was an extreme drought in South Wales. During the summer of 1887, Cardiff Corporation had to cut off domestic water supplies between 5.30 pm and 4.30 am each night and discontinue supplies to trade customers. The water stored in Llanishen reservoir, on top of Lisvane's supply, prevented a bad situation from becoming a disaster.

The Taf Fawr Pipeline

In 1885, before Llanishen reservoir was completed, work had also begun on the 32-mile pipeline that would connect the reservoirs in the Brecon Beacons to Llanishen. It started just above Nant Ddu in the Taf Fawr Valley and travelled all the way down to Llanishen, mainly following the route of the A470, although avoiding the centre of Merthyr. The pipes were made of cast iron and were 24in diameter from Nant Ddu to Quakers Yard, 29in diameter from Quakers Yard to Rhiwbina, and from Rhiwbina to Llanishen 24in diameter. The different sizes reflecting the pressures they had to withstand.

A further measure to regulate the pressure in the pipes was several balancing tanks that were constructed on the route of the pipeline. These were at Cefn Coed y Cymmer, Blackbrook near Quaker's Yard, and Rhiwbina. The pipeline was finished in November 1888 and could deliver up to 11.5 million gallons per day.

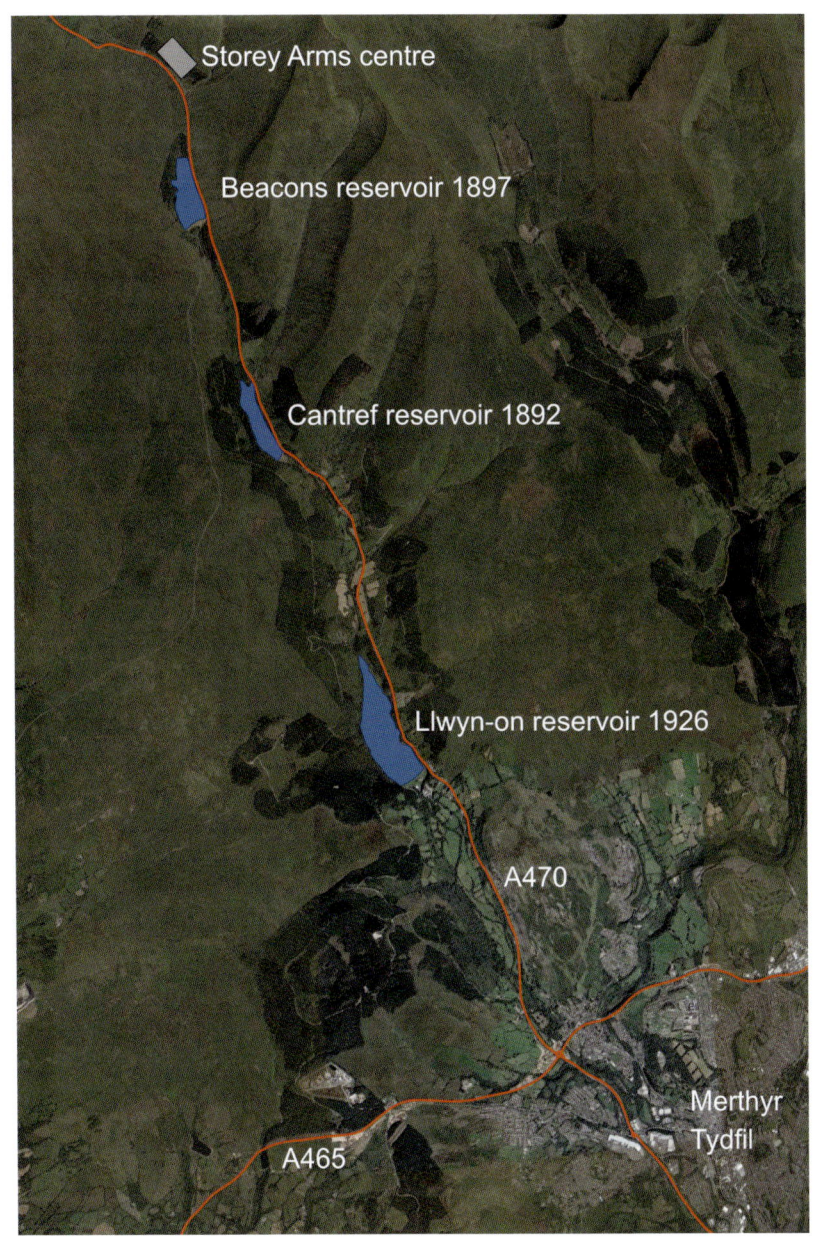

Figure 1.5. The three reservoirs in the Taf Fawr valley of the Brecon Beacons, which together with Llanishen reservoir make up the Taf Fawr Scheme. Background image from Google Earth © Maxar Technologies 2023.

Cantref Reservoir

Work on the first reservoir in the Taf Fawr Valley, Cantref reservoir, began in March 1886. Its construction took over six years, and it was not completed until September 1892, again mainly because of problems with the contractors employed. In fact, after two of the contractors became insolvent, employees of the Cardiff Corporation finished the project.

The reservoir was constructed by building a dam across the valley immediately north of the Nant Ddu shooting lodge, which is now a well-known hotel. Here the valley was narrow, with the hills rising steeply on either side. The dam was 120 ft in height, and the resulting reservoir was about 3/4 of a mile in length, 82 ft maximum depth and contained around 322 million gallons of water. The catchment area of this reservoir came directly from the Brecon Beacons, and the resulting water was extremely pure and soft as the water percolated through the peat on the hills. About three million gallons of water per day were discharged from the reservoir into the river Taf to compensate for the flow into the river from the catchment area.

Although the reservoir was officially opened on 14th September 1892, about a year earlier, on 13th October 1891, there had been the first test flow of water from Cantref down the 32-mile pipeline to Llanishen. Llanishen reservoir was gradually filled to its total capacity, and the Taf Fawr supply system became fully operational in 1892.

Beacons Reservoir

In the 1890s, Cardiff continued to grow at a fast rate. As soon as Cantref reservoir was completed, work began on the Beacons reservoir to the north. This time the Corporation did not bother advertising for contractors but used their own men who had just finished work at Cantref and had all the necessary plant and machinery *in situ*. They worked under the direct supervision of the Waterworks Engineer, J.A.B. Williams.

When the design for the Beacons reservoir was being refined, Mr Williams realised that the capacity of the proposed reservoir could be more than doubled by building the dam a little higher up the valley, where there was also a better rock foundation. Accordingly, the Council had to obtain the necessary powers for this alteration, which was achieved through the Cardiff Corporation Act 1894.

Work on the Beacons reservoir began in April 1893, and the Chairman of the Waterworks Committee, Alderman David Jones JP, opened the reservoir on 30th September 1897. The surface area of the reservoir was 52 acres, the maximum depth 52 ft, and it contained 345 million gallons of water. It was connected to Cantref via a series of 20-inch diameter cast iron pipes. When the Beacons reservoir was completed, the Corporation needed to give further compensation water to the river Taf, which was increased to 4.75 million gallons per day.

Llwyn-on Reservoir

Following the completion of the Beacons reservoir, it was envisaged that there would now be sufficient capacity to keep Cardiff supplied with water for a considerable number of years. However, the city continued to grow rapidly. In 1902, Charles Priestley, the new waterworks engineer who had taken over when J.A.B. Williams retired in 1901, first recommended that the final part of the original Taf Fawr scheme should be implemented.

The Council was initially reluctant to invest in another large reservoir, but it finally agreed in 1908, after the demand for water became more urgent. Again the main dam was re-sited to accommodate a much larger reservoir that could hold 1,260 million gallons.

In November 1910, a contract for the construction of the reservoir was let to Mr L. P. Nott of Bristol. The contract was for £201,000 and ran over six years. Unfortunately, in 1915 the First World War intervened, and the contract was suspended. It was agreed that by this time, roughly half the work had been completed, and Mr Nott was paid accordingly. However, Mr Nott was not happy with this settlement and began litigation. Although he died in 1916, a friend took up his cause, and after an appeal against the outcome of arbitration by the Corporation, the House of Lords eventually ruled in favour of Nott. Cardiff Corporation Waterworks Committee never seemed to get on well with its contractors!

After the war, in 1919, work resumed, but this time it was carried out by labourers employed by Cardiff Corporation under the direct supervision of Mr Priestley. The completion of the work cost a further £258,000. The reservoir was completed in June 1926 when the Lord Mayor of Cardiff finally closed the valves. The water levels reached their top height in November 1926, but the final commissioning did not take place until May 1927.

Cantref Roughing Filter and the Second Pipeline

While Llwyn-on reservoir was being completed, a problem had become apparent with the pipeline carrying water down to Cardiff. The carrying capacity had suffered from encrustation on the cast iron interior, and its original capacity had reduced by about a third. So a second pipeline was constructed using 27-in. diameter steel pipes lined with concrete. It was laid along the same general route as the first pipeline but not directly adjacent to it. The capacity of this new pipeline was 15 million gallons per day.

In order to solve the problem of encrustation, a filtration plant was also constructed just below the Cantref dam. This 'roughing filter' used filtration media of different sizes to remove any sediment, which protected the new water main and prevented any further reduction in the capacity of the original pipeline. The Cantref roughing filter was opened in June 1926, and the second pipeline was completed in 1930.

Finally, J.A.B. Williams' original plans for the Taf Fawr water supply system were realised. The total storage capacity of the scheme was 2,245 million gallons, and water could be delivered to Cardiff at a rate of 22 million gallons per day. It was an amazing feat of engineering and continued to supply water to Cardiff for the next 40 years!

Chapter 2

The History of the Reservoirs in the 20th Century

The Taf Fawr system continued to supply water to Llanishen without interruption between 1892 and 1929, but in the early 1920s, it became apparent that much debris and silt were also coming down the Taf Fawr pipeline and accumulating in Llanishen reservoir. The Cantref roughing filter had been installed in 1926 and was designed, in part, to address this problem, but it was decided that the reservoir needed to be dredged of the deposits that had already built up there.

Cleaning Llanishen Reservoir 1929

In late June 1929, the outlet from the Taf Fawr pipeline was closed off, and the water in Llanishen reservoir was gradually used during July, leading to the reservoir being empty for cleaning by 19th August. Fishing continued up until this point when the remaining fish were transferred to Lisvane reservoir. Lisvane reservoir had also been drained and cleaned of silt a year earlier but had now been refilled. The draining of Llanishen reservoir was an ideal time to make any structural modifications, and a new screening chamber was installed. The valve shaft of the reservoir was cleaned, the valves were overhauled, and other working parts were renewed. In addition, the operating floor of the valve tower was raised so as to be above the adjacent ground level.

Figure 2.1. Kerr Stuart 4161. This engine was owned by Cardiff Corporation and used to carry silt out of Llanishen reservoir in 1929. Photo by Frank Jones, courtesy of the Industrial Locomotive Society.

At the end of August, a start was made removing the weeds, silt and peat deposits on the inner slopes and floor of Llanishen reservoir. To aid this work, two incline roads from the reservoir bed to the east and west side of the reservoir were constructed, and a 2ft gauge portable railway was installed with a small Kerr Stuart 'Wren' class locomotive, which the Corporation owned. Up to 100 men were employed on the dredging work. About 5,340 cubic yards of peaty deposits were removed and tipped outside the embankment on the low-lying ground to the east and west of the reservoir. Then about 4,320 cubic yards of clay and marl were removed from the bottom of the reservoir near the scour outlet and tipped on the bottom of the reservoir near the main embankment. This covered up thick deposits of peat that it had not been possible to take out. The dredging and repairs were finished by the end of the year, and the refill of the reservoir from the Taf Fawr pipeline began on 1st January 1930. By 31st March, it contained 287 million gallons and was fully operational again.

Water Supply to East Moors Steelworks

A few years later, there was a major change in the role of Lisvane reservoir, which would have far-reaching consequences 80 years later. In 1934, the Corporation Waterworks Committee received a request from the British Iron and Steel Company (Guest, Keen and Baldwins) to provide them with a supply of commercial water from Lisvane reservoir. The company was in the process of a major £3 million refit of the East Moors steelworks in Tremorfa that involved the construction of a rod and bar mill at what became known as the Castle Works. The rod and bar mill was built in 1935 and started production early in 1936. The Corporation contracted to provide water for the works from the 1st January 1936, and the agreed rate was 6d (2.5p) for 1000 gallons with a minimum annual payment of £3000. This agreement involved laying new mains from Lisvane reservoir to the steelworks, and a new 30-inch commercial supply main was laid from Lisvane through the western bank of Llanishen reservoir. In 1938, the Corporation decided to supply only commercial water from Lisvane and the outlets to the ordinary domestic supply were disconnected. However, a new 12-inch inlet was also added from the Taf Fawr conduit so that in times of drought, the water in Lisvane reservoir could be augmented by the Taf Fawr supply.

The Second World War

A year later saw preparations for the Second World War. It was apparent by April 1939 that war was imminent, and the Corporation had set up an 'Air Raid Precautions Committee'. One of its remits was to look at how best to protect the city's water supply, and it recommended changes that would allow water from Llanishen reservoir to be taken directly into the city in case the Heath filters were damaged and rendered 'out of service' by enemy action. This was achieved by making a connection between the 26-inch main from Llanishen reservoir and the 20-inch Taf Fawr by-pass main under Rhyd-y-penau crossroads.

On the outbreak of war in September, all fishing permits were cancelled, and watchmen were installed at all the reservoirs and other

Corporation water works to guard against unauthorised access and saboteurs. On Llanishen and Lisvane reservoirs, steel bars or shackles were driven into the surrounding embankments, and cables stretched across the water, buoyed by empty 100-gallon drums so that no enemy float planes could land on the water. There are no reports of any damage to the reservoirs during the war, although there are local reports of a bomb falling on Llanishen reservoir that failed to explode. As far as I know, when the reservoir was drained in 2010, no sign of this was found.

Figure 2.2. Mr John Stevens who was the reservoir keeper during the war years. (Photo courtesy of Denise Dalley.)

Llandegfedd Reservoir

The Taf Fawr system continued to supply water to Cardiff without major problems until the 1950s. Then a series of dry summers in the early 1950s led to a more severe drought in 1955. An official period of drought was declared on 24th April and persisted through the summer until, by the end of August, there was talk of the water supply being cut off for the first time in the city's history. By this time, the city's population was around a quarter of a million, and water was being used at a rate of 14 million gallons per day. The three Beacons reservoirs were less than half full, and in theory, only 40 days supply remained, although, in practice, the engineers thought that much of this would be unusable. Fortunately, the drought ended before such drastic measures had to be taken, but it focused the minds of the Corporation Waterworks Committee on the urgent need for additional water supplies.

One of the first options they considered was building two new reservoirs in the Taf Fawr Valley to supplement the existing three reservoirs. This would have cost £2.6 million and would supply an extra 6.5 million gallons daily. However, at this time, there was a growing recognition that it would be better to manage water resources on a regional basis rather than every Town Council pursuing its own independent scheme. The Welsh Board of Health were keen to promote this idea. It called a meeting early in 1956 of local water authorities who might be interested in building a large reservoir at Llandegfedd in Monmouthshire.

The Llandegfedd scheme involved building a dam and flooding the Sor Valley east of Pontypool. The resulting reservoir would cover 174 ha and be capable of holding 5,390 million gallons at an estimated cost of £2.1 million. Water could be supplied to Cardiff at a rate of 9 million gallons per day. This scheme was better value than the additional Taf Fawr reservoirs, so Cardiff Corporation opted for Llandegfedd.

Although Cardiff acted as the leading promoter of the Llandegfedd scheme, an agreement was reached with Newport Corporation, Pontypool Water Company and Abertillery Water Board that water would also be provided to these local authorities. There was also the possibility of a new steelworks being built at Llanwern, and the proposed new reservoir could potentially provide the works with water.

Construction of the reservoir started in April 1961, and the filling of the reservoir commenced in October 1963. The first supplies of water were provided to the associated local authorities on 9th March 1964, and the final completion of the project took place in 1965. Water from the river Usk is pumped into the reservoir, and raw water is pumped up from the reservoir to the adjacent Sluvad treatment works, from where it flows, by gravity, to Cardiff, Pontypool and Abertillery. A separate supply goes to Newport and the Llanwern steelworks.

Decommissioning of Heath Filters and Llanishen Reservoir

A few years later, in 1968, the Heath filters were decommissioned. The reason for closing the Heath filters was twofold. Llanishen reservoir, which fed the Heath filters by gravity, was not high enough to supply large parts of the expanding city of Cardiff, and the filter beds themselves had become choked with decaying vegetable matter and needed completely stripping and re-sanding. Given the new supply of treated water coming from Llandegfedd, it was decided that this was not a worthwhile investment and that the filters had come to the end of their useful life. They were drained and later demolished. Water was then pumped from Llanishen to the Wenallt reservoir in Rhiwbina, from where it passed through micro-strainers before being used to supply Cardiff. Two pumping engines were installed at the southern end of Llanishen reservoir, each capable of pumping 1.5 million gallons per day.

As Llanishen reservoir was then only capable of providing a maximum of three million gallons of water per day and the new supply from Llandegfedd was backed up by a vast storage reservoir, it was decided in the early 1970s that Llanishen reservoir had come to the end of its useful life. It was not drained of water but ceased to receive water from the Taf Fawr pipeline and was simply kept topped up by rainwater thereafter. As a result, the water in Llanishen reservoir remained pure and low in nutrients, coming originally from water filtered through the peat beds of the Brecon Beacons and subsequently topped up by 'distilled' rainwater. This meant that the reservoir was ideal for recreational uses such as sailing and fly fishing, which will be covered in the next chapter. It was also left to provide a backup water supply in case of emergency.

Changes of Ownership

Since Llanishen reservoir was built in 1886, it had been owned by Cardiff Corporation, but in the early 1970s, this was about to change.

The UK government finally recognised the logic of managing water and sewerage resources on a regional basis. The Water Act of 1973 set up ten regional water authorities and came into effect on 1st April 1974. This led to all of Cardiff Corporation's waterworks assets being passed to the Welsh National Water Development Authority. The latter changed its name in 1984 to the Welsh Water Authority, which was often referred to simply as Welsh Water. But the changes did not stop there.

In 1989, the Conservative Government of Margaret Thatcher privatised the ten regional water authorities by stock market flotation. This allowed the newly privatised companies to expand into other areas outside of their core business, and Welsh Water diversified into a wide range of sectors, including hotels, IT and construction. In 1996, it took over the local electricity supply company SWALEC with the aim of becoming a multi-utility company and renamed itself Hyder. However, it is generally agreed that Hyder paid over the odds for SWALEC, and it accrued debts of £1.9 bn, making it vulnerable to external shocks. In 1998, the new Labour government introduced a windfall tax on the privatised utilities. In 1999, price cuts required by Ofwat, the water regulator, added to its woes. Hyder's share price plummeted, as did its pre-tax profits, and made it vulnerable to a takeover bid.

There was a four-month takeover battle in the summer of 2000, resulting in Hyder being acquired by Western Power Distribution, which was itself a subsidiary of a US Company called the Pennsylvania Power and Light Corporation. Western Power was mainly interested in Hyder's electricity distribution network, which it integrated with its own operation in the South West of England. The water and sewerage side of Hyder's business was sold on to a newly formed 'not for profit' company called Glas Cymru.

Glas Cymru had been formed by Nigel Annett and Chris Jones in 2000 with the purpose of acquiring and managing Welsh Water. They were financed by a £1.9 billion bond issue and eventually acquired Hyder's water infrastructure business for £1, along with £1.85 billion of Hyder debt in May 2001. Glas Cymru has no share capital, and it is owned and controlled by members who do not receive dividends or have any other financial interest in the company. Any financial surpluses are used to benefit Welsh Water, its customers and the environment. Since the water company was acquired by Glas Cymru, it has been known as Dŵr Cymru / Welsh Water and is often referred to by the initials DCWW.

Like the rest of Wales' water infrastructure, Llanishen and Lisvane reservoirs had passed through a number of hands since the 1970s and now ended up being owned by DCWW. But what we didn't know at the time was that Western Power Distribution retained an interest in the reservoirs. At the time of the sale of its water assets to Glas Cymru, Western Power had identified several sites that it thought had potential for residential development. A clause was included in the sale agreement that gave Western Power the right to repurchase these assets from Dŵr Cymru at some unspecified time in the future. Unfortunately, one of the prime sites Western Power had identified for such development was Llanishen and Lisvane reservoirs, which led to their re-acquisition in 2004. But more about that later.

Figure 2.3. Keeper's cottage was built shortly after Llanishen reservoir. It was sited at the end of the lane from Rhyd-y-penau Rd. This photo was taken in the early 1940s. Photo provided by Denise Dalley.

Chapter 3

Recreational Use

Over the years, the reservoirs have had a number of recreational uses, including fishing, sailing, bird watching and the quiet enjoyment of walking in a tranquil environment surrounded by nature. I will be dealing with the wildlife of the reservoirs in the next chapter, so here I will consider fishing and sailing.

Fishing

Fishing at the reservoirs began shortly after Lisvane reservoir was first opened in 1865, as evidenced by this correspondence in the South Wales Daily News (28/11/1892):

> 'When the landowner passed over his right in the land to the then Waterworks Company, he reserved the right of fishing to himself and his friends – the proprietors of the Waterworks sharing this right with him. This right, of course, passed to the new owners, the ratepayers of Cardiff, when the Corporation bought the waterworks, and for a statutory period the waters have been fished under these conditions.'

The Waterworks Company, including Lisvane reservoir, was bought by Cardiff Corporation on Christmas Eve 1879, and the first mention of fishing occurs in the Council Minutes of 5th March 1880. Captain Montgomery of the 41st Regiment (the Welch Regiment of Foot based at Maindy Barracks) was quick off the mark and wrote to the newly formed Corporation Waterworks Committee asking for permission to fish in Lisvane Reservoir. The committee agreed and resolved that *'all persons desirous of fishing in the reservoir must obtain a non-transferable ticket from the Council's Financial Clerk, costing 2s 6d per day'*. (The equivalent of about £13 today).

When Llanishen reservoir was built, fishing also quickly got established there. By 1890, a system of day permits was clearly in place, as a deputation from the Cardiff Angling Association approached the Waterworks Committee and asked it to consider issuing season permits as well. After inquiring about the policies adopted by other Councils, the committee agreed, and it became possible to purchase a day ticket for 2s 6d or a season ticket for a guinea (£111 today).

The first record of the reservoirs being stocked for fishing occurred in 1899. The Western Mail (02/05/1899) reported that Alderman David Jones, Chairman of the Waterworks Committee, placed some 7,000 young trout in Lisvane reservoir and that this was the first time that artificially bred fish, spawned and reared in the borough, had been deposited in Corporation water. The fish had been reared by two members of the Cardiff Piscatorial Society: Mr Mander and Mr Watkins. The enterprising Mr Mander had two or three slate trays in a small bathroom in the back premises of the Rising Sun Hotel in the Hayes, where he raised the young trout (Pettigrew 1902). Not the

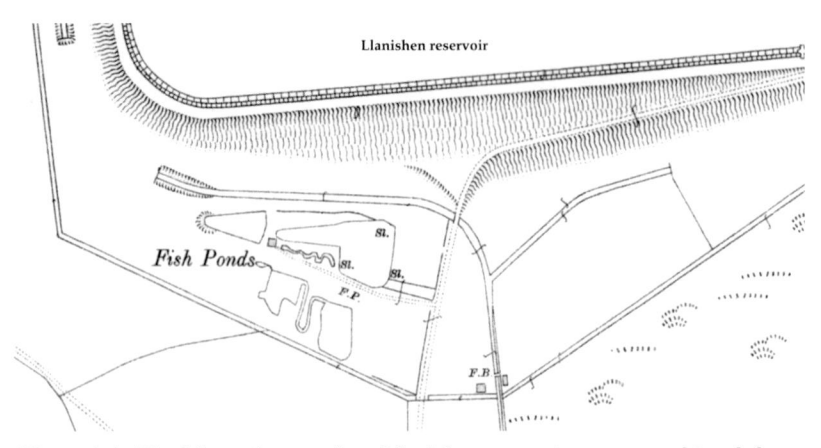

Figure 3.1. The fish rearing ponds at Llanishen reservoir, constructed just below the main southern dam. (From 1920 Ordnance Survey map).

usual place you would expect to find a fish hatchery, but then he was the hotel's licensee!

Early in 1900, a successful fish hatchery was established at Roath Park Lake (in the current wild gardens), and a few years afterwards, around 1909, the Corporation constructed a series of fish-rearing ponds below the main dam of Llanishen reservoir (see Figure 3.1). These stone-lined ponds were gravity fed by channels from the adjacent Nant Fawr stream, and the clean, well-oxygenated water from the Nant Fawr was ideal for rearing young brown trout. As the young trout grew, they were moved to successive pools until they were large enough to be placed in the adjacent reservoirs. However, after only a few years of operation, at the start of the First World War in 1915, the fish hatchery fell into disuse and was never re-opened after the war.

In 1906, after representations from the Cardiff Piscatorial Society, the price of annual season tickets for fishing in Llanishen and Lisvane reservoirs was reduced to 10s 6d (£51 today), but at the same time, fishing became restricted to three days per week. The permit could also be extended to cover Cantref and The Beacons reservoir in the Taf Valley for a further guinea.

At the start of the First World War in 1915, all fishing was stopped in the reservoir, and a military guard was stationed there to prevent any unauthorised access. After the war, the reservoirs were restocked, and fishing resumed.

In the 1931 season, tickets cost one guinea (£59 today) for ratepayers of Cardiff and £1 10s (£84 today) for non-ratepayers. As before, fishing was only allowed on three days a week, with no fishing on Sundays. A catch limit was also imposed for each day, which allowed three fish to be taken from each reservoir. In 1934, the Corporation considered re-opening the fish hatchery at Llanishen, but in the end, decided to establish a new hatchery adjacent to the Nant Ddu stream by Cantref reservoir in the Taf Valley.

When the Second World War started in September 1939, once again, all fishing permits were cancelled. However, in April 1942, it was decided to open up the reservoirs for fishing again. Unfortunately for the fishermen, this did not last long as in January 1943, there was an outbreak of an unspecified fish disease in both reservoirs and fishing was halted on the instructions of the Medical Officer of Health. This persisted for the next two seasons, and in 1945, the Corporation attempted to remove all the fish from both Llanishen and Lisvane reservoirs and, after an appropriate period of time, to restock them.

This was clearly successful as, in November 1948, the Cardiff Reservoirs Fly Fishing Club was founded. (The rest of this account is based primarily on the booklet summarising the club's history, published by the late Fred Davies in 2015).

The Cardiff Reservoirs Fly Fishing Club had its inaugural meeting at Rhyd-y-penau School and was attended by over 50 anglers who joined for an annual subscription of 5 shillings (25p). Mr William Earle was elected as the club's first Chairman. At this meeting, it was reported that 2000 9-inch brown trout and 1000 5-inch brown trout had been put into Llanishen and Lisvane reservoirs, respectively. The club went on to lobby for better facilities for fishermen at the reservoirs, and in response, the Cardiff Waterworks Committee granted use of the first-floor room of the building next to Keeper's cottage as a clubroom. Shelters for anglers were also established in the old pump house and the meter house on the west side of Llanishen reservoir.

By the 1950s, the club had over 150 members, and the summer evenings became a popular time for fishing. Both Lisvane and Llanishen reservoirs were regularly fished. The usual practice was for each reservoir to be stocked with 1000 fish at the end of the fishing season in October. Interestingly, fish grew almost twice as fast in Lisvane reservoir, which was fed by the Nant Fawr and had a higher nutrient load. Llanishen water originated from the Brecon Beacons and was soft and low in nutrients. This meant that it had a lower biological productivity, and the fish did not grow so quickly.

In 1961, the stocking regime run by the Waterworks Committee changed. Two stockings of fish in October and June were introduced in each reservoir, but at least 75% of the fish were now rainbow trout.

This is a non-native species from North America, but one that tends to grow faster and larger and is reportedly easier to catch. In 1963 there was a record catch of 3,558 fish in the two reservoirs. A further innovation in 1968 was boat fishing. The fly fishing club was allowed the use of a single boat on Llanishen and another on Lisvane. Members could hire these boats, although the fishing on Llanishen reservoir was not very successful due to its size and depth.

Following the Water Act 1973, the ownership of the reservoirs changed from Cardiff Corporation to the Welsh National Water Development Authority, which later became known as the Welsh Water Authority. Immediately after this change of ownership, things continued much the same as before. However, some years later, in the 1980s, it appeared to the Fly Fishing Club that Welsh Water was becoming less enthusiastic about managing smaller reservoirs as trout fisheries and the price of permits rose. At the same time, the number of fish stocked declined. This culminated in 1990 with the cessation of season permits and the introduction of a 'Day Ticket only' regime. The fishing club eventually responded by offering to lease the fishing rights from Welsh Water and managing the fishery themselves. A limited company was formed called Cardiff Fly Fishing Ltd., which purchased the fishing lease for £3000 per annum. Season tickets were offered to members of the fishing club based on the number of fish that could be caught. For example, a licence to take up to 100 fish per year cost £210. Day tickets were also made available for £12 and covered up to four fish. The money raised through the permits was spent on stocking the two reservoirs. Volunteers from the club acted as bailiffs and checked the number of fish caught by fishermen daily.

This scheme worked well, and fishing at the reservoirs prospered with good stocking levels and most fishermen being able to catch the number of fish allocated by their permit. The company also managed to make a small profit each year. This situation continued for six years until, at the end of the season in 1998, Hyder, as Welsh Water had been renamed, suddenly announced that it would not renew the lease and would take the management of the fishing back 'in house'. No explanation was given for this change of policy.

The fishery returned to being managed by Hyder in 1999, and initially, there was a good level of stocking, albeit with increased permit prices. However, around this time, rumours began to circulate that other plans were afoot regarding the reservoirs, and in 2001 came the news of plans to build houses there.

In the next couple of seasons, fishing continued, despite the threat of development by Western Power Distribution and its first planning application, which was submitted in December 2002. However, the stocking levels by Hyder started to decrease and become increasingly haphazard.

A major blow for the fishermen occurred almost a year later, on 3rd December 2003, when the building where their clubroom was based caught fire during the night and was completely gutted. The club lost most of its records and mementoes. It was later discovered to be a case of arson, although no one was caught. The remains of the building were declared to be unsafe, and it was demolished. Several members of the local community commented that it was convenient for Western Power to see the Fishing Club's premises disappear from the reservoir site.

The last season that fishing took place at the reservoirs was in 2004, although by this time, stocking was sporadic, and only a handful of the most dedicated fishermen remained. In October 2004, Western Power Distribution took over ownership of the reservoirs, and from 1st January 2005, all members of the public, including the fishermen, were stopped from entering the site. Fishing was never reinstated.

Figure 3.2. The building containing the Fishermen's HQ was destroyed by fire in December 2003.

Sailing

The first report of sailing on the reservoirs was in 1958, but surprisingly, sailing started on the much smaller Lisvane reservoir. In 1958, 1962 and 1966, the University of Wales Sailing Championships were held there, hosted by the University College of Cardiff.

The Waterworks Committee was reluctant to allow sailing on Llanishen reservoir as it provided drinking water for domestic use. In May 1965, the Corporation's Director of Education had written asking that the Youth Committee be allowed to hold sailing courses on Llanishen reservoir on two evenings a week, but this was turned down by the Waterworks Committee. When asked to reconsider, the Committee agreed to do so in twelve months' time. Approval finally came early in 1967 when it was agreed that sailing would be allowed on Llanishen reservoir in the summer months but would be limited to a maximum of 40 boats. As well as the Youth Committee, permission was granted to several local scout troops, Sea Ranger girl guides, the Reardon Smith Nautical College, and the Cardiff Medical and Dental Students' sailing club. In 1968, the landing jetty was constructed, and shortly afterwards, a compound for storing boats and a storage facility for equipment was also built. By this time, a 'Sailing Master' for the reservoir, Mr Coke, had been appointed, and shortly afterwards, under his supervision, the Cardiff Education Authority set up the sailing centre. In the 1969 season, 200 young people passed through the sailing centre, and about 25 went on to take the Royal Yachting Association Proficiency Certificate.

In 1974, two wooden bungalows near the Lisvane car park, formerly occupied by reservoir staff, had been leased from the newly formed Welsh National Water Development Authority and converted to changing accommodation and social facilities for the sailing centre. By this time, there were two full-time staff members: Wally Medland and Jim Dunn. The other instructors at the centre were mainly experienced volunteers. The initial programme involved beginners' sessions on weekday evenings for 12-16 year-olds, with classes for improvers and more advanced sailors on Saturday and Sunday mornings.

Figure 3.3. Optimist dinghies being launched at Llanishen reservoir.

The centre also catered for other groups. In the summer term, school groups came for tuition during the day, and five-day courses were held for adults, usually at Easter, Whitsun and during the school summer holidays. The sailing club of University College Cardiff used the facilities on Wednesday afternoons and at weekends between September and March. At this time, the sailing centre fleet consisted of 25 Mirror dinghies, six 420 dinghies, five Wayfarers and one Wanderer.

The winter months are not ideal for sailing tuition, and the wooden Mirror dinghies were stored in workshops at Gladstone Primary School. However, the staff also ran boat maintenance courses over the winter and built more Mirror dinghies from kits with local secondary school children.

A key element of the centre's success was becoming recognised by the Royal Yachting Association (RYA), which meant that all courses followed the syllabus of the RYA Dinghy Sailing Scheme. The volunteers who helped with the tuition were also encouraged to train to become RYA qualified instructors, and over the years, more than 100 people gained this qualification.

At the end of the 1970s, Wally Medland retired as the principal instructor, and Jim Dunn took over this role. Frances Hurley filled the vacated post of chief instructor. Frances was keen to get race training included in the activities covered by the centre and started to take young sailors to youth and schools championships. This proved to be a great success, and youngsters from the centre began to get selected for the national team. Sadly, towards the end of the 1980s, Jim Dunn died, and Frances Hurley took over as principal.

At the start of the 1990s, Frances was the principal, and Anne Curtis had become the Chief Instructor. The Welsh Yachting Association (WYA) had recently been promoting Optimist dinghies, which had specifically been designed for children to learn to sail singlehanded but could also be used for racing. The centre bought six of these and decided to lower the entry age of children to eight years. This was quite a controversial decision at the time but one that was to prove successful. The period during which sailing was offered was also extended to eleven months of the year. The focus on racing continued to pay dividends, with many young sailors from the centre ending up representing both Wales and Great Britain in international competitions. The most notable was Hannah Mills, who went on to win gold medals in the 2016 and 2020 Olympics and is now recognised as the most successful female sailor in Olympic history. Others included Emily Penn, who became the first female winner of the Royal Yachting Association's 'Yachts-person of the Year'; Mark Nichols, who became the RYA's Youth Racing Manager; and Nathan Bailey, who is now the Sailing Director of the Royal Bermudan Yacht Club.

Another milestone for the centre was in 2001 when it became the sailing venue for the Special Olympics. This is a UK-wide event for young people and adults with learning disabilities and is held every four years. As well as athletes from the UK, teams from Austria, Belgium, Germany, Hungary and Switzerland took part. In 2002, Llanishen Sailing Centre was recognised by being designated as a Volvo RYA Champion Club - the first in South Wales and only the second in Wales.

In 2003, there were several notable changes in the running of the centre. The Cardiff Bay Barrage had been finished in 1999, and Cardiff Council was awarded a contract to manage the barrage. To this end, they set up the Cardiff Harbour Authority. Some elements in the Council were keen to see the sailing centre at Llanishen moved down to the bay, possibly in a bid to help justify the large sums of money that were being spent in maintaining the barrage and the artificial lake created there. The Sailing Centre staff resisted this, not least because of ongoing issues with water quality in the bay, squally wind conditions due to wind shadows from high buildings like the St. David's hotel, and the potential for collisions with larger boats using the waterway. Nevertheless, the pressure remained, and responsibility for the Llanishen Sailing Centre was transferred from the Education Department to the Cardiff Bay Harbour Authority. Around this time, Frances Hurley went on long-term sick leave and, after almost a year of ill health, took early retirement. In 2004, Anne Curtis was promoted to principal, and Ben Smith became the chief instructor.

Figure 3.4. Wayfarer dinghies were often used for adult sailing courses.

Recreational Use

The Centre continued to operate successfully for a number of years, but pressure continued to mount both from the Harbour Authority and also from changes made by Western Power Distribution once it had purchased the reservoir site from Welsh Water in October 2004. Anne carried on for a couple of years but resigned in March 2006 when it became clear that it would only be a matter of time before the sailing activities were transferred to the bay. Ben Smith took over the running of the centre, but the sailing centre eventually closed, and its activities were moved to Cardiff Bay when Western Power started draining the reservoir in 2010.

As well as training many exceptionally gifted young sailors, many children (and adults) in Cardiff had their first experience of sailing at Llanishen. The local community held the centre in high regard, and this undoubtedly helped fuel the anger that was felt when plans to drain Llanishen reservoir and build houses on the site were first mooted in 2001. This anger led to the formation of the Reservoir Action Group, which went on to campaign to save Llanishen reservoir for the next fifteen years.

Chapter 4

Wildlife at the Reservoirs

Since they were built, the reservoirs have attracted a wide range of wildlife. Partly because they have been largely undisturbed but also because there is a range of different habitats in a relatively small area. However, it is perhaps only in recent years that the true significance of the site in terms of its biodiversity has been appreciated. I'll deal with each of the major groups of animals and plants found there in turn. To aid readability, I have left out scientific names but included a list in Appendix 2 at the end of the book.

Birds

Many species of birds are attracted to water, and this has made the reservoirs a good haunt for birdwatchers. In 1967, the reservoirs were mentioned in the first edition of John Gooders' seminal book 'Where to Watch Birds', which covered the main birding hotspots throughout the UK.

The main interest over the years has been in diving ducks, particularly pochard and tufted duck, which are found mainly on Lisvane reservoir. In the past, they have occurred in considerable numbers, and it was for this reason that Lisvane reservoir was designated as a Site of Special Scientific Interest (SSSI) in 1972. Over the years, the numbers have decreased, which is thought to be mainly due to the milder winters we now experience, with many species of duck staying more on the eastern side of the UK rather than moving to the west in cold weather. Other species of waterbird that can be seen most days at the reservoirs during the winter include mallard, coot, moorhen, great crested grebe, little grebe, cormorant, mute swan, grey heron and more recently, Canada goose. Then, of course, there are the gulls. These tend to be found on the larger Llanishen reservoir, where they bathe in the fresh water and roost at night. Lesser black-backed gulls, herring gulls and black-headed gulls are common, along with a few common gulls, which, ironically, are now one of the less frequent species. Earlier in the twentieth century, common gulls used to live up to their name, with up to 300 being seen at the reservoirs on occasion (Ingram and Salmon 1929).

One of the big attractions of bird watching at reservoirs, however, is that in hard weather and during migration periods, all sorts of species might drop in. Sometimes other wildfowl species turn up, although often just for a few days. These include diving ducks such as scaup, long-tailed duck, common scoter, goldeneye and goosander; various species of divers and some of the rarer grebes; and sometimes a few dabbling ducks such as wigeon, shoveler, teal, gadwall, and pintail. The reservoirs aren't really suitable for dabbling ducks, however, as they generally feed in shallow water where they graze by upending, and the reservoirs are too deep for them. However, if the water levels get low, as they sometimes do in Lisvane reservoir, dabbling ducks are more likely to be seen.

The early spring and late summer are exciting times when more unusual species may appear on passage. Although the reservoirs aren't really suitable for wading birds, as they have no exposed mud, migrating common sandpipers often stop to feed at the water's edge. Other waders, such as redshank, green sandpiper, and dunlin, also make occasional visits. Late summer is often a good time to see migrants such as common tern, arctic tern and, occasionally, black tern. Wagtails like to feed on the stone pitching of the reservoir, and small numbers of pied and grey wagtails are present pretty much all year round. Some years they are also joined by migrating yellow wagtails, although this is another species whose numbers have declined dramatically in recent years. Another regular migrant seen during spring and late summer, but usually found higher up on the top of the embankments, are wheatears, which stop briefly to refuel en route to and from their breeding grounds.

The other group worth mentioning are the hirundines: the swifts, swallows and martins. Although they do not breed at the reservoirs, they are aerial feeders and are attracted to the insects that have aquatic nymphs and larvae, like mayflies and caddis flies. These may emerge from the water surface in large numbers in spring and summer. When the birds first arrive back from their wintering grounds, they are often first seen over lakes and reservoirs where they can build up their food reserves rapidly from these emerging insects. Sand martins usually arrive first towards the end of March, followed by swallows a few days later, then house martins around the second week of April, and finally swifts towards the end of April.

As well as the birds attracted by the water, the woods and hedgerows around the reservoirs attract a different range of species, many of which are familiar from our gardens. Species like the blue tit, great tit, coal tit, long-tailed tit, chaffinch, greenfinch, goldfinch, siskin, nuthatch, robin, dunnock, wren, goldcrest, and blackbird are all common. Greater spotted woodpeckers can frequently be heard drumming in the neighbouring woods in the spring, and green woodpeckers are often sighted searching for ants in the short grass on top of the embankments. In the summer months, these resident species are joined by summer migrants who come to the woods and hedgerows around the reservoirs to breed. These include species such as chiff-chaff, willow warbler, blackcap and whitethroat. The last of these used to be a common breeding species in the hedgerows but suffered big population crashes on their migration through the Sahel desert in northern Nigeria in the spring of 1969 and some subsequent years. They are now seen and heard relatively infrequently.

Corvids are abundant at the reservoirs, with carrion crows, magpies and jackdaws being seen on almost any visit. Jays are also encountered regularly and breed in the surrounding woods. Ravens sometimes fly overhead. Perhaps the most spectacular corvid displays occur in winter when jackdaws gather in a pre-roost assembly in the trees on both sides of the reservoir. The birds start congregating in the late afternoon on winter days and are very evident in swirling, noisy flocks. There can be hundreds of birds, and just before it gets dark, they all

Figure 4.1. Some of the birds of Llanishen and Lisvane reservoirs. Left, top down: mute swan, great crested grebe, black headed gull in winter plumage; Right, top down: tufted duck, pochard and spotted sandpiper. The sandpiper is a rare vagrant from America that visited for several months in 2008. Photo credits: great crested grebe and tufted duck by Andrew Crowder, spotted sandpiper by Bill Symondson; others by the author.

depart in a westerly direction. Possibly to spend the night in the wooded area of Llanishen Park, just north of the tax offices.

The reservoirs are also a good place to see birds of prey. Buzzards have bred in Gwern-y-Bendy, which is a wood now forming part of the reservoir grounds, for the last fifteen years. Usually, one or two can be seen floating over the woods or flying over the reservoirs. Sparrow-hawks are also common in the area and are regularly seen hunting. Kestrels appear occasionally, as do peregrine falcons, and hobbies are sometimes recorded in the summer. There are even a few records of ospreys visiting briefly for a spot of fishing, possibly en route to and from their breeding sites in other parts of Wales.

Changes in the bird populations of the reservoirs

The first recorded account of the birds at the reservoirs was published in the Transactions of the Cardiff Naturalists' Society in 1929 by Col. Morrey Salmon and his friend Geoffrey Ingram.

Morrey Salmon was born in 1891, raised in Whitchurch, and was one of the most celebrated ornithologists of his generation in Wales, as well as being a pioneer of bird photography. For much of his life, he lived at 24 Bryngwyn Road, Cyncoed, only a short walk away from the reservoirs, which became his local bird-watching patch.

Ingram and Salmon's (1929) record of birds at the reservoirs is, in many respects, similar to one that could be produced now. For example, they recorded common pochard and tufted duck as the most frequent ducks in winter, with 60 pochard and 120 tufted ducks being typical. There was also a small resident population of mallard and coot, although sometimes, in winter, the number of coot could rise up to 600 individuals. The other common species were gulls, which, as today, often used the reservoirs for fresh-water bathing and as a safe place to roost overnight. Black-headed gulls, herring gulls, lesser black-backed gulls, common gulls and the occasional great black-backed gull are all mentioned as occurring, with numbers peaking in winter.

Perhaps the most interesting aspect of their account is some of the species they recorded but which have now disappeared from the area. Yellowhammers were mentioned as breeding in the 'rough field' south of the main dam, as were grasshopper warbler, stonechat and red-backed shrike. A pair of skylarks sometimes bred in the reservoir grounds. Nightingales could usually be heard singing in May and June and nested nearby.

More recent accounts of the birds at the reservoirs were produced by Steve Young (1972) and Nigel Odin (1984). Both were reports published by the Cardiff Naturalists' Society Ornithological Section. Interestingly, some of the main changes since Ingram and Salmon's account involve the number of diving ducks. In the early 1970s, the flock of tufted duck, which wintered mainly on Lisvane reservoir, was well over 250 in most years and in 1970 reached 400. Similarly, pochard reached flock sizes of 200 in the early 1970s. It was mainly as a result of these increases that Lisvane reservoir was notified as an SSSI for wintering waterfowl in 1972. This increase continued throughout the 1970s, but then in the mid-1980s, numbers started to fall away (Odin 1984), and this decline has been particularly marked in recent years. By 2010 only about 100 tufted duck were regularly occurring in mid-winter, along with about 30 pochard (Buisson 2017). As mentioned earlier, this may be due to changes in their national distribution and possibly to increased disturbance at the reservoirs in recent years.

Mammals

Quite a few mammal species are found at the reservoirs, although they were more abundant in the days before Western Power took ownership and dog-walking became more frequent.

In the late 1990s, rabbits were common, most noticeably on the stretch of embankment adjacent to the South Rise allotments. Probably, as a result, foxes were also frequently seen and used to breed at the end of one of the gardens in South Rise. Unfortunately, a few years later, there was a severe outbreak of rabbit haemorrhagic disease, which seems to have wiped the rabbits out. One advantage of the rabbit grazing was that it kept the grass on the embankments short and possibly encouraged the grassland fungi to flourish, along with a more diverse flora.

There was great excitement in May 2003 when an Environment Agency survey found evidence of otters using the Nant Fawr stream alongside the reservoirs, or as the South Wales Echo headline put it 'The heated campaign to save a Cardiff beauty spot just got 'otter'. Otters were once widespread in the UK, but during the early part of the twentieth century, their populations dramatically declined, reaching an all-time low in the 1960s. They disappeared across much of their former range due to the combined effects of water pollution with persistent chemicals such as DDT, habitat destruction and hunting. The 1980s were a turning point: the persecution of otters was banned by the Wildlife and Countryside Act 1981, efforts were made to reduce water pollution, and there was an active campaign to reintroduce them to their former haunts. By the start of the twenty-first century, otters were returning to South Wales and had started spreading through the streams and rivers of Cardiff.

Otters are extremely difficult to see, being shy and mainly nocturnal. Evidence of them can usually be found in the form of their 'spraints' or droppings, which are left in prominent positions as they are used to mark out territories and inform other otters of the territory holder's presence. A thorough survey in the spring of 2003 found otter spraints on the whole length of the Nant Fawr stream and around both reservoirs. There were also signs of otters using some sections of large concrete pipes that had been abandoned in a few places around the site. These pipes appear to have been used for relatively short periods, such as laying up during the day, and there have been no confirmed records of otters breeding at the reservoirs.

The other larger mammal that can be found at the reservoirs are badgers. The first indications were of badger hairs caught on the bottom strands of a barbed wire fence around part of the site in 2001. Badgers spend much of their time feeding on earthworms, and therefore, habitats such as the unimproved grassland on the reservoir embankments provide an ideal spot for them to forage. Since Welsh Water took over the site in 2016, better perimeter fencing has been installed, and trespassing has been controlled more effectively. As a result, there has been less disturbance and more evidence of badgers using the area.

Another notable group of mammals using the reservoirs are bats, and just as the emerging aquatic insects attract lots of insectivorous birds during the day, at night, they attract lots of bats. This is particularly true in the late summer / early autumn when the bats are feeding actively to lay down fat stores for hibernation. A number of bat surveys have been conducted over the years using ultrasonic detectors to identify them from their calls. A total of seven species have been identified: noctule, common pipistrelle, soprano pipistrelle, Nathusius' pipistrelle, whiskered bat, Daubenton's bat and brown long-eared bat.

The pipistrelles are by far the commonest species at the reservoirs, as they are in general. The Nathusius' pipistrelle, however, is particularly interesting. This is a species that is quite common in continental Europe but was only sporadically recorded as a vagrant in the UK prior to 1995. Since then, however, it has become increasingly common, although principally as a migrant species, travelling here to breed in the summer. Most of the breeding records are from the SE of England, but it is now increasingly being recorded in South Wales, particularly over water bodies. It was first recorded at the reservoirs in 2011, which now appear to be a particularly important site for it.

As far as I know, there have been no systematic attempts to sample smaller mammal populations at the reservoir, with the exception of hazel dormice. There are quite healthy populations of dormice in woodlands not too far away, and there is plenty of hazel and bramble in the hedgerows and woodlands surrounding the reservoir embankments. Surveys have been conducted using small plastic roosting tubes attached to the branches, but so far, none have turned up any evidence of dormice. However, there are casual records of other species of smaller mammal using the site, including mink, weasel, grey squirrel, hedgehog, mole, bank vole, field vole and brown rat. A harvest mouse nest has also been found just outside the reservoir boundary in the

Nant Fawr meadows. There are also likely to be other small mammal species in the woodland areas, such as common shrew and wood mouse.

Reptiles and Amphibians

Figure 4.2. Common toads in 'amplexus' or mating. The smaller male is on the back of the female, which is laying strings of eggs.

People living near the reservoirs may well be aware that there is a large population of common toads breeding there. Toads spend most of the year away from water, but each spring, towards the end of March, they migrate to traditional breeding sites, which are usually in large reservoirs or lakes. Here, over a few weeks, they mate, and the females lay their long strings of eggs amongst the aquatic plants. Once they have done this, the adult toads leave the water and migrate back to the damp shady spots in gardens and allotments where they live for the rest of the year. The spawn hatches after about three weeks, and the tadpoles feed by grazing on algae in the shallow waters. During this period, they gradually undergo metamorphosis: they develop legs, and their tails drop off. After about 12 weeks, they have developed as fully formed little toadlets and usually emerge from the reservoir on warm, damp evenings in early July.

I have visited Llanishen reservoir in early July, on the morning after one of these emergences, when there were thousands of little toads hopping around on the embankments. There were so many that there was a danger of crushing two or three underfoot with every step that you took. After they leave the reservoir, the little toads slowly make their way into the surrounding fields, woods and gardens where they set up home, only returning to the reservoir to breed.

Reservoir Wildlife

In 2008 Cardiff Council ecologists undertook a survey of the toad population at Llanishen reservoir and concluded that it was 'exceptional' with an estimate of around 1000 breeding individuals. Interestingly, Lisvane reservoir did not seem to attract anywhere like the same number of toads, perhaps due to its poorer water quality.

Clearly, the draining of Llanishen reservoir in 2010 led to a dramatic decrease in the toad population, although some may have relocated to Lisvane. Fortunately, since the reservoir has been refilled, more young toads are appearing again in the summer, although it may take some time for the population to build up to its former levels.

Despite extensive searches, no other amphibians have been found using Llanishen or Lisvane reservoirs, although the old fish ponds, in the woods just below the main dam, have a good population of palmate newts. Some of the wet areas in these woods also support a few common frogs, and their spawn is sometimes found in the smaller pools. Unfortunately, and despite our best efforts, no great crested newts, a European-protected species, have been found on the site.

The large population of toads in Llanishen reservoir means the surrounding grasslands are a good place to find one of their main predators: grass snakes. Grass snakes feed mainly on amphibians, and they can swim well, which means they are often found near water. There is known to be a good population at the reservoirs, although they are difficult to see. Often, you just hear a rustle and see them slithering away into the long grass. There are also some casual observations that suggest the grass snakes may use crevices between the stone pitching surrounding Llanishen reservoir as a hibernation site in winter.

Figure 4.3. Dr Rhys Jones at the reservoirs in 2003 with a young grass snake.

The only other reptile to be found at the reservoirs is the slow worm. These are not 'worms' at all but legless lizards. It is unusual to see them out and about, but they can usually be found sheltering under discarded objects such as flat pieces of corrugated iron and plastic. There seems to be quite a healthy population on the west side of Llanishen reservoir that extends into the allotments behind South Rise.

Two more species of reptile that might be present are adders and common lizards, both of which occur relatively close by on Caerphilly Mountain just north of Parc Cefn Onn. However, despite extensive searches over the years, neither species has been found at the reservoirs.

Insects

There have been no systematic studies of insects at the reservoirs, and what we know comes mainly from casual records.

Butterflies are probably one of the best-recorded groups, and in the past, there were good populations of several common species. I remember visiting Lisvane reservoir in late May 2002 and walking through clouds of common blue butterflies, presumably attracted by the large patches of their food plant, birds-foot trefoil, on the pitching of Lisvane reservoir. Small coppers, orange tips, gatekeepers, small skippers and meadow browns were also common in the embankment grasslands. Although difficult to see close up, there was a thriving population of purple hairstreak butterflies which could be seen through binoculars fluttering around the tops of oak trees beside Lisvane reservoir. Unfortunately, they rarely come down to ground level. Other species that regularly occur include small tortoiseshell, small, large and green-veined whites, red admiral, peacock, comma, brimstone, holly blue and, in some years, large numbers of painted lady. Near the woodland margins, speckled woods are also common. Unfortunately, many of our butterfly populations have declined dramatically in recent years, so it remains to be seen which species will still be around when the reservoirs finally reopen to the public.

Reservoir Wildlife

Figure 4.4. Some common butterflies and moths at the reservoirs. Top row, L-R: common blue, small skipper, painted lady. Middle row L-R: gatekeeper, orange tip. Bottom row, L-R: mating small coppers, cinnabar moth caterpillars, six-spot burnet moth.

Another group of conspicuous insects are the *Odonata* or dragonflies and damselflies. Although the relatively steep sides of the reservoirs can make them quite difficult to observe closely, some of the larger species, such as the emperor dragonfly and southern hawker, can be seen patrolling over the water on Lisvane reservoir. Common, ruddy and red-veined darter have also been seen there, and in some years, black-tailed skimmers are abundant. The smaller species of damselfly can often be found on the vegetation surrounding the Nant Fawr stream, which runs through the site. Species such as banded and beautiful demoiselle, as well as common blue damselfly, azure damselfly, blue-tailed damselfly and large red damselfly, have all been recorded.

One of the most notable insects that was formerly present at the reservoirs in considerable numbers were glow-worms. They are actually beetles, and it is the female that 'glows' in an attempt to attract males when she is ready to mate, usually on warm nights in July and August. Their larvae can also glow to a certain extent. I have spoken to fishermen at the reservoirs who recollect times in the 1980s when they would see hundreds of glow-worms in the grasslands around the reservoirs, but they have now all but disappeared. A few of us conducted a survey for glow-worms, one night in July 2002 but found only two individuals in the southwest corner of Llanishen reservoir and another down in the woods near the old fish ponds. A more recent survey in 2018, carried out by ecologist Peter Sturgess, found two adult females again in the southwest corner of Llanishen reservoir, showing that the species is still present, but the small population must be very vulnerable to going extinct. Glow-worms are declining across the UK, and it is not clear why. Factors may include habitat loss, use of pesticides and light pollution. It has been suggested that males are attracted to artificial lighting, such as street lights, and this may distract them when looking for females.

Plants

The reservoirs support a diverse flora, with over 400 species of flowering plants having been recorded. In spring, the embankments are covered in large drifts of woodland plants such as bluebells, wood

Reservoir Wildlife

Figure 4.5. Some of the plants found at the reservoirs. Top row, L-R: the embankments of Llanishen in spring, common spotted orchid, bugle. Middle row, L-R: common centuary, wood anemone, greater twayblade orchid. Bottom row, L-R: early purple orchid, yellow flag iris, green-winged orchid.

anemones and primroses. Later in the summer, quite a few orchid species can be found, including common spotted orchid, twayblade orchid, early purple orchid, bee orchid and occasionally green-winged orchid. There are many other plants at the reservoirs that are uncommon in Cardiff, such as adder's-tongue fern, betony, bristle clubrush, burnet saxifrage, devil's bit scabious, heath woodrush, meadow thistle, quaking grass, restharrow, sneezewort, yellow rattle, and water figwort.

Fungi

The reservoir embankments have turned out to be an exceptional site for grassland fungi, which are typical of grazed, unimproved grassland. Unfortunately, most of these fungi are intolerant of the artificial fertilisers that have been widely applied to agricultural land since the 1950s, and their numbers throughout Europe have plummeted. Typical fungi in this category are waxcaps, clubs, pinkgills and earth-tongues. A full list of the grassland fungi found at the reservoirs is included in Appendix 3, but given that they played such an important part in the RAG campaign to save the reservoirs from development, they have two chapters of their own later on.

Part Two

*The Reservoir Action Group
and the Campaign to Save
the Reservoirs.*

Chapter 5

The Formation of the Reservoir Action Group

RAG - the very beginning

I first started visiting the reservoirs regularly in the late 1990s. I had a largely sedentary job and thought I could do with a bit more exercise. As I have always been keen on nature and live near the reservoirs, I thought it would be a good place for an early morning walk. I soon got into the habit of walking from my house and doing a lap of both reservoirs before heading off to work.

The reservoirs in the early morning were an absolute delight. It was unusual to see more than a couple of other people there, and these would usually be solitary bird-watchers or, in summer, a few early fishermen. It was also always a pleasure to bump into Dennis Moore, the Welsh Water Ranger who usually opened the site in the morning and was one of those cheery people who could always brighten up your day.

There was always some interesting wildlife to see at the reservoirs, and my pre-work visits became the

Figure 5.1. Dennis Moore the Welsh Water ranger at the reservoirs.

highlight of my day. It was an unwelcome surprise, therefore, to arrive at the reservoir one day in July 2001 and see a newspaper cutting in the window of Dennis' cabin. The article was from the Western Mail Business News, with the headline '£1m-a-mansion housing estate for reservoir site'. It explained how an American-owned company, Western Power Distribution, was in discussions with interested developers over the future of Llanishen reservoir and planned to build exclusive homes on the site.

Over the summer, I thought about the article whenever I visited the reservoirs and discussed the proposed development with friends and neighbours, most of whom shared my concerns. In early September 2001, a letter from the Labour Councillors in Llanishen Ward to local residents provided more information. They mentioned that surveyors working on behalf of Western Power had been seen on the Council-owned meadows behind Rhyd-y-penau Road. They reported that no planning application had been received at this stage and pointed out that the reservoirs formed an integral part of the Nant Fawr green corridor, which had been identified as a strategic wildlife corridor in the Council's Unitary Development Plan. Because of this, they thought the developers would have problems obtaining planning permission, but the local Councillors planned to meet with senior Council officers in the next few weeks to seek reassurances regarding the Council's position on the development.

I certainly wasn't reassured by this and, a few days later, was speaking to an acquaintance called Pat Bishop, who lived in Black Oak Road on the northeast side of the Nant Fawr meadows. Pat told me that their local Neighbourhood Watch Coordinator, Ted Thurgood, was keen to start a group to oppose the proposed development, and she gave me his contact details. I gave Ted a ring, and he invited me to his house to discuss how we might try and start a local community campaign.

I met with Ted and Mike Walker, another concerned resident, towards the end of September 2001. We talked about what we knew of the proposals and how we might start to organise a campaign against them. Ted was just the person for the job, as although he was now retired and in his early seventies, he had previously worked as the

Conservative Party Central Office Agent for Wales. He was a born organiser and knew the political system inside out. Ted suggested that we should form an 'organising group' by recruiting other residents who were concerned about the proposals and who had expertise that might be useful. For example, people with experience of organising similar campaigns or with a background in planning, public relations or sailing etc. We agreed to keep in touch and to start sounding out others to see if there was much support for forming a group to oppose the development.

Figure 5.2. Ted Thurgood, who became RAG's first Chairman. Photo provided by his daughter, Diana Pierce.

It quickly became apparent that there was widespread support for the idea, and at our next meeting, in mid-October, we talked about organising a public meeting. We drafted a flyer, which we circulated in late October in the roads immediately adjacent to the reservoir. This asked people to contact Ted if they were worried about the planned development and would be interested in joining a group to oppose it. Ted's 'phone didn't stop ringing all week, and some of those who responded to this initial leaflet were to become key members of our team.

The next time I saw Ted was on 2nd November 2001. He had arranged a meeting with Sue Essex, the Labour Assembly Member for Cardiff North, her assistant Danny Bethel and Councillor Garry Hunt. Garry had recently attended another meeting between local councillors and a group calling themselves 'Llanishen Water'. At this meeting, they were told more about the proposed development, and he provided us with a summary.

On the 'Llanishen Water' group were two representatives of Western Power, an architect, a consultant from the Wildfowl and Wetlands Trust, a planning agent called Phillipa Cole and Tony Dudley, the other Welsh Water ranger at the reservoirs. They had expressed the view that the reservoirs had reached the end of their 'natural life' and were not sustainable into the future. Their plans consisted of two main clusters of houses: one on the Cyncoed side comprising 120 houses and the other on the Llanishen side of 60 houses. There would also be a three-story block of 60 apartments near the Lisvane car park overlooking Lisvane reservoir. The houses on the Cyncoed side extended onto the Nant Fawr meadows, which surprised us as the meadows belonged to Cardiff Council. Lisvane reservoir was to be left as it was, presumably because it was a Site of Special Scientific Interest, and the water area of Llanishen would be much reduced with 'peninsulas' of houses extending out into the remaining water. At the north end of Llanishen reservoir, there would be an area of marsh and small pools designed to attract wildlife. It was envisaged that the houses on the Nant Fawr meadows would be terraces of 'affordable housing', whilst the waterside houses on the reservoir site would be more expensive (around £750,000). The 'sweeteners' that the developers were offering included free public access around the new lake, cycle paths, enhanced habitat for wildlife, and a new cricket pitch, plus changing rooms on the playing fields in Rhyd-y-penau Park. Garry had been told that the developers would consult with users and local interest groups in the next few weeks and that a planning application would likely be submitted towards the end of November 2001.

At the end of Garry's report, we discussed how we might best oppose this application in relation to the Council's current planning policies. We agreed to meet again in a few weeks. Later, Ted sketched out a plan based on what we had heard (see Figure 5.3 opposite).

A few days later, on 6th November 2001, Ted and I met with a rapidly expanding 'organising group'. The new members were people who had contacted Ted and whom he thought might have relevant experience to aid our developing campaign. They included Geraint Evans, a chartered surveyor with links to the sailing school on Llanishen reservoir; Ruth Jenkins, a local teacher who had campaigned against a housing development on the Llanishen Rugby Club ground; Neil Ashton, a solicitor who lived on Fidlas Road; and Bert Williams, a retired customs officer who lived close to Ted and had offered to help

The Formation of RAG

with administrative tasks. Ted also mentioned Ewart Parkinson, who lived in South Rise and was keen to help us but wanted to stay in the background. Ewart was appointed as Cardiff's first city planning officer in 1964 and subsequently became Director of Planning and Environment for South Glamorgan County Council. He did much to devise the current city plan for Cardiff. Over the years, Ewart was to prove to be an influential and wise adviser to the RAG campaign, and Ted always referred to him as 'my planning guru'.

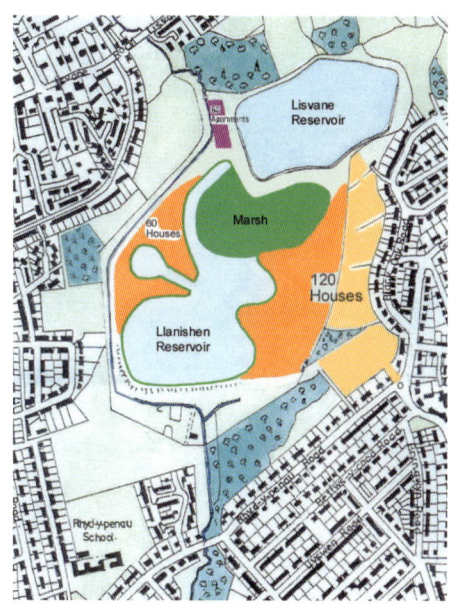

Figure 5.3. Ted's original sketch map of Western Power's plans, based on Garry Hunt's report.

Ted and I described to this group what we had learned from our meeting with Sue Essex and Garry Hunt. Everyone was surprised to hear that Western Power's plans included homes on the Nant Fawr meadows behind Black Oak Road, which belonged to the Council. Garry had also mentioned that Western Power had been discussing the development with Council Officers since March. As a result, Ted was worried that the Labour Council was supporting the developers and that any eventual application might have an easy passage through the Council's Planning Committee.

The main focus of the meeting, however, was the launch of the group that we planned to set up to oppose the development. A launch date had been set for Tuesday, 4th December 2001, and Ted had booked the main hall at Rhyd-y-penau primary school. This would accommodate about 200 people, which we thought would be more than adequate. Ted offered to draft a flyer that could be delivered in the local area, and we also planned to put up notices in local shops in Cyncoed, Rhyd-y-penau crossroads and Llanishen village.

We started to parcel out some of the main jobs that needed to be done. I offered to look into the ecological impact of the proposed development, Bert was happy to deal with the administrative side of things, Geraint would look into the planning aspects, and Ruth had her arm twisted to act as secretary, possibly because Ted seemed to have a fairly unreconstructed view of women's roles!

After the meeting, I began looking into the ecological issues and rapidly discovered that Western Power had already embarked on a charm offensive with various local wildlife organisations, including the Glamorgan Bird Club, the Cardiff Naturalists' Society and the local Wildlife Trust. Fairly regular meetings had been taking place in recent weeks, probably because Western Power recognised the ecological sensitivity of the site and realised how important it was to get such groups onside from the outset. The involvement of these organisations is described in Chapter 8, but suffice it to say here that it looked as though Western Power had been making considerable headway with some of them.

Another group that Western Power realised it would need to persuade were 'The Friends of Nant Fawr', but they proved to be a more critical audience. 'The Friends' are a community group who look after the meadows and woodland running alongside the reservoir site, which are owned by the Council. It was on these meadows that the developers wished to build their affordable homes. Representatives of Western Power made a presentation to the 'Friends' on 26th November. Their presentation reviewed the history of the reservoirs and pointed out that Llanishen reservoir had been 'decommissioned' in the early 1970s. They also claimed that the lease to supply water from Lisvane reservoir to the steelworks in Cardiff Bay was about to end, and therefore, the whole site would become redundant. They stressed the involvement of the Wildfowl and Wetland Trust and pointed to their experience in converting abandoned reservoirs to wildlife sites and used their London Wetland Centre as a prime example. They claimed that they had first gone to the Council with the plans 18 months

The Formation of RAG

earlier and that senior Council staff supported the scheme, as well as Derek Moore, the Chief Executive of the Glamorgan Wildlife Trust. Many members of the Friends of Nant Fawr expressed their opposition to building houses on the meadows behind Black-Oak Road, but the Western Power representatives claimed that the scheme was not commercially viable without the meadows and that the alternative was having to build houses all over the drained reservoirs, leaving no space for wildlife.

In the run-up to our inaugural meeting, Ted continued to recruit people to the 'organising group'. These included Justin Cooper, a traffic expert, and Ceri Davies, who had recently retired as a senior planner from the Council Planning Department. Together with Geraint Evans and Ewart Parkinson, they formed a planning sub-group. Ted had also linked up with the local Liberal-Democrat team, who offered to help with the inaugural meeting and publicise it in their local magazine, *Focus*, which had a wide distribution in the Cyncoed area.

A few days before the meeting, the 'organising group' met again to make the final preparations. Lib-Dem. Wendy Congreve had offered to chair the meeting, and we had organised stewards to man the door and hand out membership forms. The final thing we needed to do was to decide on a name for the new group. Several suggestions were proposed, including.

- Friends of Llanishen Reservoir
- Campaign to Save Llanishen Reservoir
- Cyncoed and Llanishen Residents Association
- Llanishen Reservoir Action Group
- Residents Against Greed and Exploitation (RAGE)
- Residents Against Development at Reservoir (RADAR)
- Nant Fawr Green Corridor Protection Society

In the end, we decided to propose calling it the 'Reservoir Action Group'. This avoided any direct reference to residents as we wanted the group to have as wide an appeal as possible; it had the word 'action', which suggested dynamism; and had a short, memorable abbreviation - RAG.

The Inaugural Meeting of RAG (4th Dec. 2001)

On the evening of the meeting, which was due to start at 7.15 pm, those of us from the organising group got there at about 6.30 pm and put out 150 chairs, which we thought would be sufficient. We had a stack of RAG membership forms at the door, along with some collection plates for donations. But it was a cold, dark December evening, and we wondered how many people would turn up.

The first trickle of people started to arrive at 7 pm, which was encouraging, and ten minutes later, the trickle had turned into a steady stream. By 7.15 pm, all the seats we put out had been taken, and the people who were still arriving started standing at the back of the hall. Towards 7.30 pm, people were still flooding in, and every available space in the hall was taken. We estimated that there were almost 400 people in the hall, but there was also still a huge queue at the door. We decided we couldn't let any more people in on safety grounds, so the marshals had to start turning people away. They estimated that there were at least 200 further people who wanted to get into the hall.

All this caused a delay, but the meeting eventually got underway, and the first speaker was Councillor Owen Pryce, who had been at a recent presentation by Western Power to Council members. He outlined the proposed plans.

Next to speak was Jenny Randerson, the Assembly Member for Cardiff Central. She expressed her concern about the effects of the development on the Council's sailing school and the Cardiff Reservoirs Fly Fishing Club, both of which had been running for many years and provided recreational facilities for local people. She was also concerned about the effect of the development on local traffic and concluded by saying she was totally opposed to the proposed development.

It was then Ted Thurgood's turn to take to the floor. Ted mentioned that since we had started distributing leaflets about this meeting, he had received over 350 'phone calls from local residents who were strongly opposed to the idea of building on the reservoirs. He thanked

The Formation of RAG

Cllr. Owen Pryce and Mrs Randerson for taking a lead in opposing the proposed development and mentioned that he had also received the support of all the local MPs, AMs, and Councillors of all the main political parties. Ted suggested we needed to set up a campaigning organisation to spearhead the campaign to defeat the planning application and that we form a steering committee to draw up a constitution for the proposed 'Reservoir Action Group'. This was approved by an overwhelming majority of those present, and as Ted had conveniently produced a list of potential nominees, the following people were elected to the steering committee:

Chair:	Ted Thurgood	Committee	Geraint Evans
Vice Chair:	Richard Cowie	Members:	Bert Williams
Secretary:	Ruth Jenkins		Ceri Davies
Treasurer:	Rhys Thomas		Vernon Hale
Liaison Officer:	Mike Walker		

It was also agreed that the steering committee would have the power to: co-opt additional members and set up sub-committees; charge a subscription fee for members that was provisionally set at £5; open a bank account in the name of the group; and draft a constitution to be approved at the first Annual General Meeting of the group, which would be held within three months.

The meeting was then thrown open to questions and comments from the floor. Some 20 people asked questions about the development or proposed ways in which it could be opposed. Only one person spoke out in favour of Western Power's plans, which was brave considering the general tone of the meeting. The meeting finished at 9 pm, and those of us who had organised it were delighted that the local community had clearly engaged with the idea of defeating the development proposal.

The days following the meeting were pretty hectic. First, we wrote a Press Release to announce the formation of the Reservoir Action Group, which was duly reported in the South Wales Echo on 6th December 2001.

As so many people had turned up and failed to get into the meeting, we produced the first RAG Newsletter on 7th December. This was sent out with a membership form to all houses in Cyncoed, Llanishen and Lisvane. The form also included a section where people could indicate how they were prepared to help the campaign, which other relevant organisations they belonged to, and whether they had any specialist knowledge or expertise that might be useful to the campaign. Ted asked people who had volunteered to help with leafleting at the inaugural meeting to distribute the newsletter, but it took some time to deliver, and it was clear we needed a more efficient local distribution system.

A week after the first meeting, on Tuesday, 11th December, a second meeting was held at Christ the King Primary School in Everest Avenue, Llanishen. This was organised by the Labour Councillors in the North Cardiff ward, and again Ted was invited to speak. This meeting had not been publicised as far in advance, and the attendance was lower, but a further 200 people attended. Sue Essex AM expressed her concerns about the effect of the proposed development on the Nant Fawr green corridor, which runs from the north of Lisvane through the reservoirs and Roath Park to Waterloo Gardens. Again the attendees endorsed the idea of setting up the Reservoir Action Group, but as Ted pointed out at the close of the meeting, it was likely to be a long, hard and expensive campaign. I'm sure even he didn't realise at the time just how prophetic his words were and how long it would take!

RAG – Getting Organised

After the inaugural meeting, we set to work getting RAG up and running. One of the first things we wanted to do was to create an eye-catching logo. We finally settled on a tufted duck. It was one of the species for which Lisvane reservoir had been declared a Site of Special Scientific Interest, and more pragmatically, it was black and white and would reproduce well on photocopies etc.

Over the Christmas period in 2001, we also started work on a RAG website. The World Wide Web was at a fairly early stage then, and many organisations did not yet have websites, but we realised that it was becoming increasingly important. None of us had the necessary expertise in website design, but my son John did, and he offered to set up a site for us. We collated information about the reservoirs and got messages of support from local politicians across the political spectrum. The website went live on 16th January 2002.

Ted and Bert set to work on another important aspect, developing an efficient system for distributing information, such as newsletters. We couldn't afford to send information out by post every time, but at the two inaugural meetings, many people volunteered to help distribute leaflets. Displaying his political roots, the first thing that Ted did was to go and buy copies of the electoral registers for Cyncoed, Llanishen and Lisvane. In those days, people were less concerned about confidentiality and most householders were included on the registers. Ted divided up all these areas based on the electoral wards and turned to the list of people who had volunteered to help with deliveries at one of the inaugural meetings. He then rang around until he found one person in each electoral ward who was prepared to act as a 'Ward Organiser'. These Ward Organisers were then given a list of other people in their ward who had also volunteered to help. The idea was that when there was a newsletter to go out, Ted would deliver the appropriate number of newsletters to the Ward Organiser, who would then ring around the other volunteers in the ward and get them to deliver the newsletters to each household in their own street or others nearby. This system proved to be effective, and we could get information out quickly either to members or all households in the area. We used it throughout the RAG campaign.

Bert also took responsibility for creating a membership database using Excel. Every morning Bert visited Ted's house and picked up the latest batch of membership forms that had arrived. He then entered the information into the database. Given the number of people who were joining in those first few weeks, it was a major job. However, it gave us the ability to produce lists of members quickly, based either on their addresses or some other attribute, such as whether they had volunteered to help with a particular task, such as letter writing or fund-raising. Of course, we asked people if they minded us keeping an electronic copy of their details, but with only a handful of exceptions, they were happy for us to do so.

The first meeting of the RAG Steering Committee took place on Tuesday, 8th January, at Ted's house. Ted began by introducing Geoff Roberts, whom he had recruited as RAG's press officer. Before he retired, Geoff had been Director of Information at the Welsh Office, so he was well-connected with the local media. We also had an update on the membership and finances: by 7th January, we had 327 paid-up members, and through membership fees and donations, we already had £3,430.85 in the bank. Enough to get things rolling! Ceri Davies also reported as the lead of the planning group. They had already decided that the main thrust of our objection on planning grounds should be the integrity of the Nant Fawr river corridor. This was one of the four main river corridors that lead into the centre of the city, and several local planning policies expressed a presumption against building on them. They had also highlighted several related issues that needed further investigation, such as the Council's nature conservation policies and the legal ownership of the land surrounding the reservoir. At this meeting, we also started to look at a draft constitution that Bert had drawn up with input from Ted.

We didn't manage to get through everything on the Agenda at that meeting, so we decided to reconvene a week later on 15th January. By then, Ted was able to announce that he had arranged the first Annual General Meeting of RAG for 26th February 2002 at Rhyd-y-penau school. We also discussed ways of publicising the RAG campaign and producing posters. The first RAG posters were A0 and A1 black and white photocopies, which were hand-coloured and then laminated. They featured the RAG slogan of 'Save Our Reservoirs', the RAG tufted duck logo, and Ted's telephone number for people to call if they were interested in joining. We agreed to spend up to £100, which would cover four A0 posters and eight A1 ones, which would be put up in members' gardens close to the reservoir entrances and near major road intersections.

Towards the end of January 2002, we produced our second newsletter, which was delivered using our new distribution system to all houses in the neighbourhoods of Cyncoed, Llanishen and Lisvane that surrounded the reservoirs. This advertised the forthcoming AGM but also reported on the latest developments. We had heard that Western Power was planning to open an exhibition about its housing plans in a vacant shop in Llanishen village and had scheduled a press conference on Wednesday, 11th December, a few days after RAG's launch. However, this press conference was cancelled at short notice after the RAG meeting, and their exhibition never materialised. Rumours also began to circulate that Western Power was undertaking a major revision of its plans and that a planning application was not now expected imminently.

Further RAG Steering Committee meetings were held on 29th January and 19th February; both mainly focused on making the final arrangements for the forthcoming AGM and finalising the details of the RAG Constitution.

Around this time, another important issue arose, which was the ownership of the reservoirs. We had assumed up until this point that they now belonged to Western Power Distribution, but one of our members, Ivor Lippett, had the foresight to check with OFWAT, the Water Services Regulation Authority. He discovered that the reservoirs were still currently owned by Dŵr Cymru / Welsh Water and that Western Power was seeking planning permission for development on a site they did not yet own. This gave us a whole new avenue to explore, as if we could block the sale of the reservoir to Western Power, we could scupper the whole scheme. At the time, we were not aware of the 'buy back' arrangement that had been agreed between Glas Cymru and Western Power when the former company was set up (see Chapter 2).

The First RAG Annual General Meeting

The first RAG AGM was held on 26th February 2002. Only paid-up RAG members could attend, although we had a desk at the door where non-members could join on the spot. We had over 200 members attending. Ted was adept at running meetings, and we rattled through the business. The Constitution was approved, and most steering committee members were elected to the first RAG committee. Geoff Roberts was elected to the new post of Press Officer, and Geraint Evans had decided that he did not want to be on the main committee but was happy to stay on the Planning sub-committee. Instead, Peter Gretton, a retired banker, was elected as a Committee Member. Peter lived on Lisvane Road and was well-known in the Lisvane area, which improved the scope of our coverage. It was reported at the AGM that, as of 25th February 2002, RAG had 602 paid-up members and £6,244.64 in the bank, which was an encouraging start for an organisation that had been formed only ten weeks previously.

In what has now become a familiar pattern, after the formal business, Ted gave an update on the progress of the campaign and reported on rumours that Western Power might be ditching its plans to build on the meadows behind Black Oak Road. There had also been a suggestion that Western Power would submit a formal planning application on 7th March 2002. However, Ted stressed that this was all hearsay and might come to nothing.

I gave a brief report as Chair of the Ecology sub-committee and summarised what we knew about the biodiversity aspects at the time. It also included a plea for anyone with specialist knowledge of the site to let us know, as well as any interesting biological records that people might have.

Ceri Davies followed this up as Chair of the Planning sub-committee. He mentioned that this group now included himself, Ewart Parkinson, Geraint Evans, Justin Cooper and Andrew Hill. Andrew was a relatively new recruit to the planning team who worked as an architectural conservator and was interested in developing alternative plans for the reservoirs and surrounding area. Ceri stressed the importance of the river corridors and pointed out that the Cardiff Local Plan was about to be replaced by a new Unitary Development Plan. He argued that it was important for us to try and get this new plan to define clearly the river corridors and make sure the Council strengthened their protected status.

Following these presentations, there were a large number of questions and observations from members. Ted eventually brought the meeting to a close with a request for volunteers to collect signatures for a petition against the planning application; to write letters to Councillors, Assembly Members and MPs; and for members to allow RAG to put up a poster in their front gardens.

Time to Prepare

At the time of the AGM, we were expecting that the planning application from Western Power would be submitted any day. Nothing materialised on 7th March, and then we heard that it would likely be late April. Still nothing. This waiting game went on for the rest of the year, and the application didn't appear until December. The advantage of this was that it gave us more time to prepare.

From the outset, we realised that not only would we have to defeat Western Power's plans but also present an alternative vision for the reservoirs. This became a priority for Ceri Davies and the planning group. At a RAG Committee meeting in September, they presented a draft document entitled 'A Better Way for Llanishen Reservoir', which described a way of keeping the reservoirs as an integral part of the Nant Fawr river corridor and enhancing their value for nature conservation and recreational use. It also involved the building of a new visitor/sailing centre and provided proposals for financing and management of the new facility. Perhaps this now sounds familiar? It was eventually published as a glossy report in March 2003 called 'The Cardiff Reservoirs Country Park'.

The delay in the arrival of the planning application also enabled much more information to be collated regarding the site's conservation value. This allowed us to establish that glow-worms were still present on the embankments, albeit in low numbers, and to make the all-important discovery of waxcap fungi in November 2002. This later became a key aspect of our campaign, which I will describe in Chapter 7.

The other aspect that we had time to organise were poster boards to publicise the RAG campaign. Ted was keen on having signs that could go in members' front gardens to demonstrate the strength of local support. He thought the type of boards used by estate agents would be ideal, but they were expensive to have printed. The rest of us weren't sure that they justified the cost, but Ted was adamant and eventually convinced us that it was a good idea. Ted designed the signs with the help of his son-in-law John and arranged to have them printed.

Teams were organised to put up the 'estate agent' boards, and they went up over a couple of weekends in December 2002 and January 2003. We concentrated them on main roads such as Fidlas Road, Rhyd-y-penau Road, Cyncoed Road and Station Road in Llanishen, where they would be most visible. The impact was dramatic and

Figure 5.4. RAG boards on Fidlas Road in January 2003. Photo courtesy of Media Wales/Reachplc.

provided an enormous boost to public awareness of our campaign. We should have trusted Ted's political instincts from the outset!

The planning application finally arrived on 17th December 2002, just before the Christmas Holidays. Another unexpected element was that two days later, leaflets were distributed throughout north Cardiff describing the scheme and bearing the logos of Llanishen Water and the local Wildlife Trust. Much emphasis in this leaflet was placed on describing the proposed development as a new nature reserve rather than a new housing estate! This is something I will return to in Chapter 8, but in the next two chapters, I will describe the plans and how, to quote Rabbie Burns, *'the best-laid schemes of mice and men often go awry'*.

Chapter 6

The First Planning Application

The first planning application was broadly as we had anticipated, but fortunately, the rumours about the proposed houses on the Nant Fawr meadows were correct, and these had been omitted from the final plans. So much for Western Power's earlier claims that they were indispensable. The application was for 346 dwellings consisting of 99 detached houses, 52 town houses and 195 apartments. The development was split into two main halves (see Figure 6.1).

On the eastern side of the reservoir, the plan was to have 52 town houses, 31 detached houses and 87 apartments. These would be accessed by a new road that would cross the Nant Fawr meadows and link the roundabout at the top of Rhyd-y-penau road with the reservoir entrance. Western Power had purchased three houses beside the roundabout, which would be knocked down to make this access possible.

On the western side would be the remaining 68 detached houses, with 108 apartments leading up to the location of the current Lisvane reservoir car park. These apartment blocks would be four storeys high and comprise a mixture of 1, 2 and 3 bedroomed flats. This side of the development would be accessed from Lisvane Road.

Although there was a road linking the two sides of the development, it was intended that this would be closed off with barriers to prevent people from using it to take a shortcut from Lisvane to Cyncoed and vice versa. Only buses and emergency vehicles would be able to access one side of the development from the other.

The First Planning Application

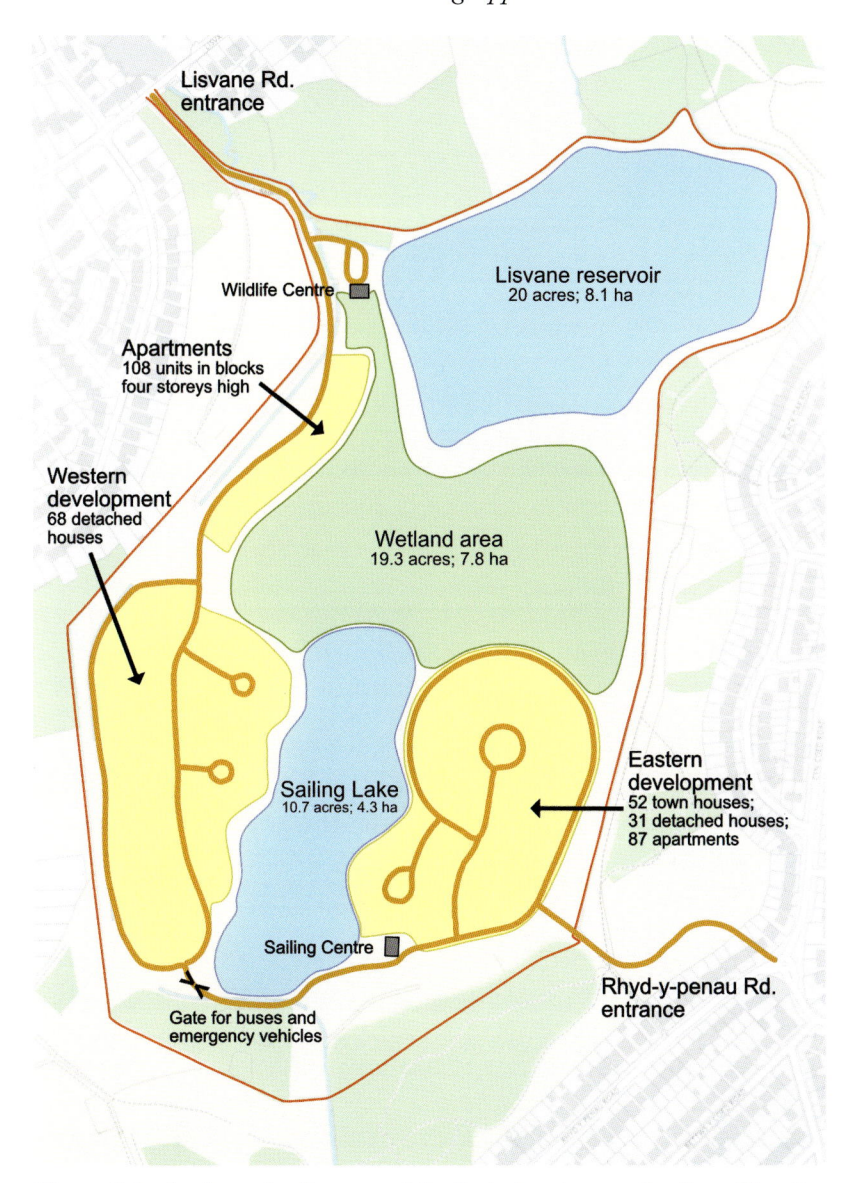

Figure 6.1. A schematic diagram of the first planning application. The site boundary is shown in red, the roads in brown and the proposed residential developments are shaded yellow.

In the middle of the two housing developments was a much-reduced sailing lake, referred to as 'Llanishen Water'. I think this had two purposes. The first was to enable the adjacent houses to be sold at a premium as 'waterside properties', and the second was to allow at least some sailing still to take place. To this end, a sailing centre was planned in the southeast corner of the lake adjacent to the housing development. However, due to the water area being only one-fifth that of the existing reservoir, it was proposed that only basic tuition for beginners would occur there.

The other major feature of the development was a wetland area just to the north of the lake and adjacent to Lisvane reservoir. This would contain reed beds, a number of pools of different depths and have the Nant Fawr stream flowing through it. The expressed hope was that it might attract wildlife such as water voles, grass snakes, amphibians and new bird species.

The only other amenity was a Wildlife / Community Centre on the existing Lisvane reservoir car park. This would be run by the Wildlife Trust of South and West Wales, who would be involved in the long-term management of the site once the developers had departed. It was envisaged that the wetland centre would provide educational displays about the various wildlife found on the site and could be a useful resource for local schools.

The planning application did not include Lisvane reservoir, which was already a Site of Special Scientific Interest (SSSI) for its over-wintering wildfowl. Presumably, because even Western Power realised that it would be unlikely to get planning permission for a development that had a potentially negative effect on an SSSI.

Western Power tried to make the most of what it claimed would be positive effects of the development on wildlife. These mostly centred on the small area of marshland to the north of Llanishen Water. Admittedly a greater variety of wetland habitats like reed beds and shallow lagoons would be likely to attract a greater range of species to the reservoirs, and the developers liked to compare their proposals to the successful London Wetland Centre in Barnes (see Chapter 8).

The First Planning Application

However, the big problem was one of scale. Given average occupancy, building 346 houses and apartments was likely to bring over 900 people to live on the site, which was only 110 acres in total. There were no plans to separate people and wildlife, and a network of paths across the whole area was shown on the plans. In our opinion, the adverse effects of this potential disturbance on any remaining wildlife would far outweigh the benefits of any extra habitat creation.

Western Power also faced another biodiversity issue, although it did not know it at the time. Around the same time that its first planning application was submitted, rare waxcap fungi were discovered on the reservoir embankments. Its plans involved infilling a large part of Llanishen reservoir by bulldozing the existing embankments into the reservoir bowl and re-profiling the whole area. This would be likely to obliterate the fungi completely.

Another major issue for RAG was that local planning policies provided a presumption against developing the four main river corridors in Cardiff, of which the Nant Fawr is one. The others are the Taff, the Ely and the Rhymney. These river corridors had been specifically protected in the overall City plan to provide green spaces linking the centre of the city with the surrounding countryside. RAG viewed the reservoirs as being an integral part of the Nant Fawr river corridor, and the proposed development and its roads would completely bisect it, let alone bringing 900 people to live bang in the middle of it.

Our other concern was the loss of public amenities provided by the reservoirs. Since they were built, the reservoirs had provided enjoyment to generations of fly fishermen and, from the 1970s, had been the base for a very successful sailing school that had given many children a great introduction to water sports. Not to mention the peace and tranquillity many found from walking around the reservoirs amongst the abundant flora and fauna.

Chapter 7

Waxcap Fungi (Part 1)

Western Power was unlucky. A month before it submitted its first planning application, some unusual fungi were discovered at the reservoirs. It didn't pay much attention to this at first, but the fungi were to become a major problem for the developer.

The Discovery of the Waxcaps

On Friday, 15th November 2002, I visited the reservoirs for my usual early morning walk before going to work. When I arrived, Dennis Moore told me that Peter Sturgess, the ecologist doing surveys for Western Power, had been at the reservoirs the day before and seemed pleased to find some brightly coloured mushrooms. Fred Slater, a work colleague, had advised me to look out for waxcap fungi, which are well-known for being colourful, so I abandoned my walk and went home to collect a fungi field guide and some polythene bags. When I got back, it did not take long to find a variety of likely-looking fungi, and I collected one or two specimens of each.

Later that day, I showed them to Juliet Preston-Mafham, a postgraduate student at Cardiff University, doing research on grassland fungi. She immediately identified one specimen as a pink meadow waxcap *Hygrocybe calyptriformis* and

Figure 7.1. Pink meadow waxcap (Hygrocybe calyptriformis).

another as a crimson waxcap *H. punicea*. The rest, which were mainly a variety of shades of yellow and orange, were trickier to identify, and Juliet took them away to examine in more detail. She promised to let me have the results in a couple of days' time.

That evening I read up about waxcap fungi. One of the first things I discovered was that the pink meadow waxcap (Figure 7.1) was a UK Biodiversity Action Plan priority species. These are species that have been identified as being the most threatened in the UK and requiring particular conservation action. This seemed like a good species to find at the reservoirs!

In the following week, my morning walks became fungal forays. I collected more specimens and took them to Juliet to identify. She enlisted the help of Alan Orange at the National Museum of Wales, who was a lower plant, lichen and fungi specialist, and by the 22nd November, they had identified 12 species of waxcaps from the embankments of Llanishen reservoir.

I contacted Vaughan Grantham, Cardiff Council's ecologist, with news of our discovery, but he told me he already knew about them and that any waxcap records would be included in the developer's environmental statement. The RAG Committee, however, was worried that there might be some attempt by Western Power to downplay the presence of the waxcaps, so we decided to go public. We sent a press release to the South Wales Echo, along with a photograph of a pink meadow waxcap taken at the reservoirs. They carried the story on 28th November, along with the picture of a waxcap on the front page with the headline 'Could this mushroom save Llanishen Reservoir from the developer's bulldozers?' Hopefully, this guaranteed that the fungi couldn't be ignored.

One of the most useful outcomes of the article in the Echo was that the next day, I got a telephone call from Roy Perry. Although by this time he had retired, Roy previously worked at the National Museum of Wales and was one of the most knowledgeable people in South Wales when it came to identifying fungi. He had recently been contacted by Western Power and asked to help Peter Sturgess with the fungal surveys. I had met Roy several times in the past, and we were on friendly terms. We arranged to meet at the reservoirs to look for waxcaps together. We visited on Tuesday, 3rd December. Roy was much more experienced at finding and identifying fungi, and by the end of the morning's outing, we had identified another five new species, bringing the grand total to 17. A few days afterwards, Western Power somehow discovered that Roy and I had done a joint survey. Roy was told in no uncertain terms that he should not have any further contact with me nor share any information with me. Fortunately, he was the sort of person who didn't like being told what he could and couldn't do, so we were more discreet and continued to collaborate by occasionally meeting for lunch and comparing notes.

By mid-December, the waxcap season was well and truly over, as there had already been some hard frosts, and no more fungi were appearing. Also, on 17th December 2002, Western Power's first planning application had been lodged with Cardiff Council, and in the run-up to Christmas, there was much to do putting together RAG's response.

Waxcap Primer

At this stage, providing more background information about waxcap fungi and their conservation importance would probably be helpful.

Waxcaps occur predominantly in long-established, nutrient-poor grassland that has not been fertilised with chemicals. They were once widespread throughout northern Europe, but with the spread of intensive agriculture since the 1950s and the use of fertilisers to increase agricultural yields, they have become increasingly scarce (McHugh et al. 2001). Recently, conservationists have recognised the value of waxcap species as bio-indicators of good quality unimproved grassland habitats, which not only have a rich diversity of fungi but also a wide array of flowering plants (Griffiths et al. 2004). Like most fungi, waxcaps spend most of the year underground, where their thread-like hyphae penetrate throughout the soil. It is only in the autumn when their fruiting bodies, or what we generally call 'fungi', appear above the ground. These fruiting bodies release millions of microscopic spores, which fall from the gills and are dispersed by air currents. Waxcaps are striking because their fruiting bodies tend to be brightly coloured. However, like many fungi, their delicate structures cannot withstand freezing, and they are destroyed by frost. Therefore, the time when they can be found is quite limited. They tend to appear in the late summer and autumn, often when there has been a dry spell followed by a period of damp, wet weather with cool but not freezing temperatures. In some years, when the weather conditions are right, they can appear in huge numbers; in other years, when the weather is not suitable, or frosts come early, few are seen. Surprisingly, waxcaps were not found at the reservoirs until mid-November, which is approaching the end of the season, and by all accounts, 2002 was not a good year for fungi.

Llanishen and Lisvane reservoirs are likely to be good for waxcaps as a result of two factors. Firstly, the reservoir embankments, not being used for agriculture, have never been treated with chemical fertilisers. Secondly, waxcaps like short grass, which normally occurs as a result of grazing by animals. Although not grazed, the reservoir embankments are mown regularly so engineers can check for leaks and earth movements. This mowing simulates grazing and, together with the lack of chemical fertilisers, provides ideal conditions for the waxcaps.

A variety of systems have used been used to assess the importance of sites for grassland fungi. Rald (1985) proposed a system based on the number of waxcap species, which was modified later by Vesterholt et al. (1999). They considered sites with 17-21 species of waxcap to be nationally important, with sites having 22 or more species as being of international importance. Boertmann (1995) also concluded, from his studies in Denmark, that sites with more than 17 waxcap species should be considered as being of national importance. McHugh et al. (2001) came up with a numerical scoring system after studying a wide range of Irish grassland sites. This system awards different scores for different species, depending on their rarity and includes a number of other grassland fungi species besides waxcaps. In Ireland, sites with a score of more than 30 points are considered to be of national importance, and the scores for species we had recorded at the Cardiff reservoirs in 2002 added up to exactly 30! As we had reached this after discovering waxcaps late in the season and may have missed species that were fruiting earlier, a case could be made for the site being one of national importance for grassland fungi, whichever system is used.

SSSI Designation Request

Being a site of national importance for a particular species or group of species is one of the key criteria for its designation as a Site of Special Scientific Interest (SSSI). At the time, these designations were made by the Countryside Council for Wales (CCW), so in early January 2003, I decided to make a formal request for the reservoir embankments to be designated as an SSSI for grassland fungi. I wrote to this effect to Dr Sue Howard, who was the CCW Team Leader covering Cardiff and Newport. She replied to say that they would consider the request to notify the embankments but that they would need to establish the site's relative importance, which might take some time.

In fact, it did not take too long. On Thursday, 6th March, we received the good news that the CCW agreed that the embankments of Lisvane and Llanishen reservoirs were probably of SSSI quality for their grassland fungi and that the site had been added to a list of candidate SSSIs. However, the CCW said it wanted more information before proceeding to a formal SSSI notification, which would involve collecting data for another field season from October to December 2003.

Waxcaps (Part 1)

Figure 7.2. A selection of waxcaps photographed at Llanishen reservoir. From left to right: (top row) meadow waxcap (Hygrocybe pratensis); scarlet waxcap (H. coccinea); (middle row) crimson waxcap (H. punicea); parrot waxcap (Gliophorus psittacinus); golden waxcap (H. chlorophana); (bottom row) blackening waxcap; (H. conica); heath waxcap (G. Laetus).

Chapter 8

Wildlife Organisations

Western Power realised at the outset that its plan to build a housing development in the middle of the Nant Fawr green corridor would likely encounter significant opposition on environmental grounds. Not only was Lisvane reservoir a Site of Special Scientific Interest for its over-wintering waterfowl, but Llanishen reservoir itself was a Site of Importance for Nature Conservation because of its unusual aquatic plant community and large breeding population of toads. From the start, Western Power sought to get the local conservation community onside with what can only be described as a propaganda campaign.

The Wildfowl and Wetlands Trust

Western Power's first good move was to engage the Wildfowl and Wetlands Trust as consultants to the project. The Wildfowl and Wetlands Trust (WWT), formerly known as the Wildfowl Trust, was set up by the ornithologist and artist Sir Peter Scott in 1946. Its headquarters is at Slimbridge on the Severn Estuary, and it is dedicated to the conservation of wetland birds and their habitats. The Wildfowl and Wetlands Trust now has nine centres throughout the UK and is one of the best-known wetland conservation charities. However, like many such charities, WWT struggles to get sufficient money to fund its conservation work and has set up a commercial consultancy. This provides habitat management advice for a fee and is a valuable source of income for the Trust. It was this consultancy that Western Power had engaged. The reason WWT was such a good source of advice for Western Power was that one of its most successful

Fig. 8.1. The London Wetland Centre is much larger, and housing is separated from the nature reserve by a security fence and deep pools.

centres, the London Wetland Centre, was developed on the site of four redundant reservoirs adjacent to the river Thames and financed by selling off some of the land for housing.

The Wildfowl and Wetlands Trust first considered opening a centre in London in 1988. The redundant reservoirs at Barn Elms in the London Borough of Richmond were ideal. They were surrounded on two sides by the river Thames and on the south side by Barnes Common. The reservoirs themselves covered 70 acres and the surrounding land a further 60 acres. At the time, Thames Water owned the site, but the reservoirs were about to become redundant for the supply of drinking water, and Thames Water was keen to dispose of them.

Although Thames Water and WWT agreed to cooperate in redeveloping the site into a wetland centre, this would cost a great deal, and that is why Berkeley Homes became involved. Part of the site was allocated for housing, the sale of which would generate enough capital to redevelop the rest of the site into a wetland reserve. In the end, 25 acres became housing, and the remaining 105 acres were completely re-profiled into a wetland reserve, with pools of different depths, surrounding wet grassland, reed beds and a visitor centre. The whole wetland area was surrounded by a high-security fence separating it from the adjacent housing.

The London Wetland Centre opened in 2000 and has been a phenomenal success. It is now one of the best bird-watching sites in the London area and, in 2012, was chosen as the UK's favourite nature reserve in the BBC Countryfile awards. It is one of the most visited of the WWT centres.

Given WWT's background in developing the London Wetland Centre, and given the similarity of the scheme in repurposing a redundant reservoir financed by building housing, it is not surprising that Western Power turned to the Wildfowl and Wetland Trust for advice. However, there are some key differences in the characteristics of the two schemes, which I will return to shortly.

Matthew Millet from the Wildfowl and Wetland's Trust consultancy was engaged to provide advice on creating a wetland area and also to get local wildlife organisations on board with the whole scheme. In the autumn of 2001, we became aware that Western Power and WWT were organising meetings with representatives from groups such as the Glamorgan Bird Club, the Glamorgan Moth Group, the Cardiff Naturalists' Society, the local Wildlife Trust and the RSPB. At these meetings, the attendees were told that the reservoirs were redundant and that Western Power couldn't afford the maintenance costs of keeping them in their present state. The development scheme was presented as Cardiff's equivalent of the London Wetland Centre. Those present were told that, as in London, the funding for this new nature reserve would have to come from some of the site being sacrificed to housing. It is clear that some groups, notably the Glamorgan Bird Club, enthusiastically embraced this argument and became vocal proponents of the scheme, perhaps because it was being fronted by such a well-respected conservation organisation as the WWT. Others, however, were more sceptical and were more sympathetic to the general aims of RAG, which was getting established around this

Wildlife Organisations

time. Therefore they ensured that we were kept updated about discussions at these meetings as, not surprisingly, representatives of RAG were not invited to attend. In fact, I was told that while the participants were waiting for these meetings to start, there were often jibes and ridicule directed against members of RAG, emanating mainly from representatives of the Glamorgan Bird Club.

In the autumn of 2001, when we were setting up RAG, we realised that the wildlife aspects of the site would be significant. When we designed our initial membership form, we asked people to indicate whether they were also members of the Wildfowl and Wetland Trust, the RSPB or the Glamorgan Wildlife Trust. By the end of February 2002, RAG had 600 paid-up members, and we had a significant number who also belonged to these other organisations.

In early March 2002, when the extent of the involvement of the Wildfowl and Wetland Trust was becoming apparent, we decided to tackle the issue head-on. A group of RAG members who were also Wildfowl and Wetland Trust members wrote to Hugh Mellor, the Chairman of the WWT trustees. We wanted to ensure that the Trustees were aware that WWT staff were actively promoting the reservoir development to wildlife groups on behalf of Western Power and that this development was happening in one of Cardiff's key river corridors, which was designated in the Local Plan as being of key conservation value. We also wanted them to know about the scale of opposition to the scheme amongst the local community and the potential damage that could be done to the reputation of the WWT. This letter resulted in a series of emails and further letters between us and Tony Richardson, the Managing Director of WWT, in which he defended the Trust's involvement and assured us that senior management had taken the decision with the trustees' full approval. Again he likened the scheme to that at the London Wetland Centre.

Our view was that the Cardiff scheme was completely different. The London site was larger, and a smaller proportion of it was allocated to housing, which was all concentrated to the north of the wetland area. More importantly, the wetland site in London was completely discrete and separated from the housing by a tall security fence. It could only be entered via the visitor centre, which was restricted to WWT members or those paying an entrance fee. Therefore visitors could be carefully controlled and limited to certain areas of the site. From what we knew of Western Power's plans, there was to be no physical separation between the housing and the proposed 'nature reserve' at Llanishen. Also, the proportion of the site allocated to housing was more extensive, and the main housing complex was located in the middle of the scheme. Therefore, there would be constant disturbance of the wildlife by residents going about their daily business. Western Power was proposing 346 homes ranging from large detached houses to apartments. Given average occupancy rates, this would mean somewhere in excess of 900 people coming to live in the middle of a site of high conservation value along with their pets, cars and other trappings of suburban life.

Whilst we were clearly not going to make any further headway with the WWT, those of us who were members thought we had done our duty by making the Trust aware of the significant opposition to the scheme and the potential reputational damage to their organisation.

The Wildlife Trust of South and West Wales

We also approached other organisations that had been attending the meetings organised by the Wildfowl and Wetlands Trust, such as the RSPB and the Wildlife Trust of South and West Wales. They either sat on the fence and said they would wait for a planning application to be made before coming to any decision (RSPB), or in the case of the Wildlife Trust, the Chief Executive stated that "at this stage, I do not believe there is an opportunity to submit a plan for this site other than one which contains some development". This sounded ominous.

Our fears were confirmed when Western Power submitted its first planning application in December 2002. It was calling its development scheme 'Llanishen Water'. At the same time as the planning application was submitted to the Council, a glossy brochure dropped through the letterbox of every household in Cyncoed, Llanishen and Lisvane. This had two logos on the front, that of Llanishen Water and

Wildlife Organisations

also of the Wildlife Trust of South and West Wales. The brochure explained that the site would become a new nature reserve, which would be gifted to the Wildlife Trust as well as funds for its long-term management. It mentioned briefly, almost as an aside, that a fifth of the site would be used for quality houses and apartments, whilst it focused mainly on the benefits to wildlife, outdoor activities and educational facilities. Nowhere did it mention that the scheme involved 346 homes and all the infrastructure that goes with them, such as roads, garages and parking areas. It was a classic exercise in spin.

As a member of the Wildlife Trust, I was outraged to see the extent to which the Trust was involved. This was compounded by an article on the BBC Wales news website published later the same day, which included a quote from Derek Moore, the Chief Executive of the Wildlife Trust, who said: "We came into the equation to ensure that the concerns of local people and naturalists were addressed". My concerns were certainly not being addressed, and I found it infuriating that an organisation meant to promote nature conservation was apparently doing precisely the opposite.

Over Christmas 2022, I contacted other RAG members who were also members of the Wildlife Trust. All were equally dismayed that the Wildlife Trust had allowed themselves to become involved, although one or two suggested that it was not surprising as the Trust stood to gain a new 'nature reserve', a new visitor centre and funds to run both. All the Trust needed to provide was its support. Nevertheless, none of us were convinced that Western Power's proposals would be good for wildlife, given the number of houses that were planned and the disturbance that would be caused.

In early January 2003, twenty Wildlife Trust members who lived in North Cardiff signed a letter to Roy Jones, Chairman of the Trustees of the Wildlife Trust. The letter pointed out that Llanishen reservoir was itself a Site of Nature Conservation Importance and that 17 species of waxcap fungi had recently been discovered on the embankments making it a potential candidate as a Site of Special Scientific Interest for grassland fungi. We expressed dismay that the Trust was aligning itself with a development that involved destroying these embankments. We also expressed our concern that the Trust's association with the project would damage its reputation and good name. We asked the Trustees to disassociate the Trust from the Llanishen Water development publicly and instead consider an alternative plan that RAG had proposed for a green wildlife corridor in northeast Cardiff, incorporating the reservoirs and the surrounding fields north to Lisvane.

A few days later, Roy Jones replied, inviting all the signatories of the letter to a meeting that would include himself and senior staff from the Trust. He indicated that the professional advice he had received from the Trust staff and 'other experts' contradicted the case we had made. He mentioned that both Julie Morgan MP and Jenny Randerson AM had also asked for meetings with Derek Moore to find out why the Trust had managed to upset so many of their local constituents. The meeting was subsequently arranged for the evening of Tuesday, 21st January 2003, in a seminar room at Cardiff University's Centre for Lifelong Learning.

Almost all the 20 signatories of the letter attended the meeting, and the Wildlife Trust was represented by Derek Moore (Chief Executive), Madeleine Havard (Director of Operations), Roy Jones (Chairman of the Trustees) and Roger Turner (Vice Chairman of the Trustees). Roy Jones chaired the meeting, but Derek Moore did most of the talking. I did not warm to Derek Moore. He was well regarded in bird-watching circles, but he seemed rather patronising and presented himself as the ultimate authority on conservation matters.

He began by saying that the Wildlife Trust was supporting the application but was not promoting it. He explained that they weren't aware that the Trust's logo was going to be included on the Western Power brochure. Given that the main thrust of the brochure was to describe the development as a new nature reserve, this seemed disingenuous and also because the article on the BBC news website quoted him as saying that the Trust joined the project to ensure the concerns of local people were addressed. The brochure had given the clear impression that the Wildlife Trust were promoting the scheme as equal partners to Western Power.

Wildlife Organisations

Derek Moore reiterated that the scheme would be good for wildlife and claimed that birds such as little ringed plover, lapwing, and redshank would end up nesting there, along with otters and water voles. We countered that on the small wetland area proposed, this was extremely unlikely given up to 900 people living in close proximity and the resultant high population of predators such as domestic cats. We also mentioned the significant population of crows that bred in the trees surrounding the reservoirs and were likely to predate the nests of wading birds. On the other hand, the housing development would entirely obliterate the rare waxcap fungi on the embankments, which in conservation terms, were the most significant species at the site.

We asked if the Wildlife Trust would consider our alternative plan for a green wildlife corridor in North Cardiff incorporating the reservoirs, but Derek Moore said our proposal was unrealistic as we wouldn't be able to afford to buy the reservoirs. We pointed out that if Western Power's planning application was refused, the land would have a nominal value, but he wouldn't accept this proposition. (In fact, Western Power eventually sold the reservoirs for £1, but we will come to that much later).

The meeting could best be described, using the usual euphemism, as 'robust'. Eventually, we agreed that the Trust would issue a press release pointing out that it was not promoting the development, just supporting it, and that it would write to those householders who had received the brochure to the same effect. The Trust also agreed to meet with members of the RAG committee to discuss our alternative plans.

When I got home that evening, I emailed a report of the meeting to the rest of the RAG Committee so that they knew what had happened. The next morning I was telephoned by a reporter from the South Wales Echo, who seemed to know pretty much everything about the meeting. I guessed that someone from the RAG Committee had been in touch with the Echo, even though I had expected my email would be treated in confidence. When I spoke to Ted Thurgood later, he admitted that he had been the source of the leak, but he was quite unapologetic and said he had done it for the good of the RAG campaign. Ted could be infuriating at times, and for the first time in my life, I put the 'phone down on someone because I knew that if I continued, I would say something I would probably regret.

Fairly predictably, I got a letter from Roy Jones at The Wildlife Trust a few days later, saying how disappointed he was that someone had gone to the press following the meeting. In my reply, I admitted that the press had contacted me and I had answered their questions, but I didn't reveal what Ted had done. The article in the Echo was very critical of the stance taken by the Wildlife Trust, and as a result of my apparent betrayal, he said they would reconsider the actions we had agreed at the meeting. In fact, they did not follow through on any of their promises.

The Wildlife Trust management seemed rattled following the meeting due to the bad publicity it had started to attract, but also because they were being taken to task by our local Assembly Members. Many Cardiff members of the Trust who were against the reservoir development began writing to them, and some cancelled their membership.

However, a few of us decided that it might be more productive to remain as members and try to persuade the charity's Trustees, who had overall responsibility for the Trust, to stop supporting Western Power's development. We reasoned that when they first decided to get involved, they did not know about the waxcaps and the importance of the embankments for grassland fungi. Once they knew more about this, perhaps they would change their mind?

At the time, the Wildlife Trust had quite a progressive policy that allowed members to attend Trustees' meetings as observers and then to raise any local issues of concern at the end of the meeting. We decided to take advantage of this and to make our case directly to the full Board of Trustees.

The next meeting of the Trustees was held in Swansea on the 24th June 2003. Nine of us from Cardiff travelled down to attend. We sat through a pretty boring meeting, at which there was only passing mention of the reservoirs. We did learn, however, that the Trust's current financial situation was precarious. When the meeting finished, we had the opportunity to address the Trustees. I read a prepared statement to the meeting. It described the current wildlife interest of the reservoirs, including the 300+ species of flowering plants that had been recorded on the embankments and the spectacular diversity of rare waxcap fungi. We also made it clear that the reservoirs were important to the local community for recreational uses such as fly-fishing, sail training for children, and the general enjoyment of a tranquil and peaceful oasis within the city boundary. We described how damaging Western Power's development proposal would be to the wildlife interest and asked the Trustees to support RAG's alternative vision for the reservoirs as a Country Park. Our presentation was listened to in stony silence, and no questions were put to us at the end. The Chairman perfunctorily thanked us for our input, and that was that. Interestingly, the policy of allowing members to attend Trustees' meetings was stopped at the next meeting!

Although we didn't achieve much, we had alerted the Trustees directly to the potential damage that the development scheme at the reservoirs would do to biodiversity. They were also left in no doubt about the strength of feeling amongst many of the local Trust members.

Before we gave up on the Wildlife Trust, we had one last attempt. At the earlier meeting in January, we had asked why the Wildlife Trust had not consulted their local members to gauge their views before getting involved with the development. We were told that the reason was that there was no local members' group in Cardiff. As the Trust covers a large swathe of south and west Wales from Cardiff to Aberystwyth, local members groups had been set up across the area to provide an opportunity for members to meet. There were groups in Swansea, Bridgend, Carmarthenshire, Ceredigion, Pembrokeshire etc., but currently no such group in Cardiff, and therefore, they claimed, no one to consult. It occurred to us that perhaps we should set one up.

It took some time to organise over the summer and autumn of 2003, and the Trust were rightly wary of our motives, but they couldn't really refuse local members wanting to set up a local group. We did everything by the book and had our inaugural meeting on 6th January

Save our Reservoirs

2004 in Lisvane Memorial Hall. We even invited Derek Moore along to give the first talk! At least as the official Cardiff Group, we now had a platform within the Trust to try and persuade the Trustees to change their stance in supporting the reservoir project.

Derek Moore retired as Chief Executive of the Trust in 2004, and his deputy, Madeleine Havard, took over. Unfortunately, this did not lead to a change in policy. Throughout this period, the Cardiff Local Group took every opportunity to lobby against the Trust's involvement at the reservoirs, but it wasn't until 2009, when the Trust got into serious financial difficulties, that there was a real prospect of change. Madeleine Havard and many of the original Trustees resigned, and a new Chief Executive and Trustees took over. The new team, led by Sarah Kessell (Chief Executive) and Prof. Lynda Warren (Chair of Trustees), adopted a much more enlightened approach, and the Trust finally disassociated itself from the reservoir development.

Although Derek Moore retired from the Wildlife Trust in 2004, his involvement with Western Power and the reservoirs was not over. We can look forward to coming across him again.

Chapter 9

The Campaign Ramps Up (2003 - 2005)

After something of a digression into the discovery of the waxcaps and the role of the Wildlife Trust, it's time to return to the main story. In late December 2002, Western Power had just submitted its first planning application.

The early part of 2003 was, therefore, a busy time for the RAG Committee. Now that we knew exactly what Western Power was planning, we had something concrete to oppose.

Public Meeting at the Heath Hospital

Groups of us started going through the application documents in detail and planning our response. We also decided to hold a public meeting for our members so that we could brief them on the application and suggest points that they should make in letters of objection. RAG had over 1200 members by this stage, so we would need a pretty big venue. We explored several options and finally plumped for the 500-seat lecture theatre at the Heath Hospital, which is normally used for teaching medical students. We also booked an adjacent smaller lecture theatre with a video link in case not everyone could be accommodated in the main venue. The date was set for the evening of Tuesday, 28th January 2003.

The day before this meeting, we had another important breakthrough. On the 23rd January, the South Wales Echo published an article in which Western Power was asked to state its case for the development, and RAG was given the opportunity of presenting its arguments against. Both agreed. Then, the paper invited readers to participate in a 'phone poll' to indicate whether or not they supported Western Power's plans. Over 3,800 people responded to the poll, and 72% were against the development. On 27th January, on the strength of this result, the Echo threw its weight behind the RAG campaign. The Echo became a staunch supporter of our cause, and it is hard to overstate the influence that this had over the years.

On the evening of the public meeting, the main Lecture Theatre was packed (see Figure 9.1), and the smaller overflow lecture theatre also had to be used. We estimated that 700 people attended altogether.

Ted chaired the event and began by thanking the South Wales Echo for its recently declared support. He went on to introduce Ceri Davies, who described the proposed development and put it into the context of the local planning policies. He stressed the importance of members writing individually to the planning authority, listing their reasons against the development, and promised that RAG would shortly be circulating a guide to letter writing that would outline the most effective arguments to use. Next up, I described the importance of the site for biodiversity and argued that although the developers intended to create some new wetland habitats, the benefits arising from these would be massively outweighed by the harm caused by

Figure 9.1. The RAG meeting at the Heath Hospital. Photo courtesy of Media Wales/Reachplc.

bringing so many people to live on such a biologically sensitive area. Although the developers had tried to describe their scheme as a 'new nature reserve', this was a travesty of the truth.

The RAG contribution was followed by some of the local politicians. Jenny Randerson (AM for Cardiff Central) and Sue Essex (AM for Cardiff North) both expressed their opposition to the development. They urged protestors to write not only to Cardiff Council but also to other bodies such as the Countryside Council for Wales and the Water Regulator (OFWAT). They both expressed their delight that the campaign to save the reservoirs had ignited the enthusiasm and support of so many local people.

Chris Basten of the Welsh Yachting Association, Ivor Lippett of the Friends of Nant Fawr, and Cllr David Walker of Lisvane made further contributions, all expressing opposition to Western Power's plans.

The meeting was a great morale boost and provided a good start to our efforts to have the planning application turned down.

RAG's Response to the First Planning Application

Next, we produced two glossy reports in quick succession. The first was RAG's response to the planning application, which was submitted to the local planning authority, and pointed out how the proposed development ran counter to many of the Council's own planning policies, particularly those concerning open space, the river corridors and nature conservation. Many residents were also concerned about the proposed development's effects on local traffic, especially as the surrounding main roads were already choked with traffic during rush hours. However, the RAG planning group had already decided it would be best to steer clear of traffic issues and to focus on the Council's stated planning policies, as the Council's general view seemed to be that more traffic congestion would lead to more use of public transport, which they wanted to encourage.

The second report described RAG's alternative vision for the reservoirs, as we recognised the need to present a viable alternative to the housing development. Our plan was for the whole area to be developed as a country park. In the report, we laid out strategies for conservation, recreational use, management and finances. In all this, we were greatly aided by Ewart Parkinson, the former Director of Planning for South Glamorgan, who led the conversion of some abandoned limestone quarries to the current country park at Cosmeston on the outskirts of Penarth.

The Council's Response to the First Planning Application

Normally, when a planning application on the scale of Western Power's is submitted, the Planning Committee has a period of 16 weeks to decide on the application. However, the application at the reservoirs was unusually complex as it involved both an existing SSSI at Lisvane reservoir and a candidate SSSI in the case of the embankments and grassland fungi. Western Power's plans involved flattening the embankments around Llanishen, and using the resulting spoil to infill much of the reservoir, which would destroy a large part of the candidate SSSI. Furthermore, the whole reservoir issue had become something of a *cause célèbre* in North Cardiff and was a politically sensitive issue in a marginal seat. As a result, the Planning Committee failed to reach a decision within the 16-week period.

There were no significant developments over the spring and summer of 2003, but on 1st October, Western Power appealed to the Welsh Government over the non-determination of its planning application within the specified period. If the Welsh Government agreed, this would result in a public planning inquiry led by a planning inspector who would consider all the relevant evidence and make a recommendation to the Minister for Environment, Sustainability and Housing as to whether to accept or decline the appeal. The Minister would then have to decide whether or not to grant planning permission based on the inspector's recommendation.

However, on 5th November 2003, just a month after its appeal was lodged, Western Power surprised us all by submitting a second planning application. It had recognised that the waxcap fungi were going to be a major problem and that if the Countryside Council went as far as declaring an SSSI on the embankments, it was likely to scotch the chances of the first application altogether.

Bizarrely, the Council's Planning Committee met on 19th November to decide what decision they would have come to on the first application if they had made a decision within the statutory period. They determined that they would have refused the planning application on 12 separate grounds. The three major ones were based on: nature conservation issues; the effect of the development on sail training because the proposed sailing lake was so limited in size; and the suitability of bringing a significant amount of traffic from the development out onto a narrow part of the Lisvane Road. Interestingly, Western Power had addressed most of these issues in the second planning application, suggesting it was already aware of the Council's concerns.

The Second Planning Application

The second application was similar to the first but had a number of modifications to try and head off some of the criticisms levelled at the previous application.

The number of dwellings had been reduced from 346 to 326, and the resulting extra space was used to make the sailing lake slightly wider at its southern end (See Figure 9.2). The road arrangement had also been changed so that now all the houses on both the east and west sides of the reservoirs would access the site from Rhyd-y-penau Road. Only the apartments on the west side would have their access from Lisvane Road. The road and buildings on the west side had also been shifted in towards the lake so that some of the western embankments would remain intact. This was the area where the greatest concentration of waxcap fungi had been found, and Western Power apparently hoped it would be enough to placate the Countryside Council for Wales.

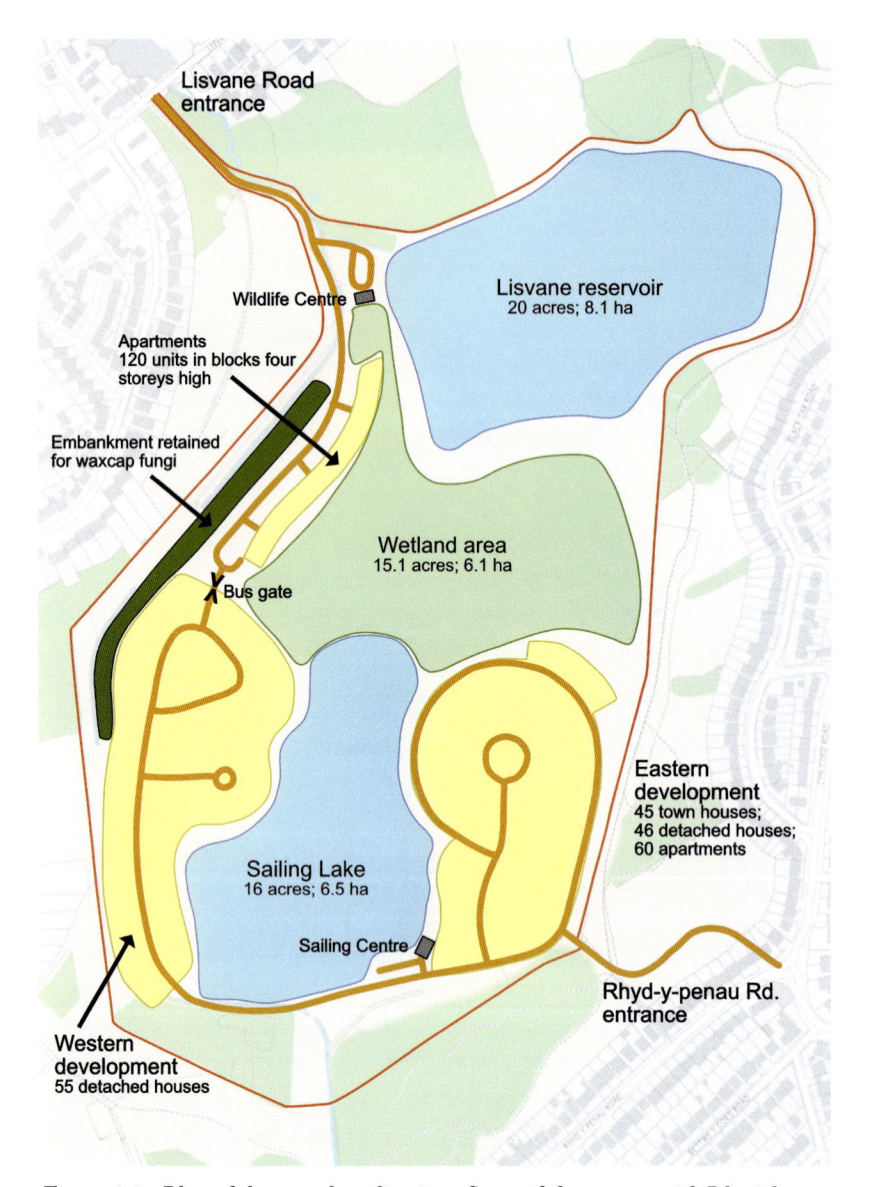

Figure 9.2. Plan of the second application. Some of the waxcap rich Llanishen embankments were retained (shown in dark green) by moving the western housing development eastwards. The sailing lake was also enlarged by slightly reducing the number of houses.

The second application put unwelcome pressure on RAG. At the time, we were concentrating on our response to the Council's new Unitary Development Plan, which had gone on deposit on 28th October. This important document spelt out the local authority's planning policies for 20 years from 2006. We wanted to ensure that the policies regarding the protection of the river corridors were strengthened and that the corridors were shown clearly on the proposals map. We also made a strong case for the part of the corridor around the reservoirs to be designated as a country park.

Once this document was out of the way, the RAG planning sub-group turned to the second application. Although the scheme had been tweaked a bit, our main objections to the first application still stood. The new application still ran counter to the Council's stated policies on open space, recreation, conservation, and the protection of the river corridors. Western Power was also now arguing that the reservoirs were a 'brownfield' site and should therefore be a priority for development. However, the RAG planning group pointed out that 'brownfield' land in Planning Policy Wales specifically excludes previously developed land later put to amenity use and land that has a high nature conservation value. We also pointed to many shortcomings in the Environmental Statement submitted by the developer. We submitted our response just before Christmas 2003.

Western Power Buys Llanishen Reservoir

The RAG campaign, I suspect, like many others, was typified by periods when not much happened, followed by periods of frantic activity. Two thousand and four started off quietly. The only notable event was that Western Power scored a significant own goal in April. One of their employees, a former ranger for Welsh Water, started going around the local primary schools offering to give talks about wildlife. Several schools accepted his offer, but the talks turned out to be a thinly disguised propaganda campaign for Western Power. In the sessions, Western Power's plans were presented and the children told that they would be good for wildlife. Reportedly, it was then suggested that the children should go home and encourage their parents to support

Save our Reservoirs

the development. Several parents contacted us, outraged that their children, some as young as nine, should be used in this way. When it came to the attention of the press, Western Power claimed that its representatives had been invited to go into the schools to talk about the development, but this was refuted by the head teacher of Coed Glas school in Llanishen, who had no idea the speaker was associated with the company.

Apart from this, not much happened until 11th October 2004 when Welsh Water sold the reservoirs to Western Power Distribution for £4 million. There were no immediate changes, but shortly afterwards, Western Power announced that both Llanishen and Lisvane reservoirs would be closed to the public from 1st January 2005.

It was lucky that the site did not close immediately, as 2004 turned out to be a bumper year for waxcap fungi, and we could still access the reservoirs during the crucial autumn period. By the end of the year, 28 species of waxcap had been found, indicating that the site was now one of international importance for grassland fungi and, therefore, much more likely to be designated as an SSSI (See Chapter 7).

Figure 9.3. The rally at the gates of the reservoirs.

The Campaign Ramps Up

Figure 9.4. Part of the crowd attending the rally at the gates.

On Thursday, 30th December 2004, RAG held a rally at the gates of the reservoir led by Ted Thurgood. It was attended by 300 residents and local politicians, including Julie Morgan MP (Cardiff North, Lab), Sue Essex AM (Cardiff North, Lab), Jon Owen Jones MP (Cardiff Central, Lab), Jenny Randerson AM (Cardiff Central, Lib-Dem) and Jonathan Morgan AM (South Wales Central, Con). The politicians all condemned Western Power's plans for developing the reservoirs and pledged their wholehearted support for the continuing RAG Campaign.

Western Power Takes Over

Western Power was true to its word. The gates to the reservoir shut on 1st January 2005, and it started to install a 1.8m high galvanised metal palisade fence around the perimeter of Llanishen reservoir. (Figure 9.5). What was once a lovely open vista came to look more like a prison camp. When challenged about the need for this, Western Power responded that its Health and Safety advisors had deemed it necessary to prevent the risk of people falling into the reservoir.

Figure 9.5. The fence erected around Llanishen reservoir.

Interestingly, it did not consider such a measure necessary for Lisvane reservoir, which has much steeper banks faced in smooth cement. The fence was only installed around Llanishen. Many people thought this was done purely out of spite, to spoil the reservoir's appearance.

Fishing also ended on 1st January, but sailing continued for the time being as Cardiff Council had a lease that gave them the right to run sailing courses on the reservoir. A month later, Lisvane reservoir was re-opened for public access, but Llanishen reservoir remained closed. At least closed in theory, as Western Power appeared to take a relaxed view of people trespassing on the site, and there were several gaps in the boundary fence. The reservoirs continued to attract many people, particularly dog walkers, who made the reservoir embankments a regular part of their daily walks.

Application to Cadw for Listing

In June 2005, one of our more enterprising members commenced a new line of attack against Western Power's plans. Andrew Hill had been a member of our planning group since its formation in 2001. By training, Andrew was an architect who specialised in historic buildings and structures. For 25 years, he was Historic Buildings Architect and Conservation Officer for Cardiff City Council and later Cardiff County Council. Naturally, Andrew was curious about the background of the Cardiff reservoirs and began to look into their history.

Andrew identified the importance of Lisvane and Llanishen reservoirs in providing a clean water supply to the growing town of Cardiff in the second half of the nineteenth century. He also recognised the significance of the plan devised in 1881 by Borough Engineer J.A.B. Williams to pipe water 32 miles from reservoirs in the Taf Fawr Valley of the Brecon Beacons to the new storage reservoir at Llanishen (See Chapter 1).

Andrew discovered that Cadw, the Welsh Government agency that protects Wales' historic environment, had listed the Cantref and Llwyn-on reservoir dams in the Beacons in 2002 as structures of historical importance because they were associated with the Victorian water supply scheme to Cardiff. He wondered why, if these components of the project had been listed, had Llanishen reservoir been ignored, as it was an integral part of the same system.

Andrew's concern about Llanishen and Lisvane reservoirs stemmed from the imminent threat from Western Power's planning application, which would involve bulldozing the embankments of Llanishen reservoir to accommodate its housing development. He also knew that a Cadw listing should not only protect the reservoir structure itself from damage but also its 'setting'. A good argument could be made for the 'setting' of the reservoir being one that involved water rather than houses! If achieved, a listing could mean the end of Western Power's scheme to develop the site.

On 21st June 2005, Andrew arranged for Dr Stuart Owen-Jones, a well-known expert on Wales' industrial heritage and former Director of the Welsh Industrial and Maritime Museum, to submit a request to Cadw that Lisvane and Llanishen reservoirs should be listed. Andrew wrote a letter in support and arranged for various local historians, architects, engineers and town planners to send letters as well.

One of the most significant was from Denys Morgan, the Wales Manager of the Institution of Civil Engineers. He pointed out that while the dams in the Brecon Beacons looked impressive because of their height, they were actually quite short in length, simply damming up the lower end of a steep-sided valley. Llanishen, on the other hand, was encircled by a continuous clay-cored earth dam, 1.3 kilometres long, which was the longest embankment dam in Wales.

Unfortunately, Cadw was not impressed. It sent its decision back on 8th November 2005. It did not consider that Llanishen and Lisvane reservoirs met the criteria to be listed. It argued that Llanishen and Lisvane reservoirs were mainly functional in character and had no special architectural interest, such as eye-catching valve towers, monumental retaining walls or architectural masonry detailing. Therefore, they could not be classed as having 'special interest'. It pointed out that a great number of civic buildings were erected in the Victorian era and that only buildings of outstanding character and quality were listed. In its opinion, Llanishen and Lisvane did not pass this test. This was disappointing, but Andrew was still convinced that the reservoirs merited listing because of their significance in the history of Cardiff.

Chapter 10

Waxcap Fungi (Part 2)

In March 2003, the Countryside Council for Wales (CCW) had put the embankments of both Lisvane and Llanishen reservoirs on a list of candidate Sites of Special Scientific Interest (SSSIs). However, before they formally notified the site, they wanted further surveys in the autumn of 2003 to confirm that it was indeed a site of national importance for grassland fungi.

Unfortunately, the 2003 field season turned out to be a disaster. The previous year was, by all accounts, a poor one for fungi, but 2003 was even worse. September and October were very dry, and shortly after it finally rained, there was a series of hard frosts. At the reservoirs, although we found a few of the species from the previous year, only one new one turned up, a rather small, orangey species called *Hygrocybe mucronella*, whose main characteristic is its bitter taste. We now had 18 waxcap species recorded at the site, but this was not enough to persuade the CCW to proceed with the SSSI notification. We would have to wait another year, which increased the risk that Western Power would receive approval for its development plans before we had a full appreciation of the importance of the embankments for fungi.

Fortunately, this did not happen, and the autumn of 2004 was worth the wait. It was generally mild and wet throughout September and October, with no hard frosts until the middle of December. Fungi began appearing everywhere, in enormous quantities. I was keen to get Ray Woods, the CCW's fungi expert, to visit the site and see it for himself. I took advantage of the fact that he was due to give a talk on grassland fungi on the morning of Friday, 5th December, to ecology students at Cardiff University. That afternoon, in conjunction with my colleague Fred Slater, we managed to get him to run a practical session for the students up at the reservoirs. When we got there, Ray strode around, reeling off the names of fungi as he went while the rest of us struggled to keep up with him. We managed to identify four new species at the reservoirs that afternoon. I think the sheer number and variety of fungi impressed Ray, and he was very animated on our way back to the university.

The following week I found another two new waxcap species, bringing us to a total of 24 waxcaps and 48 points on the McHugh et al. scoring system. Both of these indicators pointed to the fact that we were now looking at a site of international rather than national importance. I really hoped that this, along with Ray's now evident support, would finally persuade the CCW to go ahead and notify the SSSI.

Early in March 2005, the news got even better. Western Power published an addendum to its Environmental Statement, which included details of the fungal survey carried out in the autumn of 2004 by Roy Perry and Peter Sturgess. As well as confirming the 24 species we had found, they had an additional four species, bringing the grand total of waxcaps to 28 and a grassland fungi score of 60. The evidence for this being an internationally important site now seemed incontrovertible.

The first indication that the CCW was finally going to act came late in April 2005 when it lodged a formal objection to Western Power's second planning application. During the autumn of 2004, the CCW had evidently commissioned surveys to be undertaken at a number of other sites throughout Wales, which enabled the relative importance of the reservoirs to be assessed with more accuracy. On the basis of this, it had recognised that Llanishen and Lisvane Reservoir embankments ranked as the sixth most important site for grassland fungi in Wales and the best site in the former county of Glamorgan. Therefore it decided to progress with designating the embankments as an SSSI. It finished by saying it hoped to be in a position to notify the SSSI within the next month and had already contacted the owners about the implications of this designation. Hooray!

In practice, one month stretched out to five, and it wasn't until 26th September 2005 that the SSSI notification was finally announced. This was a major step forward in our campaign to save the reservoirs. However, the SSSI status wasn't a completely done deal yet. Western Power had until 6th January to lodge objections to the designation, and these would be considered along with the case for notification at the next meeting of the CCW's Council in Cardiff, which wasn't scheduled until 6th February 2006. Western Power would be able to attend this meeting and make representations to the Council members directly. However, the meetings were also open to the public, and although we wouldn't be able to speak ourselves, at least we could go and observe the proceedings.

The autumn of 2005 was frustrating as I wanted to go and look for more fungi, but the reservoirs were now owned by Western Power and had been closed to the public. Although there were plenty of unofficial entrances in the surrounding fence, I didn't think it would be good publicity for RAG's Vice-Chairman to be caught trespassing! Instead, I busied myself thinking about how I could help ensure that the SSSI notification was confirmed at the forthcoming CCW Council meeting. I decided to try and get support for the SSSI designation from well-regarded fungi experts or mycologists. I wrote to all the members of the Conservation Committee of the British Mycological Society, to the President and Conservation Officer of the European Mycological Society, and to some of the leading grassland fungi experts at British universities. I explained the situation at the reservoirs and asked them to write to the CCW to support its decision to notify the reservoirs as an SSSI. Eight of them wrote letters of support to the CCW, and I received encouraging replies from Peter Marren, David Boertmann, Professor Bruce Ing, and Dr David Minter, amongst others.

There was a final interesting twist before the meeting. Western Power made more or less continuous Freedom of Information requests to the CCW and got access to any correspondence that the latter had received regarding the reservoirs. This included the letters of support written by the mycologists. At the end of January 2006, Mr Charl Oosthuizen, the Finance Director of Western Power, wrote personally to each of these scientists and asked them to withdraw their letters of support. He claimed that it was untrue that Western Power's development plans would destroy the waxcap habitat and that they would create lots of new habitats to encourage biodiversity, which the Wildlife Trust would manage. He made no mention of the 326 houses and apartments that would be built on the site, along with roads and other infrastructure. Fortunately, most of the mycologists emailed me on receipt of this letter, and I was able to explain exactly what Western Power was planning. I don't know of any that retracted their letters.

The Countryside Council for Wales Meeting

CCW Council meetings are normally fairly staid affairs, attended by the Council Members themselves, a few CCW staff, and one or two interested members of the public. They are held throughout Wales, usually in small village halls or local leisure centres. The Cardiff meeting on 6th February 2006 was quite different. The CCW had booked a large ground-floor meeting room in the plush MacDonald Holland House Hotel in Newport Road. There was a large group of tables pushed together in the middle of the room, around which sat the CCW Council members, a number of senior CCW staff, and a team from Western Power. The rest of us, who were merely observers, sat on one side of the room. There was only one item on the agenda: the confirmation of Llanishen and Lisvane reservoir embankments as a Site of Special Scientific Interest.

The Chairman of the CCW, John Lloyd-Jones, opened the meeting and stated that the representatives of the developers would be able to give an oral presentation and that normally the time allowed for this was ten minutes. However, the developers had asked that they be allowed to speak for up to one hour. Given the sensitivity of the issue, he agreed to this request. First, the CCW Officers would be asked to present their case, followed by the representatives of Western Power. After each presentation, Council members would be able to ask questions. There would then be a general discussion between Council members, after which they would have the opportunity to go back to either side for clarification. Finally, the Council would come to a

Waxcaps (Part 2)

decision as to whether or not to confirm the SSSI designation. The Chairman also stated that the meeting would be recorded.

It appeared that they were being careful to do everything by the book and to give Western Power no grounds to appeal afterwards if the decision did not go its way.

Jessica Poole, a Senior Conservation Officer, led the presentation for the CCW, supported by Ray Woods for his specialist knowledge of grassland fungi. They made the case with which we are already well acquainted, namely that 28 species of waxcap fungi had been found on the embankments and that the site had a 'modified McHugh grassland fungi score' of 60, compared to the normal minimum of 30 points usually used for SSSI designation. Jessica then dealt with a number of points that Western Power had raised in objection to the notification of the site. After her presentation concluded, the Council Members asked a large number of technical questions about the assessment of waxcap sites that were mainly dealt with by Ray Woods. Ray made the point that it was not the scarcity of any particular species found at the reservoirs that was important but the extraordinary diversity of waxcap fungi on such a small site.

Next, it was the turn of Western Power. Its case was presented by Mr John Steel QC, a leading London barrister whom we would come to know well over the next few years. John Steel was urbane, suave, experienced, and, no doubt, expensive. He was supported by another barrister, Mr Robert Palmer, and by Mr Charles Felgate, the instructing solicitor from Geldards LLP. They also had with them Mr Peter Waldren from RPS Planners, one of the largest Planning Consultancies in the UK, and Dr Charles Gibson, Managing Director of Bioscan, the ecological consultants used by Western Power. So, all-in-all, a pretty high-powered team.

Mr Steel's arguments against the notification of the SSSI centred around three main points:

- First, he criticised the scoring system used to assess the quality of grassland fungi sites and the fact that it did not take into account the number of times a site had been visited. He pointed out that there had been a large number of fungal surveys done at the reservoirs over the last four years and that, inevitably, more species were likely to be found there than at sites visited less frequently. He pointed to a site at Rhyd-y-car near Merthyr, where waxcaps had recently been discovered and 24 species found on the first visit. He went on to complain that the CCW hadn't been very cooperative in helping to identify other good waxcaps sites and argued that there were probably sites much better than Llanishen and Lisvane but that it was just a case of there having been insufficient attempts to find them. Therefore, he was arguing that the reservoirs shouldn't be notified, even though they had a high diversity of waxcaps, because there might just be better sites elsewhere. (Mind you, if this were a good reason, many SSSIs would probably never have been declared!)

- His next line of attack was to argue that factors other than the overall diversity of fungi seemed to be taken into account when declaring a site as an SSSI for grassland fungi and that one of these factors was whether the CCW thought the owner was sympathetic to conserving the fungi. For example, the Mynydd Epynt in the Brecon Beacons had not been declared an SSSI but was on land owned by the Ministry of Defence. Another, Llanerchaeron in Ceredigion, was owned by the National Trust, and a third, at Gilfach Farm in Radnorshire, was owned by the Radnorshire Wildlife Trust. He implied that the site at Llanishen and Lisvane was being treated as a special case by the CCW as it was seen as at potential risk from development.

- The final point he made was that the northern and eastern embankments of the reservoirs had lower densities of waxcaps and, therefore, shouldn't be included in the area covered by any SSSI designation.

The members of the CCW Council proceeded to ask a number of questions of clarification, which were fielded by Mr Steel and his ecologist, Dr Gibson. One of the issues that was picked up by the

Council members was to do with the mowing of the embankments. During Welsh Water's ownership of the reservoirs, the embankments had been mown at least twice and often three times a year. However, since Western Power took over management of the site in January 2005, the embankments hadn't been mown at all. This was likely to have a detrimental effect on the waxcaps because, as already mentioned, they prosper on sites where the grass is grazed and kept short. The implication was that Western Power was making the embankments less suitable for waxcaps to flourish. Its representatives could not explain why this change in management had occurred. The discussion also focused again on the scoring system for waxcap fungi that had been used and whether it represented the best way of assessing the quality of a site, and whether other sites of equal or better quality might become apparent with time. Ray Woods stated quite categorically that even if they did, he still thought this site warranted its designation as an SSSI and that if better sites were eventually found, he would argue for them to be designated as well.

By now, the meeting had lasted over four hours, and the Chairman had to bring it to a close and decide whether to notify the site on the basis of the evidence heard. Each of the Council members was asked to express their views, and their unanimous decision was that the reservoir embankments should be designated as an SSSI with the proposed boundaries unaltered.

Result! We now had a second SSSI registered on the site and one that would prevent Western Power from building on the embankments, as there is a presumption in Welsh Planning Policy against any development proposals that would damage an SSSI. Afterwards, the RAG members present held an impromptu celebration on the veranda of the Holland House Hotel, which was duly reported by the South Wales Echo the following evening (see Figure 10.1).

But that was not quite the end of the waxcap story. As we were to discover repeatedly, Western Power did not take well to its plans being thwarted. Although the CCW had taken all the correct steps in notifying the SSSI and had given Western Power an extended opportunity to present its case at the Council meeting on 6th February, Western

Figure 10.1. RAG members celebrate the declaration of the SSSI outside the MacDonald Holland House Hotel after the CCW Council meeting. Photo courtesy of Media Wales/Reachplc.

Power was not prepared to accept the decision and challenged it in the High Court in London. The case was heard ten months later on the 13th & 14th December 2006, with Mr Justice Collins presiding. Again Mr John Steel QC and Mr Robert Palmer presented the case for Western Power, while Mr John Howell QC and Mrs Jane Collier represented the Countryside Council for Wales.

John Steel raised the same objections as he did at the Council meeting, namely that the CCW had shown a failure to try and identify alternative sites in South Wales that might be better than Llanishen and that they had notified the site, in part because it was under threat from development. In his detailed judgement, which was delivered on 26th January 2007, Justice Collins rejected this claim and concluded that the CCW had acted entirely within the law. The notification of the reservoir embankments as an SSSI for grassland fungi would remain, and there was nothing further that Western Power could do about it.

Chapter 11

The Third and Fourth Planning Applications

Western Power had anticipated that the Embankments SSSI would be confirmed at the Countryside Council for Wales meeting in February 2006. Shortly after the SSSI had first been notified the previous September, it withdrew its first application, which would have resulted in the complete destruction of the embankments around Llanishen reservoir. This left only the second application, which spared one section of the embankments. However, the developers were obviously concerned that this would not be enough to satisfy the CCW and had been working on two new applications.

The Third Application

On 13th April 2006, Western Power submitted its third planning application. This spared most of the embankments around Llanishen reservoir apart from a small section of the east embankment where waxcap density was lowest. The rest of the development was sunk down in the reservoir bowl surrounded by the remaining embankments. The developers planned to pierce the embankments in two places for road access but claimed that these access points and the limited amount of building would only damage 9% of the SSSI.

The Fourth Application

Clearly, they doubted that they would even get away with this, and one month later, on 12th May, Western Power submitted a fourth applica-

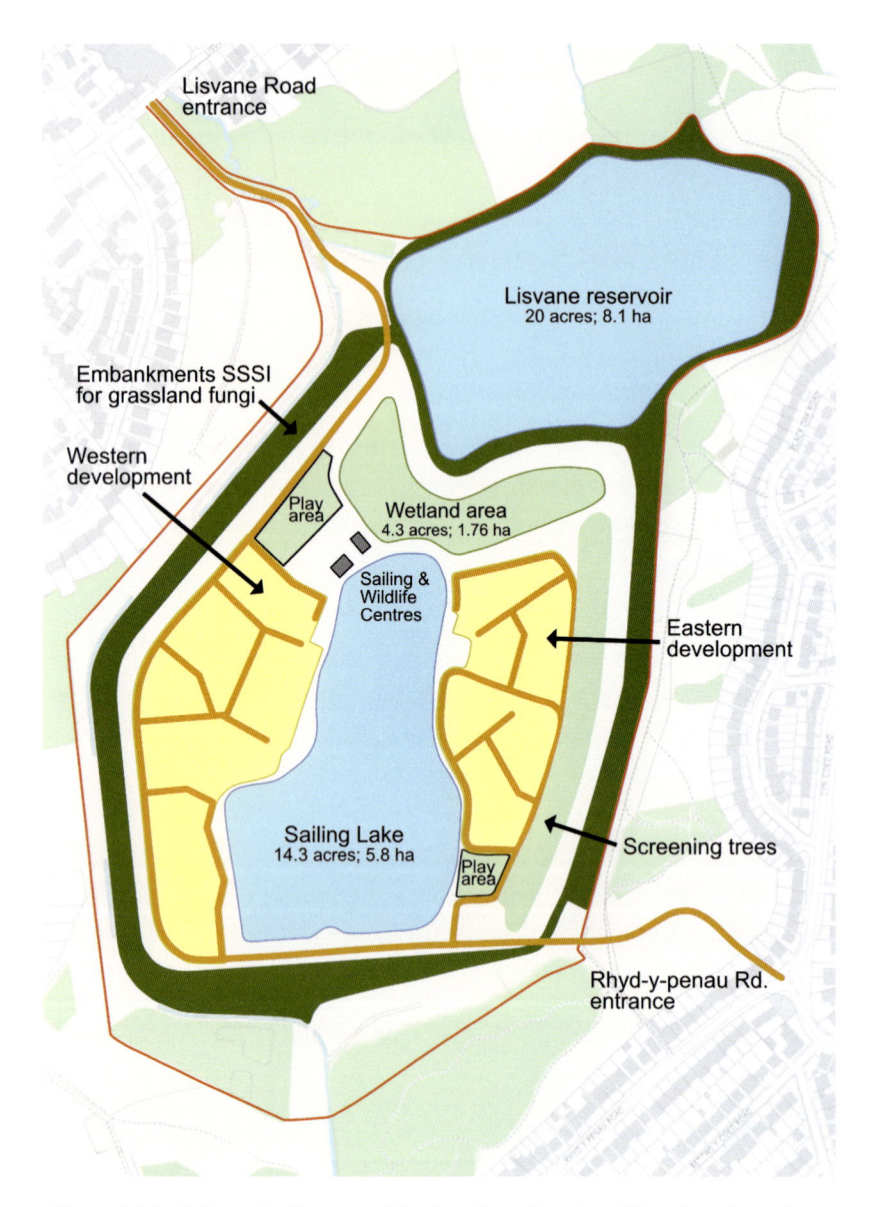

Figure 11.1. Schematic diagram of the fourth application. Note that the majority of the embankments with their grassland fungi, shown in dark green, are left intact and the wetland area has been much reduced in size.

tion which had the whole development within the reservoir bowl with only the two access roads cutting through the embankments. (See Figure 11.1). Although the houses and flats would be sunken in the bowl, there were still 161 detached houses, 97 apartments and 66 town houses. As a result, the wetland area had been drastically reduced in size to just 4.3 acres, and the sailing lake was slightly smaller at 14.3 acres. The Sailing and Wildlife Centres had been amalgamated into one area, which was now on the western side, and a children's play area had been included. Western Power claimed that this scheme would destroy only 1% of the Embankments SSSI.

In this first iteration of the fourth application, it was envisaged that all the residential properties and the sailing centre would be accessed from the Rhyd-y-penau side and that only emergency vehicles and buses would have access from Lisvane Road. However, by the time the application finally reached a public inquiry, there were two additional access options being touted: one was for all the access to be from the Lisvane side; the other was for the use of both sides.

Responses to the New Applications

Although the fourth application was less disastrous in terms of its effects on the Embankments SSSI, most of our objections still stood: principally the impact of the development on the integrity of the Nant Fawr river corridor and the disturbance to wildlife by bringing c900 people to live in the middle of a site of such biodiversity sensitivity. It was also hard to imagine that people would find it enticing to live in a bowl surrounded by high embankments. The sailing lake would be sheltered from the prevailing wind, and there was the possibility of an increased risk of flooding when extreme rainfall events occurred.

At the time, we were rather thrown by the arrival of these two new applications as we were putting most of our effort into preparing for the long-awaited public inquiry on the second application, which was due to open on 31st October 2006. RAG asked the Welsh Planning Inspectorate to 'call in' both these new applications and hold one public inquiry to deal with all three applications together as it would be more efficient. While waiting for their decision, we learned that Western Power was seeking to challenge the SSSI designation by the CCW and that a Judicial Review at the High Court in London had been set for mid-December 2006. We wrote to the Inspectorate again and asked them to delay the inquiry until the outcome of the Judicial Review was known. They said they could not do this without the permission of Western Power.

Then, in late August, to everyone's surprise, Western Power itself appealed to the Welsh Assembly for 'non-determination' of the third application on the grounds that the Council Planning Committee had again failed to reach a decision within the prescribed 16-week period. This finally triggered the Inspectorate to cancel the October public inquiry so that a later inquiry could deal with all three applications together. Both Cardiff Council and RAG were pleased with this outcome, believing it was in everybody's interests to deal with all the applications together, but Western Power took a different view.

Shortly after it learned of the cancellation of the inquiry, its solicitors wrote to the Planning Inspectorate stating that Western Power was entitled to continue with October's inquiry on the second application, as scheduled. Again, they resorted to the High Court and asked it to review the Inspectorate's decision to cancel the public inquiry on the second application. The outcome was that the parties agreed to reinstate the inquiry for the 31st October. Within days, Western Power withdrew the third application. So at this stage, we were left with two applications. Number two, which was going to be dealt with at the October inquiry and the fourth application, which would be likely to go to another inquiry in due course.

We thought this strategy by Western Power was a deliberate policy to wage a war of attrition against us. They knew that getting professional representation at these inquiries by lawyers and expert witnesses was expensive, and we believed that they hoped to exhaust our financial resources and our will to continue. We were equally determined that this was not going to happen.

Chapter 12

The First Planning Inquiry

Despite our attempts to get it postponed, the first planning inquiry remained scheduled for 31st October 2006. A pre-inquiry meeting was held on 21st March 2006 to agree on various procedural issues. RAG had indicated that it wanted to be one of the main participants at the inquiry (known as 'Rule 6' status) and that we would be represented by a barrister, who would intend to cross-examine other parties. Fortunately, we were able to engage the services of Nick Cooke QC, who was sympathetic to our cause and kindly agreed to represent us at a reduced fee. Still, Queen's Counsels are expensive, and it would stretch RAG's financial resources to the limit. Thus the main participants in the inquiry were Western Power, Cardiff Council and ourselves.

The first Planning Inquiry opened as expected on 31st October and was held in an upstairs room in the Old Library Building on the Hayes, in the middle of Cardiff. Mr Alwyn Nixon was appointed as the Planning Inspector to conduct the inquiry.

Let me try and set the scene. The Old Library is an imposing Victorian building built in 1884, about the same time as Llanishen reservoir. The main rooms upstairs are spacious, tall and elegant. The inspector sat on his own at one end of the room with the windows behind him, facing the seating where members of the public could observe the proceedings.

On his right sat the Western Power 'team', which consisted of John Steel QC, Robert Palmer (Junior Counsel), usually at least two partners of the instructing solicitors Geldards, and finally, a couple of legal clerks, whose job it was to scurry around and provide Mr Steel with whatever document he required from their voluminous library of evidence (155 separate documents and reports).

On the inspector's left, at one table, sat the Council's legal representatives, namely Mr Mark Lowe QC and two senior staff members from the Council's legal department. As they only submitted 11 documents in evidence, they could cope with these on their own.

Also on the inspector's left, at another table, sat the RAG team, which consisted of Nicholas Cooke QC, Mike Sant from Harmer Town Planning Consultants, who were instructing the barrister, and Ted Thurgood. RAG submitted eight documents to support its case.

Behind the inspector was a low bookcase containing copies of all the documents submitted by the three parties presenting evidence. Surprisingly, Mr Nixon did not have an assistant to help him find documents. In fact, he had no help whatsoever, not even a secretary to take notes. He had to manage the inquiry, keep order, rule on various legal arguments, find the correct documents from the library behind him, and follow all the points being made whilst at the same time taking detailed notes of all that went on. It was like a court case where the judge, court officials and jury were all rolled into one person. He dealt with it all with a calm assurance, and from the outset, I was impressed that he could manage things so effectively on his own.

I warmed to him even more during the long lunch breaks. When these happened, Western Power's legal team would head off to one of Cardiff's up-market restaurants. While they trooped off, Mr Nixon would open his briefcase, take out a lunch box with his sandwiches along with a Thermos flask, and sit at his desk eating his lunch while reviewing the evidence that had been presented that morning.

Overall the inquiry lasted for 12 days, and much time was spent debating various, often rather obscure, points of planning law. If I were to give a full account of all the arguments, this would end up being a long and boring chapter. Instead, I will try to give a brief flavour of the main points made by each side.

The Case Made by Western Power

At the outset, Western Power's representatives tried to portray the reservoirs as underused and redundant. They claimed that they had been forced to close the site to the public on safety and security grounds and that if planning permission were refused, it would have to remain closed until some other use for it could be found. Alternatively, if the development were allowed to proceed, the areas not used for housing would be reopened as a public open space to benefit the local community. Sail training would be re-introduced on the remaining lake, and there would be areas of woodland and recreational space to which the public would have access. They argued that the Llanishen and Lisvane electoral wards had a shortfall of open space and that this would therefore be an advantage in planning terms. In other words, they ignored the fact that the reservoirs had been open to walkers, sailors and fishermen under the permit system administered by Welsh Water for over 25 years and presented the proposed development, with its 326 houses and flats, as being a net gain of open space for the local community!

Western Power relied on the evidence of six expert witnesses who gave evidence on a range of things from planning law, transport, tourism, and biodiversity. Not surprisingly, they all came out strongly in favour of the proposed development. For example, Professor Terry Stevens argued that the proposed development would encourage more use of Cardiff Bay for sailing and that the reduced lake at Llanishen would have better facilities for beginners and intermediate sailors. Despite the residual lake being a quarter of the size of Llanishen reservoir and hemmed in by housing on two sides, he concluded that the proposal would significantly enhance the recreational and amenity opportunities of the local area. Mr Brian Denny thought the development would improve the visual amenity of the site and its surroundings. [Perhaps by replacing a boring expanse of water with a nice new housing estate to look around?] Dr Charles Gibson suggested that the development proposals sought to minimise the harm to biodiversity and to maximise the benefits that might be achieved. Whilst acknowledging that the development would extend over the majority of the Llanishen embankments and destroy almost half of the Embankments SSSI for grassland fungi, he still seemed to think this would benefit biodiversity because the remaining areas would be better managed. He also claimed that turves from the flattened Llanishen embankments could be moved elsewhere, along with the waxcaps, although he admitted that there was no evidence that waxcaps could be relocated in this way. Both Dr Gibson and Mr Steel proposed that potential harm to the grassland fungi SSSI could be compensated by improvements made to the Lisvane reservoir SSSI for over-wintering wildfowl.

The Case Made by Cardiff Council

The Council based their objections to the planning application on two main points. The first was the harm that the development would cause to the grassland fungi and the Embankments SSSI; the second was the harm to amenity and open space. They called two expert witnesses to support their claims.

The first was Ray Woods, who had previously presented the case for declaring an SSSI at the CCW Council meeting. Since then, Ray had retired from the CCW and now worked for the conservation charity Plantlife. Ray began by again reviewing the evidence for the importance of the Embankments SSSI for grassland fungi in both a national and international context. He argued that destroying 47% of the embankments, including the parts with the highest fungal diversity, would cause the SSSI irreparable harm. Planning Policy Wales, the document that sets out national planning policy guidelines, emphasises the importance of protecting and enhancing biodiversity. As it includes a presumption against developments likely to damage an SSSI, he argued that this was completely unacceptable.

Ray also commented on Western Power's plans for mitigation of the fungi. He pointed out that there is absolutely no evidence from other studies that moving waxcaps to other sites would be successful and that it was 'entirely speculative'. Although Western Power had claimed that the rest of the embankments SSSI would be better managed if the development went ahead, Ray pointed out that the fungi seemed to be thriving under the previous management by Welsh

Water. There was no evidence to suggest that any alternative management regime would be any better.

In response to Dr Gibson's claims, Ray did not accept the argument that improvements to one SSSI could be set against harm caused to another. He thought that Western Power's proposals were unlikely to significantly benefit the populations of diving ducks that used the Lisvane reservoir SSSI. Although the numbers had decreased in recent years, he argued that this was not due to poor management of the SSSI but to national trends in the overwintering behaviour of many species of ducks. With a run of mild winters, they were staying more on the eastern side of the UK and not migrating so far west.

After giving his evidence, Ray was subjected to lengthy and, at times, rather hostile cross-examination by Mr Steel. Apart from challenging his credibility, Mr Steel tried to bring into question almost all his evidence, but Ray was an old hand at public inquiries and stood his ground. He ended up giving evidence for well over a day and a half, which must have been exhausting.

The Council's second witness was Mr Malcolm Hockaday, who was a planning consultant. He argued that the proposal would result in an unacceptable loss of amenity and open space. Much of his case centred on the importance of the river corridors in the context of Cardiff's Planning policy and that the reservoirs were an integral part of the Nant Fawr river corridor. Although a developer can offer compensatory open space, Mr Hockaday suggested that the land being lost had high nature conservation value and could not be easily replaced. Not surprisingly, Mr Steel contested this view and argued that the reservoirs were not part of the river corridor and that their scheme would lead to more accessible open space for the local community. His cross-examination of Mr Hockaday was again lengthy and spent much time dwelling on the status of the reservoir area and whether it was countryside or within the urban boundary, and therefore which planning policies might apply.

The Case Made by the Reservoir Action Group

RAG generally avoided going over the ground already covered by the Council and its witnesses, particularly regarding the Embankments SSSI. Instead, our barrister Nick Cooke QC, aided by planning consultants Mike Sant and Nigel Evers, again stressed the importance of the reservoirs in the context of the Nant Fawr river corridor and its importance in linking the heart of Cardiff with the rural countryside on the edge of the city. They also dismissed the claims made by Western Power that the reservoirs should be considered as 'previously developed land', which would make them a prime target for re-development. The RAG team pointed out that Llanishen reservoir had been used for amenity and recreational purposes, such as sailing and fishing, for the last thirty years. They pointed out that Planning Policy Wales considers developed land that has been put to amenity use is no longer classified as 'previously developed'. On Western Power's claim that it would be opening new land for public use, RAG argued that Western Power had itself restricted access after taking over the site and was now trying to claim the benefit of opening up part of it to the public again. In conclusion, RAG's case was that Western Power's proposed development conflicted with both national and local planning policy and that the appeal should be dismissed.

Other Interested Parties

Several other private individuals had also indicated that they wanted to provide oral evidence to the planning inquiry.

First up was local resident Ewart Parkinson, the former Director of Environment and Planning for South Glamorgan County Council. His main point was to reinforce the arguments that had already been made regarding the importance of the four wildlife recreational and open space corridors for the benefit they brought to the everyday life of Cardiff citizens and to the city's natural heritage. As the person who had originally developed these policies, Ewart spoke authoritatively about them and suggested future ways the reservoirs could be developed more sympathetically to benefit the city.

The First Planning Inquiry

Geraint Evans spoke on behalf of the Sailing School at Llanishen reservoir and spoke of its success in training young people to sail. Geraint paid credit to the centre's staff but also described how the physical attributes of the reservoir were important to its success: its excellent water quality, its depth, its size and its lack of wind shadows (i.e. the deflection of the wind by surrounding buildings and other physical obstacles). All of these attributes would be lost were the development to go ahead.

Mr Chris Basten, who appeared on behalf of the Welsh Yachting Association, amplified many of these points. He talked about the importance of the Llanishen Sailing Centre to the sport in Wales and how the suggested alternative in Cardiff Bay would not provide such good facilities, especially for those learning to sail. The water quality in the Bay was a particular concern.

Graham Good spoke on behalf of the Friends of Nant Fawr and talked about the damage that would be done by the proposed access road across Nant Fawr meadows, especially to wildlife and the integrity of the Nant Fawr green corridor.

Fred Davies spoke as President of the Cardiff Reservoirs Fly Fishing Club and as someone who had fished Llanishen reservoir for over 40 years. Fred's evidence was succinct and focused on the loss of recreational space for the fishermen. In his cross-examination, Mr Steel suggested that the residual lake in their development plans would make a good substitute for Llanishen reservoir, but Fred was having none of it. Whilst Steel was rather patronising in his manner, Fred adopted a series of dry, laconic replies, some of which provoked laughter amongst the audience. Fred showed that Mr Steel appeared to have little appreciation of fly fishing, the process of back-casting and the space it required. He sat down to a round of applause from the public seats.

The final person to speak was Justin Cooper, a resident who was also a transport planner. Justin spoke in detail about the proposed access road across the meadows and the effect on traffic flow on the roundabout at the top of Rhyd-y-penau Road. He thought this would cause delays and more traffic build-up at the junction, which would have an unrecognised cost due to increased travel times.

There were also many written objections from organisations that opposed the development. These included many local politicians, Sports Council Wales, the National Playing Fields Association, the Ramblers Association, the Lisvane Graig Protection Society, and the Victorian Society. In addition, several hundred letters and emails of objection were received from local residents, with only three letters of support in favour of the development. The only organisation to come out in support was the Wildlife Trust of South and West Wales.

Towards the end of the inquiry, each of the main parties made their closing statements. These went in the order of Cardiff Council, RAG and then finally Western Power. In each case, these mainly repeated the key arguments that had already been made, but Western Power pulled a stunt that seemed to annoy the inspector. On the last day of the inquiry, one of their representatives sent an email stating that if planning permission were refused, then the only viable option would be for the reservoir to be drained down. The inspector objected to this being introduced right at the end of the inquiry when there was no opportunity for the barristers representing the Council and RAG to cross-examine the proposition, and he suggested that it was simply 'more tactical posturing'.

The Inspector's Report

The inquiry closed on 21st November, and then we had to sit back and wait for the inspector's report and his decision on the appeal. If he decided in favour of Western Power's appeal, then effectively planning permission would be granted, and the development would be likely to go ahead. If he recommended rejection of the appeal, then it would not. I say 'likely' because the planning inspector's decision was not final. His recommendation would be passed to the Welsh Government Minister for Environment, Sustainability and Housing, who would make the final decision. However, it would be unusual for the Minister to reject the recommendation of a planning inspector.

Mr Nixon produced his report on 19th March 2007. From considering all the evidence, he concluded that:

- The reservoirs were not part of the countryside but were part of the urban area. This was important because it affected which planning policies applied to the land.
- That the entire reservoir, including its water area, qualified as open space under the local plan.
- That Llanishen reservoir did not constitute previously developed land.
- That the proposed development would cause serious harm to the Llanishen and Lisvane Embankments SSSI.
- That any benefits to the Lisvane reservoir SSSI for overwintering birds would not outweigh the harm caused to the Embankments SSSI and their grassland fungi.
- That Llanishen reservoir formed a key part of the Nant Fawr open space corridor and that any development within it would harm the character of the Nant Fawr open space corridor.
- That the proposed development would have a significant detrimental effect on the range of activities provided by the Llanishen Sailing Centre.
- That the intended development would cause harm to the public amenity of the existing site, which would not be offset by the various compensatory measures and the improvements proposed under the Section 106 agreement.
- That the development proposals did not accord with the Local Development Plan of Cardiff Council.

In overall conclusion, the inspector recommended that planning permission should not be granted and that Western Power's appeal should be dismissed.

This result was clearly all that we had hoped for, but we still had to wait for the Minister's final decision. Typically, the Welsh Government did not move quickly, and we had to wait until 16th August 2007 for the

Minister's pronouncement. Given Mr Nixon's damning report, we were hopeful, but it was still a relief when the Minister, Jane Davidson, agreed with his conclusions and dismissed the appeal. This time we had won, but we still had Western Power's Fourth Application to deal with and no doubt they would be better prepared next time.

Chapter 13

The Village Green Application

Andrew Hill, who had previously tried to get the reservoirs listed as historic buildings by Cadw, was nothing if not resourceful. He lived on Berrymead Road, and his garden backed onto the Nant Fawr woodlands, just where the bridge passes over the Nant Fawr stream. He and his partner Mary had several dogs that they used to walk through the woods and across the fields beside the reservoirs. There is a great camaraderie among dog walkers, which meant that Andrew and Mary were well known to those who regularly used the woodlands and meadows for this purpose.

A key component of Western Power's plans for the reservoir was an access road that would enter the reservoir site from the roundabout at the top of Rhyd-y-penau Road, where it meets Cyncoed Road. One of the first things Western Power had done after acquiring the site was to purchase three houses beside the roundabout that backed onto the meadows, reportedly by offering the owners twice the normal selling price. It planned to demolish these houses to provide access for the road across the meadows. The Council owned the meadows, but if planning permission were granted, the Council might be obliged to provide Western Power with the means to access its development and would have to sell it a strip of land across the meadows.

If this potential access route could be prevented, Western Power's proposed development would be effectively landlocked. It was unlikely that it would get permission to access the development solely from the narrow lane on the Lisvane Road side. Andrew's knowledge of planning legislation led him to the Commons Registration Act 1965. This Act allows for an area of land that has been used by a significant

Save our Reservoirs

Fig. 13.1. The Nant Fawr meadows. Photo by Wilf Ingamells.

number of local people for sports or recreational purposes for at least 20 years to be registered as a town or village green. Once a piece of land has been so registered, it is protected from any development, and in the case of the meadows, Western Power wouldn't be able to drive an access road across them.

Local people had used the Nant Fawr meadows for walking, picking blackberries, exercising their dogs and picnics etc., since it stopped being used as farmland in 1983, and therefore, it had been used for recreational purposes for more than twenty years. Another important caveat of the Common Registration Act is that people use the land 'as of right'. In a legal sense, this means that the use of the land is without the landowner's specific permission but is carried on as if it were a right. In this case, the landowner was the Council, which had purchased the land in 1948, but the Council had neither encouraged the public to use the land nor had it refused them permission to do so; it just tolerated public use as if it were their right. This may seem a somewhat esoteric point, but as we will see later, it turned out to be a vital one!

Andrew set about getting the Nant Fawr meadows registered as a village green. Shortly after Western Power had submitted its fourth planning application in June 2006, he printed about 800 copies of a letter explaining his plan. He circulated it with a simple pro-forma that people could complete if they had used the meadows for informal recreation for over twenty years or more. Andrew arranged for this to be delivered door-to-door in parts of Cyncoed close to the reservoirs and left copies in local shops. It was also widely distributed to members of RAG and the Friends of Nant Fawr. Eventually, 426 completed forms were returned to Andrew, although he had to discard 75 of them as they were made by people who lived outside Cyncoed or had not used the meadows for at least 20 years.

Knowing that time was short due to Western Power's recent submission of its third and fourth planning applications, Andrew made a formal application to Cardiff Council for the meadows to become a 'green' under the Commons Registration Act 1965 on 2nd July 2006. He submitted a sample quantity of signed statements with the formal application and promised more to come. By the autumn of 2006, 350 completed proformas had been submitted, and 35 people had written detailed letters of support, testifying to their use of the meadows for recreational purposes for over 20 years.

The Council, once satisfied that the application was legitimate, placed a public notice in the South Wales Echo on 12th October 2006, acknowledging the application and inviting anyone who would like to object to it to contact the Council's Senior Legal Manager. The application was considered by the Public Protection Committee of the Council on 7th November 2006, and it decided that the application should be considered at a non-statutory public inquiry. The reason for this approach was that the Council had a conflict of interest. On the one hand, it was the registration authority under the Commons Registration Act and had to make sure that the case was dealt with fairly. On the other hand, it owned the land in question and preferred it to remain under Council control. It was agreed that Mr Vivian Chapman QC would act as the inspector for the inquiry. The Public Protection Committee would make the final decision about the proposed Village Green once it had received his report.

Unsurprisingly, Western Power's solicitors, Geldards, were quick to register their objection to the proposed 'Village Green' once the application had been made public. They argued that the Council had purchased the land as public open space in 1948 and that the public had 'a right' to use the land, rather than it having been used 'as of right'. In support of this subtle distinction, they also pointed out that the Council had been involved in setting up the 'Friends of Nant Fawr' to help manage the area, which implied that they had given them permission to be there. On top of this, there were two signs at the entrance to Rhyd-y-penau Park, which read:

> Cardiff City Council
> Dinas Caerdydd
> Leisure and Amenities Dept.
>
> Motor Cycling, Horse Riding and the striking of Golf Balls is Prohibited within this Public Open Space
>
> IL Davies, Director

Geldards argued that this indicated that the Council viewed the whole area as Public Open Space, which again would suggest that the public had 'a right' to enter the area.

Andrew was invited to respond to these objections, and he did so. He pointed out that although the land had been bought by the Council in 1948, it had been leased out to a tenant farmer until 1983, and since that lease expired, it had never been cultivated in any way, as were other Cardiff Council parks and gardens. He also pointed out that the Friends Group was run independently of the Council and had even made a generous donation to RAG's fighting fund. As far as the signs went, he was able to refer to previous case law that demonstrated that Council signs did not prevent other applications for 'Village Green' status from being successful.

Western Power had already indicated to the inspector in its letter of objection that it wished to be represented at the inquiry by its legal team, and the Council had decided that as the landowner, it would also object to the application as it had opposed past village green applications on its land. If it didn't in this case, it might lay the Council open to a legal challenge by Western Power, who could question its impartiality. Given the array of legal power arranged against him, Andrew decided to employ his own counsel and engaged Miss Morag Ellis QC. Morag was an 'up and coming' barrister at the time who had just been appointed as a Queen's Counsel. She had previously had considerable success with 'village green' cases and was an expert in planning law. RAG offered to pay her fees, which were around £20,000, as it was unreasonable to expect Andrew to meet the considerable costs personally. If successful, the village green designation could end Western Power's plans altogether.

The scene was set for yet another dramatic legal confrontation with Western Power!

The Inquiry opens

The Village Green inquiry was scheduled for three days starting on 9th July 2007. It took place in the Scout hut, behind Christ Church, in Lake Road North and provided the setting for one of my favourite memories of the whole RAG campaign. The inspector, Mr Vivian Chapman QC, sat at the far end of the hall, with the legal teams each arranged in a row down either side in front of him. What was so incongruous was the sight of the Western Power legal team consisting of our old adversaries John Steel QC and Mr Robert Palmer, along with three or four representatives of Geldard's solicitors, all in their well-tailored suits, sitting in a neat row, behind a few rickety trestle tables, on plastic stacking chairs, underneath some rather tatty Scout posters about how to tie knots and administer CPR. Quite a change from their usual High Court appearances! On the other side of the hall were Andrew Hill and Morag Ellis, as well as the Council's counsel, Mr Robert White, and instructing solicitors from the Council's Legal Department. The part of the hall nearest to the door had chairs placed in rows facing the inspector and was packed with members of the public.

The inspector began by describing the meadows and their surroundings, as well as his understanding of the law relating to the registration of new greens. He then proceeded to interview several members of the local community who had given evidence supporting Andrew's application. They included:

Patricia Connies-Laing	Robert John	Sally Shand
Kathleen Davies	Kenneth Leonard	Fred Smith
Leslie Davies	Lisa Muller	Rosemary Temple
Vivien Davies	Owain Parry	Ted Thurgood
Christopher Fookes	Jenny Randerson AM	Michael Walker
Gerald Goodson	Colin Roberts	Elsa Wall
Andrew Hill	Susan Rosser	

All the witnesses were subjected to questioning by the inspector, as well as cross-examination by the various legal representatives. Inevitably most of the questions came from Mr Steel and focused on people's use of the meadows and what they understood as the area of Cyncoed. This is important, as the definition of a village green is one that is used by 'local' people. Without exception, all acquitted themselves well, although inevitably, opinions as to the area that constituted Cyncoed varied quite widely, as there are no clear boundaries between neighbouring districts.

A particularly interesting witness was Mr Leslie Davies, who had been the Director of Leisure and Amenities for the Council between 1980 and 1996. It was his name on the signs about prohibited activities on the public open space, which were brought up by Western Power's legal team. Mr Davies pointed out that these signs were at the entrances to Rhyd-y-penau Park and related specifically to that open space. He claimed they did not refer to the meadows, which were at some distance from the more formal park.

By the time the inquiry had dealt with all these witnesses, it had gone well past the allotted three days, even though an evening session had also been arranged on Monday, 9th July. Towards the end of the week, three witnesses were examined who appeared on behalf of the Objectors, i.e. Western Power and the Council. The first two were Western Power regulars: Mr Peter Noble of Geldards Solicitors and Mr Peter

Waldren of RPS group, its planning consultants. Neither had much by way of first-hand evidence that they could provide.

The third witness, introduced by the Council, was more dramatic. This was Mr Robert Green, the Council's Land Strategy Manager. Under cross-examination from Morag Ellis, it became clear that the Council did not have a clear idea about why the meadows were purchased in 1948 and under what legal authority the land had been purchased. There was conflicting evidence and some suggestion that Mr Green had deliberately altered a record card relating to the purchase in April 2007 on the advice of colleagues! It was also unclear why the land had been let out to a tenant farmer for 35 years if the Council had intended to buy it as public open space for recreational purposes. All of these issues had a significant bearing on whether the use of the land was 'by right' or 'as of right', which, as was becoming apparent, would be the key factor deciding the outcome of the application. This development clearly exasperated the inspector, and he really had no option but to suspend the inquiry. The Council Officers were sent off to try and sort out the documentation regarding the purchase of the land. Once they had a definitive answer and the availability of everyone involved could be confirmed, the inquiry would recommence.

The Inquiry Resumes

The inquiry finally resumed over six months later, on 26th February 2008. The Christ Church Scout Hall was not available then, so the inquiry met in the hall of Cyncoed Methodist Church. It lasted three more days.

The situation was still confused, as the 1948 conveyance of the land did not identify the Act under which it had been purchased. The lawyers had identified a number of possible statutory powers that could have been used, which included: the Public Health Act 1875; the Open Spaces Act 1906; the Local Government Act 1933; the Public Health Act 1936; the Town and Country Planning Act 1944; and the Town and Country Planning Act 1947. It is impossible to go into all the details of the legal discussion that ensued, and it would be very tedious.

The problem was that the evidence was confusing and contradictory. To give you a flavour, here are a few examples:

- The land was purchased in July 1947. The Council applied to the District Valuer for a valuation and stated that 61.03 acres of land were to be acquired for open space purposes under the Public Health Act 1936 and the Town and Country Planning Act 1944 (TCPA 1944). (Incidentally, the value placed on the land was £17,025).
- On 1st September 1947, the Town Clerk wrote to the District Valuer saying they were now thinking of purchasing the land under the new Town and Country Planning Act 1947 (TCPA 1947). The District Valuer replied, advising that he had met with the Town Clerk, and they had agreed it would be purchased under the TCPA 1944.
- On 15th September 1947, the Estates Committee minutes suggest that the land had, in fact, been bought under the TCPA 1947.
- On 5th July 1948, the Welsh Board of Health sent formal consent to the Council of a loan for £17,606 to defray the cost of purchasing land at Rhyd-y-penau Road for parks and open spaces. It stated that the loan was for land purchased under the Public Health Act 1875.
- On 15th October 1958, the City Housing and Estates Manager wrote to the Director of Parks stating that he understood the meadows to have been purchased under the Public Health Act 1936.
- The town map of 20th May 1959 showed the meadows as "Waterworks Reservation" and not "Open Space available to the public".

This last observation led Morag Ellis to propose that the meadows adjacent to the reservoirs had been bought under the Town and Country Planning Act of 1944 for purposes relating to the waterworks. This was consistent with the observation that although the land had been purchased by the Council in 1948, it was not used as public open space until 1983 when Mr Parry retired and gave up the tenancy on Rhyd-y-Blewyn farm. If the Council had purchased the land as public open space, why did it wait 35 years before allowing public access? If the land had been bought as public open space, the public would have 'a right' to use it for recreational purposes, but if it had been purchased for some other reason, they would be using it 'as of right'.

As one might imagine, such conflicting evidence provided a field day for the lawyers and much of the remaining three days of the inquiry was spent in arcane legal discussions between the various counsels.

The Outcome of the Inquiry

At the end of the day, it was left to the inspector to try and make sense of it all. This inevitably took some time, and it wasn't until 9th July 2008 that his report was published, almost two years after Andrew had made his original application! In it, the inspector concluded that the land had been bought under section 164 of the Public Health Act 1875 to provide 'public walks and pleasure grounds'. This meant that the public use of the meadows was 'a right' rather than 'as of right' under the law. Although he was completely satisfied that Andrew had shown that the meadows had been used by a significant number of local people for recreational purposes for over 20 years, 'without force, secrecy or permission', the village green application failed because of the inspector's decision regarding the Council's purchase of the land. Only land used 'as of right' could be registered as a green.

This was a blow to both Andrew and RAG, but it had some degree of silver lining. It had been established that local people could use this land as 'a right' and that the Council couldn't prevent people from using the land, even for a single day. It also meant that if the Council wished to dispose of some of this land, for example, to provide an access road to Western Power, it would only be able to do so after local people had been consulted. In some ways, the inspector's decision was achieving much the same result as having a village green!

Chapter 14

The Run-Up to the Second Public Inquiry

We have got somewhat ahead of ourselves in the main story because the Village Green application took two years to resolve, and there were several other things going on at the same time. I would like to take you back to November 2006 when the first Planning Inquiry had just closed.

Keeper's Cottage Burns Down

On Christmas Eve 2006, the residents of Rhyd-y-penau Road spotted a building on fire by the reservoir entrance at 3 am in the morning. The emergency services were notified but had difficulty reaching the fire because of a locked bollard at the end of the lane that led to the reservoir entrance. The building had been completely gutted when the fire engine finally got down there.

Keeper's cottage had been built a few years after the construction of Llanishen reservoir and for many years was home to the successive reservoir keepers and their families. More recently, an employee of Welsh Water had been living there, but in 2006 it had been unoccupied for several years. Western Power demolished the remains of the building and the adjacent store buildings in January 2007. Conveniently for Western Power, it was just where the planned access road across the Nant Fawr meadows would have entered the reservoir site!

Appeal on the Fourth Application

Apart from this, the first few months of 2007 did not start well for Western Power. First of all, the High Court upheld the CCW's designation of the reservoir embankments as an SSSI, and then the inspector from the first Public Inquiry recommended to the Welsh Ministers that they should reject the second planning application, which they did in due course.

In mid-April, Western Power appealed to the Welsh Government for non-determination of the fourth application, as again, Cardiff Council had not reached a decision within the prescribed time limit. This was understandable as the Council was waiting to hear the outcome of the SSSI appeal and the first public inquiry before considering the application. Towards the end of August, the Welsh Government 'called in' the fourth application and 'recovered' the appeal for the Welsh Ministers because of the scale and sensitivity of the proposed development. This meant that there would be another public inquiry on the fourth application led by a planning inspector and that he or she would make a recommendation, but again the appropriate Welsh Government Minister would make the final decision. This inquiry was scheduled to take place in May 2008.

Purchase of Gwern-y-Bendy wood

Little else of significance happened in 2007, except that in October, Western Power purchased a small wood beside the reservoir. This was on the west side of the reservoir and was bounded by South Rise, Rheidol Close, and what was, at the time, the pitch of Llanishen Rugby Club. Western Power bought the wood for £60,000 from landowners Stuart Wyndham Murray-Threipland and Rupert Sanders. We could not understand why Western Power had bought it, but we should have guessed that there was a good reason. It turned out to be a significant factor in the outcome of the Second Inquiry.

Chapter 15

The Second Planning Inquiry

The Preliminary Meeting

To many of us, Western Power appeared to play fast and loose from the start of the second planning inquiry. At the preliminary inquiry meeting, which was held in Cardiff City Hall on Tuesday, 18th March 2008, it indicated that it would be submitting a revised Environmental Statement in mid-April, which would have details of alternative access routes to the proposed development. The other main parties to the inquiry, Cardiff Council and RAG, were concerned about this because it was late in the day to introduce major changes to the planning application. There would be little time to assess and rebut these changes as all the final inquiry documentation had to be submitted by 7th May, but the planning inspector seemed happy to accept this revision.

The revised Environmental Statement arrived on 16th April 2008. The changes in access to the proposed development were substantial. Under the original planning application, it was proposed that most of the traffic would access the development from Rhyd-y-penau Road. In the new revised Environmental Statement, this was now listed as Option A.

There were also two other options: B & C. Option C was for a new access road that would take all the traffic from the reservoir development out onto the Lisvane Road, in the dip by the Nant Fawr bridge. Option B was an amalgam of the two, where some traffic would use the Rhyd-y-penau entrance and some traffic the Lisvane entrance.

The document did not specify which of these three options Western Power intended to pursue but effectively left all of them on the table.

Cardiff Council, RAG and Julie Morgan MP immediately objected to the changes as they represented a substantive change to the planning application just before the inquiry and one that the Council Planning Committee had not had a chance to review. We were told the inspector would address the issue at the start of the inquiry, which was due to open on 28th May.

The Second Inquiry Opens

The second public inquiry opened on schedule on Wednesday, 28th May 2008. It was held in one of the committee rooms in County Hall. The main cast list was:

> The Planning Inspector, Mr Richard Poppleton, who was an urbane and polished operator. He appeared to be well-known to Mr Steel.
>
> John Steel QC again represented Western Power, accompanied by his sidekick Robert Palmer. They were instructed by Charles Felgate and Peter Noble of Geldards solicitors. In total, they called on nine expert witnesses to give evidence to the inquiry and submitted 299 documents.
>
> The Council were represented by Mark Lowe QC, instructed by Polly Ellis, the Council's solicitor. They called five witnesses and submitted 21 documents.
>
> RAG's previous barrister, Nick Cooke QC, had recently become a judge and was therefore no longer available, so we were represented by a barrister called Clare Parry, whom Mike Sant of Harmer Planning Consultants instructed. They called six witnesses and had eight supporting documents.
>
> There were also 12 local residents who had opted to give evidence in person to the inquiry.

Mr Poppleton began the inquiry by stating that he had decided to allow Western Power to present its three different access options to the inquiry. He conceded that residents needed more time to make written responses to the proposed changes and therefore extended the deadline for people to make their views known until 1st July 2008.

It was at this point that Western Power dropped its second bombshell. It submitted new inspection reports for Llanishen and Lisvane reservoirs dated 9th May 2008. Normally, these inspections are carried out every ten years, and the last inspection was in March 2004, so another report would not normally have been due until 2014. However, Western Power decided a new report was needed because of the reservoir's proposed 'change of use'. Conveniently for Western Power, the reservoir engineer, Dr Andrew Hughes, found in his latest report that the pipework running beneath Llanishen reservoir had to be inspected on safety grounds and that this would involve draining the reservoir. Due to the powers invested in an inspecting engineer by the Reservoirs Act 1975, this conclusion could not be ignored or challenged. The Council and RAG again argued that the Public Inquiry should not consider this very late evidence, but again Mr Poppleton disagreed.

I will deal with the whole issue of the drain down of Llanishen reservoir elsewhere (See Chapter 17), but it seemed to us too much of a coincidence that this issue should come to light just a few days before the start of the inquiry. The RAG Committee was worried that Western Power had identified the Reservoirs Act as a way of getting the reservoir drained that would be difficult to challenge legally. We also feared that Dr Hughes' report saying that the reservoir needed to be drained on safety grounds could lead the Inspector to believe that the reservoir was unsafe and would have to be drained anyway. Perhaps this might make it more likely that he would recommend that Western Power's planning appeal should be granted? It was not a good start to the second planning inquiry for us.

After these somewhat lengthy initial discussions, the inquiry proper started. The barristers from each of the three main parties made their opening statements, and then Cardiff Council was the first to present their detailed evidence.

The Council's Case

Mr Mark Lowe QC, the Council's counsel, made the main presentation. He seemed affable and good-humoured but had a rather unusual manner whereby he would make a point and then grin at the whole room as if seeking everyone's approbation. I found it a little off-putting, but he was an experienced and well-respected planning barrister. The Council's case focused mainly on planning issues and the importance of the reservoirs for nature conservation and as recreational open space, especially regarding sail training. They fielded five expert witnesses. Dr Malcolm Hockaday dealt with planning policy; William Latimer with biodiversity; Peter Dawson on traffic and the controversial new access arrangements; as well as Simon Howell and John Hart on sailing issues. Much of the evidence centred around sailing and whether Cardiff Bay was a suitable substitute for the current facilities at Llanishen. The Council argued that they had a lease to sail on Llanishen reservoir and that the proposed new sailing lake was too small, too shallow, and too close to the surrounding houses, which would cause 'fluky' wind conditions. As a result, it would not be suitable for beginners learning to sail and was not a large enough area for more advanced sailors. They also argued that the housing development and access road across the meadows would cause irreversible harm to the quality, integrity and character of the strategic open space of the Nant Fawr river corridor. All of the witnesses were subjected to detailed cross-examination by Mr Steel, backed up by his own bevy of expert witnesses. Some good points were made by the Council team, but there were no knock-out blows directed at Western Power.

RAG's Case

RAG was the next party to present its case. After a brief introduction summarising RAG's case, counsel Clare Parry introduced their witnesses. Ted Thurgood first talked about RAG and the huge groundswell of local public opinion against the proposed planning application. Ewart Parkinson spoke about the fundamental importance of the four wildlife, recreational and amenity open space river corridors to the character of the whole city of Cardiff and how the proposed development would seriously impact the integrity of the Nant Fawr river corridor. Graham Good backed this up on behalf of the Friends of Nant Fawr Community Woodlands and described the hard work of the local community in maintaining this green corridor. He pointed to the damage that would be done by the proposed new access road across the Nant Fawr meadows, which would effectively divide the corridor in half. Fred Davies spoke on behalf of the Cardiff Reservoirs Fly Fishing Club about the popularity of fishing in the reservoirs and how generations of local residents had fished the waters there. He pointed out that the proposed development would seriously harm the recreational opportunities previously available to residents and contended that this ran counter to policies in Planning Policy Wales. Geraint Evans represented the users of the Llanishen Sailing Centre. He emphasised the success of the current sailing centre and how at least 25% of the young sailors now representing Wales learned to sail at the Llanishen Sailing Centre. Backing up the witnesses from the Council, he confirmed the importance of the water area currently available and the limitations of a sailing lake a quarter of that size. He also raised the issue of water quality. Since sailing started at Llanishen in the 1970s, the reservoir had only been topped up by rainwater, and therefore the water quality was excellent. On the other hand, Lisvane reservoir was fed by the Nant Fawr and suffered regular blooms of toxic blue-green algae because the water from the stream had a higher nutrient load. Western Power's plans involved the new boating lake being fed by the Nant Fawr, and therefore, it was likely the water would become too polluted for immersion water sports. RAG's submission was brought to a close by traffic expert Ron Kelly on behalf of Lisvane Community Council. He pointed out their particular concern with the recently revealed access 'Option C', which would bring all traffic from the development out onto Lisvane Road. He argued that this would have an adverse impact on the road and that local residents had not been properly consulted on the proposals. He also stated that there had been no proper modelling of the proposed new junction design and its effects on local traffic flow.

RAG's formal submission was followed by evidence from a number of local residents:

- Julia Magill, who lived opposite the proposed entrance onto Lisvane Road, spoke of the dangers of bringing more traffic onto Lisvane Road and the increased risk to neighbouring residents.
- David Evans made a wide-ranging submission covering points both for and against the proposed development and suggested a compromise solution could be sought.
- Justin Cooper, a retired transport planner, criticised many aspects of Western Power's traffic assessments and assumptions.
- Mr Cress objected to Option C and the adverse effects on the area around the proposed junction on Lisvane Road.
- Vernon Hanson expressed concern about buses turning into and out of the development onto Lisvane Road as well as construction traffic.

There were also many written objections from local politicians, councillors and over 150 members of the general public, many of whom were RAG members.

Western Power's Case

By the time RAG and local residents had finished giving their evidence, the first six days of the inquiry had gone by. The next five days were allocated to the appellants, Western Power. Given the number of their witnesses and Mr Steel's past elaborate and detailed arguments, it looked like they would need it.

Mr Steel began by reiterating his usual refrain of how the development would turn private land and a redundant reservoir into one of Cardiff's best public recreational resources. [Which is true if you ignore the fact that it had already been enjoyed for many years as a public recreational resource via a permit scheme, not to mention being used by generations of fishermen and for teaching youngsters how to sail]. He went on to describe the differences from the previous applications in that now all the houses were going to be sunken down into the bowl of the reservoir, leaving the embankments in place. This was mainly to avoid the issue of harming the embankments SSSI for grassland fungi but had the added advantage that the development would be less visible from the surrounding areas. As the embankment SSSI was to be left largely intact, Natural Resources Wales did not object to the planning application, which was a further advantage. Mr Steel then went in detail through the inspector's conclusions at the first planning inquiry and tried to persuade Mr Poppleton that they no longer applied.

The usual roster of expert witnesses was wheeled out by Western Power, most of whom we had already heard from at the first public inquiry. They all testified on their area of speciality, and all concluded that the proposed development would be a great recreational resource / great for sailing / great for wildlife / hardly noticeable / and generally wonderful for everyone. However, two witnesses were of particular interest and were not unrelated: these were Mr Derek Moore and Dr Andy Hughes. To explain the link between them, I need to provide a bit more background.

The Nant Fawr Ecology and Education Trust

In July 2006, I had written to Madeleine Havard, who was, by then, the Chief Executive of the Wildlife Trust, to point out that if the Trust took over the management of the site post development, as had been agreed with Western Power, it would assume responsibilities under the Reservoirs Act 1975. Although the proposed residual sailing lake was only one-fifth the size of Llanishen reservoir, it would still qualify as a Category A large raised reservoir under the 1975 Act. This meant that should there be a major problem with the dam or any of the infrastructure, the Wildlife Trust would be responsible for getting it repaired, and such repairs could cost hundreds of thousands of pounds. I suggested that the Trustees should get legal advice about their liabilities under the Act. This they evidently did, and later that year, they decided not to proceed with taking on the freehold of the land surrounding the development. Instead, they agreed with Western Power that they would still manage the site after completion but that another organisation would take on the freehold of the land and

The Second Planning Inquiry

responsibility under the Reservoirs Act. To this end, Western Power set up the Nant Fawr Ecology and Education Trust (NFEET) to take on the freehold and endowed it with £4.5 million. NFEET had three Trustees who were: Charl Oosthuizen, the finance director of Western Power; John James, the lead for the Llanishen Water project set up by Western Power; and Derek Moore, the former Chief Executive of the Wildlife Trust, who had been an enthusiastic supporter of Western Power's plans and was now retired.

Derek Moore was one of the expert witnesses who addressed the inquiry on behalf of Western Power. Much of his evidence was about his own past experience and achievements in nature conservation. Unsurprisingly, like his colleagues, he also thought the proposed development would be a great asset for wildlife and North Cardiff.

The link between Derek Moore and Dr Andy Hughes stems from the Nant Fawr Ecology and Education Trust. In the inquiry, there was extensive discussion about why Dr Hughes had carried out an inspection of the reservoir six years before it was due. Charles Felgate, one of the instructing solicitors for Western Power, had previously stated in a letter to the Council's solicitor that he had asked Dr Hughes to prepare the report in March 2008 after a request by Derek Moore's solicitors prior to his becoming a Trustee of NFEET. However, during Derek Moore's cross-examination by the Council's QC, it was pointed out that Dr Hughes' first inspection visit had been on 3rd January 2008, suggesting that the inspection had been arranged earlier. Mr Felgate explained in a follow-up note to the Planning Inspector that he had been anticipating a request on behalf of the new owners (NFEET) for an inspection report and that in December 2007, he had asked Dr Hughes to inspect the site with a view to preparing a report. It wasn't until March 2008 that he actually requested Dr Hughes to prepare the report. Mr Felgate was clearly someone who liked to plan well ahead.

The Inquiry Finishes

True to form, Mr Steel overran his allotted time and only finished giving evidence on Friday, 13th June, the day the inquiry was due to close. There were still the closing statements to make, but it proved difficult to schedule extra time due to the inspector's availability, the availability of the respective barristers, and the availability of a suitable venue. Eventually, Friday, 29th August, was identified, and after each main party had delivered their closing statement on that day, the inquiry closed without further incident. All that had to be done now was to sit back and wait for the inspector's decision and, ultimately, the decision of Jane Davidson AM, the Welsh Government Minister for Environment, Sustainability and Housing. It was a nail-biting time. If the decision went in our favour, Western Power would either have to give up or put in another planning application. If it went in their favour, all would be lost, and the development would go ahead.

The Decisions

Given that the inquiry closed on 29th August, Mr Poppleton was quick in preparing his report – it was published on Thursday, 13th November. It was an unmitigated disaster for us. He concluded that this application was sufficiently different from the one considered by the first planning inquiry and that it would not harm the openness, character or appearance of the Nant Fawr corridor, as well as doing little harm to the embankments SSSI. He rejected the arguments that the development would have a negative effect on the facilities for sail training in Cardiff and concluded that the development should be allowed to go ahead. It looked as though we had finally lost our long-running campaign. I imagine there were celebrations that day at Western Power and their solicitors, Geldards. Our only hope now lay with the Minister for Environment, Sustainability and Housing, although we knew that Ministers usually agree with the recommend-ations of their planning inspectors. It was a long wait for her decision.

It was nearly six months before we heard from the Minister, whose decision was published on 16th April 2009. Thankfully, the Minister,

The Second Planning Inquiry

God bless her, disagreed with the inspector's conclusions and did not accept his recommendations. She turned down the development on several grounds, mainly relating to its harmful effect on the open space of the Nant Fawr river corridor and the impact of the proposed access road crossing the meadows. She also decided that the compensatory public open space to be provided as part of the proposed development was not 'compensatory', as the areas concerned already formed part of the open space of the locality. It was our turn to break out the bubbly.

The Challenge

Unfortunately, the story of the second planning inquiry does not end there. A few weeks later, towards the end of May, we learned that Western Power's legal team had decided to challenge the Minister's decision in the High Court. They couldn't make a challenge because they disagreed with her decision, but only if they thought she had made some error in law. The main problem they identified was with the issue of compensatory open space and the Minister's contention that this had to be new open space, as well as ignoring the fact that the amenity value of existing open space could be improved. This is where the 2007 purchase of Gwern-y-Bendy wood became clear because it was part of the package of compensatory open space that Western Power had planned to provide. The challenge was due to be heard in the High Court on the 22nd and 23rd of September 2009.

On 4th September 2009, the Welsh Government lost its nerve. Having reviewed all the evidence, it decided that Western Power was likely to win its challenge, and it decided to back down. This meant that the Minister's decision was no longer valid and, therefore, there was no longer, in effect, a decision on the appeal. In due course, the Minister decided that rather than just issuing a new decision, the public inquiry should re-open, although no date was set for this to occur. It looked as though we would all have to start all over again!

Chapter 16

The Second Listing Application to Cadw

Given his long experience as an architectural conservator, Andrew Hill was still convinced that Llanishen reservoir deserved listing for its historical importance as part of the Taf Fawr water supply system. Two of the reservoirs in the Taf Fawr valley, Cantref and Llwyn Onn, had already been listed by Cadw, but Beacons reservoir hadn't, and, of course, neither had Llanishen. Although adjacent to Llanishen, Lisvane reservoir had been built 20 years earlier and was not part of the same water catchment. So this time, Andrew concentrated on getting the whole Taf Fawr system listed in recognition of it being a remarkable example of Victorian engineering and its importance to the history of Cardiff.

The Institution of Civil Engineers

Before he took on Cadw again, Andrew wanted to make sure that he could make the best possible case. In 2006, he discovered that the Institution of Civil Engineers (ICE) had a Panel for Historical Engineering Works, which maintained a register of noteworthy civil engineering projects throughout the UK. Andrew wrote to Keith Thomas, the panel member representing Wales, who happened to live in Lisvane. He suggested that the entire Taf Fawr water supply system should be added to the register and outlined its history. Keith agreed that the scheme was of such significance that it merited being included in the register and offered to make such a proposal to the ICE panel.

This process took some time, but in early February 2008, Andrew received a letter from ICE informing him that the Cardiff Water Supply system had been added to the Institution's Historical Engineering works list and that they had included all three reservoirs in the Beacons as well as Llanishen reservoir. This would form a useful precedent for the next approach to Cadw.

The Second Application

Andrew made his next application to Cadw for listing in July 2008. This time he omitted Lisvane reservoir and just included Llanishen Reservoir as well as the 'Beacons reservoir' in the Brecon Beacons. He argued that these two reservoirs were integral parts of the Taf Fawr system, which represented one of the most remarkable civil engineering feats in South Wales in the late 19th century. As before, he produced extensive historical evidence of water engineer J.A.B. Williams' concept for the whole scheme, including his original specification to Cardiff Borough Council dated 14th March 1881. Importantly, Andrew could now point to the fact that the Institution of Civil Engineers had already considered the scheme and had included it, in its entirety, in their historical register. Also, as before, Andrew recruited a bevy of local historians, civil engineers, town planners and architects to write to Cadw in support of his application.

The application sank into the depths of Cadw, and we heard nothing for a long time. Then, almost a year later, on 7th May 2009, Andrew received a letter from Mr Laurence Burr of Cadw's designation branch, saying that Cadw had recommended to the Minister of Heritage that both Llanishen and the Beacons reservoirs should be listed and that the Minister was minded to accept their recommendation. He also invited Andrew to comment on a draft of the proposed listing. Andrew suggested a few minor revisions, which were subsequently accepted, and on 24th July, he received a letter confirming that both the Beacons and Llanishen reservoirs had been formally listed as structures of historical importance to Wales.

It is difficult to overstate the delight that all of us on the RAG committee felt at this development. We had the reservoir embankments protected by the SSSI designation for their grassland fungi, and now the physical structure of Llanishen reservoir would be protected as a listed building. This listed status also usually covers the 'setting' of a historic building, so it was difficult to see how Western Power could still hope to use the reservoir basin for housing. Surely it would have to give up at this stage?

Western Power Responds

Western Power's response to the listing of Llanishen reservoir was rather less enthusiastic. At the end of September 2009, its solicitors, Geldards, wrote to the Minister for Heritage explaining why they thought the listing of Llanishen was unlawful. The points they made were as follows:

- Cadw had a policy that only the best examples of particular building types were selected for listing and that, in the case of Llanishen reservoir, it had minimal architectural interest, was purely functional in nature, and employed standard methods of construction in its day. Therefore, in their view, it was a totally unexceptional 'building'.

- That the water supply system for a particular town was not of sufficient significance in the context of national Welsh history to warrant listing and that when the previous application was assessed in November 2005, it was not considered worthy of listing then, so why should it be now?

- Llanishen reservoir had been redundant and 'divorced' from the rest of the Taf Fawr system for the last thirty years and, therefore, could not be regarded as "still being an integral part of a single engineering scheme".

Geldards stated that they expected Cadw to reconsider the request and to remove Llanishen reservoir from its list of historic buildings forthwith. They gave the Welsh Government a deadline of 15th October to reply. The Welsh Government did reply but left it until the very day of 15th October. It rejected Western Power's legal challenges and maintained that the Minister's listing decision was lawful. The stage was set for yet another legal battle.

Back to the High Court

Geldards lodged the application for a judicial review on 23rd October 2009, and the case was heard in the High Court by Judge Milwyn Jarman QC on Monday 22nd February 2010. Again, Mr John Steel QC, presented the case on behalf of Western Power, and Mr Clive Lewis QC represented the Welsh Ministers and Cadw.

Mr Steel put forward the Western Power case, as usual in considerable detail, but essentially reiterating the points made above. For his part, Mr Lewis stressed that the main reason for listing was not that the reservoir had any great architectural value or unique mode of construction but was being listed in terms of the historic interest of the Taf Fawr civil engineering project in its entirety. He also argued that this scheme was of great importance to the social and economic history of Wales and that this justified its listing.

Justice Jarman accepted Mr Lewis' arguments and noted that the Listed Buildings and Conservation Areas Act of 1990 places a statutory duty on the Welsh Ministers to have regard to either the architectural importance or the historic interest of a site when it came to listing. He was, therefore, satisfied that the Minister's decision to list based on historical interest alone was entirely lawful. He also accepted that Andrew's 2008 submission was significantly different to the one made in 2005 in that Lisvane reservoir was excluded, and the later application was based on different grounds, namely the historical importance of the entire integrated scheme. In conclusion, he rejected the appeal and awarded costs of £21,596 against Western Power.

In an overly courteous way, Mr Steel thanked Justice Jarman for his decision and also for staying on for what turned out to be a very long session in court (mainly thanks to Mr Steel's own efforts). Justice

Jarman replied, "I am not sure that everyone behind you will share your stance" [meaning Western Power's representatives], "but thank you".

For the Welsh Government and Cadw, this was a great result. For us, it was phenomenal. The High Court had roundly rejected Western Power's arguments, and there was no other way that the latter could challenge the listing. But Western Power wasn't finished yet. As the High Court challenge had been taking place, its engineers had been installing the necessary pipework to start draining all the water out of Llanishen reservoir.

Chapter 17

The Draining of Llanishen Reservoir

Western Power had ambushed us on the eve of the 2008 Public Inquiry. At the last minute, it introduced a new witness: Dr Andrew Hughes of Atkins Ltd. Dr Hughes was the reservoir engineer responsible for the condition of both Llanishen and Lisvane reservoirs. He had produced a report saying that Llanishen reservoir had to be drained to inspect a pipe running beneath it.

The Reservoirs Act 1975

To explain the significance of this, I need to go into a bit of background. Reservoirs are potentially dangerous, as was demonstrated in the summer of 2019 when there was almost a breach of the Toddbrook reservoir dam in Derbyshire. This would have caused devastation to the town of Whaley Bridge, situated in the valley just below the dam. More than 1,500 people had to be evacuated from their homes. To try to protect the public from such dangers, the Reservoirs Act had been introduced in 1975. The Act applies to any 'large raised reservoir', defined as a reservoir holding more than 25,000 cubic metres of water above the natural level of any part of the adjoining land. Llanishen reservoir holds 1,441,000 cubic metres.

Under the Act, any large raised reservoir must have an 'inspecting engineer' from a panel of reservoir engineers approved for the purpose by the Institution of Civil Engineers. These engineers are expected to produce a detailed report on the condition of the reservoir every ten years and to make any recommendations that may be required on the grounds of safety. Dr Hughes was the inspecting engineer for Llanishen and Lisvane reservoirs, appointed by Western Power.

As well as the 'inspecting engineer', the Act also stipulates that there should be an independent 'supervising engineer'. The role of the supervising engineer is to make more regular checks on the condition of the reservoir and to oversee any works specified by the inspecting engineer. The supervising engineer can also call for a reservoir to be inspected under the Act if they have any concerns about safety. The supervising engineer at Llanishen at the time was Mr Stuart Davies, who worked for United Utilities.

The other key component of the Reservoirs Act is the 'enforcement authority'. The role of the enforcement authority is to ensure that the owners or 'undertakers' of large raised reservoirs comply with the Act, in particular, to ensure that inspections are carried out at regular intervals and that any recommendations in the interest of safety are carried out promptly. In Wales, the enforcement agency is now Natural Resources Wales, but in 2008, the role was carried out by the Environment Agency, whose Dam Safety Division was based in Exeter.

As specified by the Reservoirs Act, Llanishen reservoir had been subject to detailed reports by an Inspecting Engineer every ten years. The 1994 report had been conducted by Dr Hughes, who found that the reservoir embankments were in 'generally good condition'. On safety grounds, Dr Hughes recommended that level pins be installed on the main embankment and that the flow of the main drain be measured. Otherwise, there were only a few minor recommendations relating to maintenance and monitoring.

The next inspection was carried out in 2004 by Mr Denis Earp. There were no measures required on safety grounds, and Mr Earp concluded that the reservoir 'may safely continue to be used for the storage of water up to the certified level'. He made a few minor recommendations relating to maintenance and monitoring, and therefore, the next inspection was due to take place in 2014.

The 2008 Inspection Report

All the recent reports had agreed that the reservoir was in good condition, and therefore, it was a total surprise to us when Western Power appeared with Dr Hughes and a new report on the eve of the 2008 Public Inquiry. This report was produced six years earlier than would normally have been expected. We began to be suspicious.

Dr Hughes' 2008 report found several issues. The key one was with the main pipe from Lisvane reservoir, which carries water from Lisvane down to the Celsa steelworks in Cardiff Bay and runs along the bed of Llanishen reservoir. Dr Hughes claimed that Stuart Davies, the supervising engineer, had told him that the condition of this main within the city was poor and that there had been frequent bursts. Therefore, Hughes argued that it was essential to examine the condition of the pipe and valves under Llanishen reservoir. He specified that this work should be undertaken in the interests of safety under Section 10(6) of the Reservoirs Act. In another part of the report, Hughes stated that the proposed survey of the pipe and valves would require the temporary draining of the reservoir. However, this wasn't listed specifically as one of the requirements on the grounds of safety.

As the Reservoir Act was designed to ensure public safety, it carries a lot of weight. If an inspecting engineer makes a recommendation 'on the grounds of safety', it becomes something that must be complied with by law. There can be no discussion or debate. The inspecting engineer's pronouncement is final, and the work must be carried out in the specified time period. Dr Hughes had specified that the valves and pipework be inspected within 12 months. What concerned us, however, was that although Dr Hughes had specified a temporary drain down, once Western Power had emptied the reservoir, we imagined that it might be reluctant to fill it up again. A muddy hole was likely to improve its chances of obtaining planning permission compared to a pristine reservoir with people sailing on it. In other words, we thought that Dr Hughes' untimely report and recommendations were probably just what Western Power wanted to hear!

Usually, the list of expert witnesses and their evidence is provided to all interested parties well in advance of the start of a Public Planning Inquiry. Last-minute introductions of new evidence are not allowed. However, at the start of the 2008 Planning Inquiry, the inclusion of Dr Hughes' report and his presence as a witness was allowed because of the significance of a safety recommendation under the Reservoirs Act. Making this argument to the inspector was one of John Steel QC's most successful moves. The RAG committee assumed that the introduction of the Reservoir Act report at the start of the inquiry was to influence the inspector. If he were led to believe that concerns about the safety of the reservoir meant that it would have to be drained anyway, he might be more inclined to allow Western Power's appeal, and the housing development would then go ahead.

Once the inquiry was over, there was no further mention of drain down, even though Hughes had recommended that the pipe and valve inspections needed to be carried out within 12 months. Then, in early August 2009, RAG got an anonymous tip-off that Western Power was approaching engineering firms to see if they were interested in setting up a programme for draining the reservoir. This was the first indication that the strategy of drain down was being actively pursued. By then, Andrew Hill had taken over as Chairman of RAG from Ted Thurgood. He immediately alerted the local politicians and also contacted Geoff Shimmel, the senior solicitor for Cardiff Council. The reason for this was that the Council had a lease for sailing on the reservoir, and obviously, it would not be able to exercise its right as a lessee if the reservoir was empty. Mr Shimmel was on top of the issue and was due to meet with a barrister the following Monday to discuss the implications. Unfortunately, it turned out that the terms of the lease entitled Western Power to ask the sailing centre to stop sailing in the event of a safety drain down, and in December 2009, Western Power served a notice to the Council to this effect.

Andrew also tried another tack. He consulted Anthony Dinkin QC, a well-known London barrister who specialises in Planning Law. From his own experience as an architectural conservator, Andrew knew that the listing of a building by Cadw would also extend to its 'setting'. He wondered if it could be argued that the protection afforded to a listed reservoir would also extend to the water it contained. Unfortunately, Mr Dinkin's response was pretty unequivocal: he did not think the listing of the structure would extend to the water, and he advised that this line of attack was not worth pursuing.

It seemed that any recommendation made under the Reservoir Act was not legally challengeable. However, Andrew had access to some information that Dr Hughes did not appear to have when he made his inspection report. During his research into the history of the reservoirs, which formed the basis of his application for listing to Cadw, Andrew found a copy of the original plans for the reservoir drawn up by J.A.B. Williams in 1884. This talked about the construction of the main pipeline from Lisvane reservoir that ran along the bed of Llanishen reservoir and which Hughes had decreed must be inspected on safety grounds. The original specification (p39) stated that:

> *"The Contractor shall lay and joint the 18-inch cast-iron main ...from the inner end of the scouring culvert to the north end of the present filter yard, a length of 300 yards, in the position shewn, the top of the main to be 4 feet and 6 inches below the intended bottom of Reservoir; and when ordered by the Engineer so to do, he shall connect the same with the existing 15-inch main from the present Lisvane Reservoir. The water shall be well drained off from the trench and the pipes shall be surrounded with fine concrete carried up 1 foot above the top of the pipes, and the remainder of the trench to be carefully filled in with good hard materials levelled and rammed."*

In other words, the 18-inch main was not lying on the bed of the reservoir; it was likely to be almost five feet down in a deep trench and probably surrounded by a foot of concrete. Even if the reservoir were drained, it might not be possible to inspect the main without digging down and hacking away the concrete that surrounded it. This operation in itself was highly likely to damage the pipe. Another concern with draining the reservoir was the structure of the clay core of the embankments. Like many Victorian reservoirs, the embankments had a core of puddled clay, which made them waterproof. When the reservoir is full of water, this clay core stays moist, but if the reservoir were emptied for any length of time, there is a risk that the clay cores would dry out and start to crack. If this happened, it might mean that the reservoir would no longer be safe to hold water. Hughes had estimated that once the reservoir was emptied, it would take up to eight years to refill, just relying on rainwater. This is a long time to leave a reservoir empty, and our concern was that damage could occur to the reservoir's structure.

The Binnie Report

Andrew decided to get another expert opinion, so in December 2009, he contacted another reservoir engineer, Mr Chris Binnie. Andrew commissioned him to prepare a report on RAG's behalf covering the need for emptying the reservoir, the effects of drain down, and the possibilities for refilling the reservoir. Mr Binnie was eminently qualified for the job. He had been an 'all panels' reservoir engineer for over 30 years and sat on the Institution of Civil Engineers committee that appointed engineers to this role. He was also a Past President of the Chartered Institution of Water and Environmental Management.

Chris Binnie produced his report in early February 2010. It ran to 30 pages, but the main points are summarised here.

- One of the first things Binnie did was to contact Stuart Davies, the supervising engineer. You may remember that Hughes' report stated that he had been told by Mr Davies that 'the condition of the main within the city is poor with frequent bursts', which was why the pipe running underneath Llanishen reservoir had to be inspected. However, in a previous conversation with Andrew, Mr Davies had said that he could not remember saying anything to Hughes about 'frequent bursts' and had no knowledge of any bursts on the Lisvane main. Binnie asked if there could have been a misunderstanding about this, but Mr Davies replied that there had not been, although he did add that there was a discrepancy between the outlet meter at the reservoir and the inlet meter at the steelworks. Enquiries by Andrew also could find no records held by Cardiff Council about bursts in this main. Mr Binnie, therefore, concluded that there was no good reason to question the integrity of the Lisvane main, in particular where it ran under Llanishen reservoir.

- Binnie also picked up on the fact that the main under Llanishen reservoir was buried in a trench and might be surrounded by concrete. This appeared to be something about which Dr Hughes was unaware and might make the drain down of the reservoir pointless, as it would be impossible to examine even the outside surface of the pipe.

- Binnie proposed that the other surveys that Hughes had recommended on safety grounds, to chart the layout of pipes under the reservoir and to check on the valves' condition, could easily be done by other standard methods without requiring the reservoir to be drained. Also, the current drawdown rate, which Hughes had specified needed to be increased, was considered adequate by Binnie and to the panel engineers who prepared the previous Inspection Reports. It was already about twice the rate recommended by the industry guidelines at the time.

Binnie concluded that there was no compelling reason for the reservoir to be drained. In the event that it was drained, he calculated that the reservoir would take ten years to refill by rainfall alone – hardly a 'temporary' drain down. Binnie thought this was unacceptable and could well have unpredicted consequences, including the cracking of the clay core of the dam. He suggested that if the reservoir was drained, the aim should be to refill it within six months and suggested diverting excess water from the Nant Fawr to achieve this.

Additionally, if Llanishen reservoir were to be drained, the ecosystem that had built up there since the 1880s would be lost. The water in Llanishen was soft and low in nutrients, as it had come originally from the Brecon Beacons and, since the 1970s, had just been topped up by rainwater. The plant communities that had developed there were species that thrive in low-nutrient freshwater, such as stoneworts. Llanishen was also much preferred over Lisvane reservoir by the large population of common toads that bred there every spring. Possibly because Lisvane reservoir had poorer water quality as it was fed by local streams, which contained higher levels of nutrients. Once Llanishen reservoir was drained, its fragile ecosystem, along with the toads, was likely to be lost.

Andrew sent copies of Binnie's report to Western Power, to the Chief Executive of the Pennsylvania Power and Light Corporation (the American company that owned Western Power), to Dr Hughes, and to all our local political representatives.

In mid-February, Andrew also wrote directly to Dr Hughes asking him to amend his report in light of there being no evidence of bursts in the Lisvane main down in the city and the fact that the pipe running under the reservoir was buried in a trench and likely to be covered in concrete. Hughes replied, saying that he was no longer employed by Western Power as the Inspecting Engineer and that it was impossible to amend a reservoir inspection report retrospectively. It would only be superseded when the reservoir was next inspected.

The Environment Agency

The Environment Agency wrote to Western Power on 18th February 2010, in its role as the enforcement agency under the Reservoirs Act. It pointed out that the recommendations of Dr Hughes in his 2008 report did not specifically require a drain down of the reservoir, only that the pipework and valves needed to be inspected. They also noted that articles had appeared in the press implying that the reservoir must be drained to carry out the surveys and asked Western Power to correct this 'erroneous perception' immediately. Finally, the Environment Agency pointed out that Western Power was entitled to draw off up to three metres of water from the reservoir but that if it were to drain the reservoir completely, it would require a discharge consent under the 1991 Water Resources Act. The Countryside Council for Wales would also need to be consulted about the possible effects of drain down on the Embankments SSSI.

Initial Drain Down Starts

Western Power ignored all these entreaties to reconsider the need to drain the reservoir, and on 26th February 2010, it began draining the first three metres of water from Llanishen Reservoir. Large flexible pipes were used to siphon the water over the main dam crest and into the scour channel, which runs into the Nant Fawr stream. The area was fenced off, and a temporary cabin installed. This was occupied by security staff, who were there to make sure there was no attempt by the public to interfere with the operations.

Attempts to Stop a Full Drain Down

At this stage, local politicians weighed into the debate. Julie Morgan MP had been a great supporter of RAG since the outset, and she took the opportunity of the St. David's Day debate in the House of Commons to raise the issue of the drainage of Llanishen Reservoir. She summarised the present situation, including the reports of Hughes and Binnie, and the recent letter from the Environment Agency saying that draining the reservoir was unnecessary. She also described the information that Andrew had uncovered about the pipe probably being encased in concrete, which had come to light after Hughes' initial report, as well as there being little evidence of bursts in the Lisvane main down in the city. She mentioned that Mr Binnie had contacted Dr Hughes about this new information but that Dr Hughes appeared to be disinclined to amend his report in light of the new evidence. Using Parliamentary Privilege, Julie suggested why this might be the case. She mentioned Binnie's concerns about the possible dangers to the clay core if the reservoir was allowed to remain empty for a number of years and his recommendation that the pipe should be inspected using methods that did not involve emptying the reservoir. She suggested that the Institution of Civil Engineers could appoint an independent adjudicator to consider both Hughes' and Binnie's reports. Julie asked the Secretary of State, Peter Hain, to see if there was anything he could do to help. He promised to look into the issue and raise it with Carwyn Jones, the First Minister of Wales.

Andrew also tried to prevent a complete drain down by appealing to Western Power in person. On 6th March, he went over to Bristol to Western Power's offices to meet with its Chief Executive, Robert Symonds. He described the meeting as courteous but frank. Andrew pointed out that other reservoir engineers had questioned the need for drain down and that the pipe they wanted to inspect was likely to be buried in a trench and encased in concrete. Symonds was not prepared to discuss any alternatives and simply stated that they would follow the recommendations of their consultants. Andrew also gained the impression that Western Power's intention, having drained the reservoir, was to leave it empty for as long as possible.

The Warren Report

Towards the end of March 2010, the Environment Agency engaged yet another reservoir engineer to undertake an assessment of the need to drain Llanishen reservoir. I imagine it was concerned that neither Hughes nor Binnie were completely independent, having been hired by the two opposing sides in the confrontation over the reservoir's future. It engaged Mr Alan Warren, an experienced reservoir engineer who worked for the civil engineering consultant Halcrow. Mr Warren reviewed all the relevant reports, carried out his own inspection visit to the reservoir, and corresponded with the engineer, Mr Chris Owens, whom Western Power had tasked with supervising the drain down of the reservoir.

In his report, submitted to the Environment Agency in April 2010, the first thing that Mr Warren noted was that Hughes' original report of 2008 had specified that the inspection of the pipework and valves on safety grounds should be carried out within 12 months. Almost two years had passed since then, and the work had not yet taken place, so this was clearly a breach of the Reservoir Act. He also commented on the proposed plan for draining the reservoir, concluding that the overall objectives of the work were not clear to him and that the complete emptying of the reservoir was not necessarily required. Mr Warren pointed out that Mr Owens provided little evidence as to why the reservoir needed draining in preference to other approaches that could be used to examine the pipework and valves. Finally, he commented on the risks to the clay core in draining the reservoir. He stated that the work supposedly being carried out on safety grounds was potentially being addressed in a manner that would create new risks to reservoir safety. In other words, Warren's report largely supported the views that Chris Binnie had put forward. The grounds for draining the reservoir still seemed very tenuous.

Despite all this, the Reservoir Act carries a lot of authority, and the Environment Agency did not feel that it was in a position to go against the recommendations of a supervising engineer and prevent the draining of the reservoir. Alan Warren had also been asked to produce a timetable for the drain down to occur, and following the removal of the top 3m of water, he thought it was feasible for the main drain down to begin on 19th July 2010. Assuming a flow rate of 450 litres/second, he estimated it was likely that the process would be completed by mid-September 2010. Given the subsequent inspection and any repairs that might be needed, he reckoned it should be possible to complete the work by 31st January 2011. Thereafter, the refill of the reservoir could commence.

To Parliament Again

In the general election of May 2010, Julie Morgan lost her seat in the marginal constituency of Cardiff North, and the Conservative candidate, Jonathan Evans, took over. Fortunately, all the main political parties were opposed to the development at the reservoirs, and Jonathan used his maiden speech in the House of Commons on 6th July to raise the issue of Llanishen reservoir again. He outlined the whole situation in detail and pointed out the absurdity of the fact that the Environment Agency, which considered the drain down of the reservoir as being unnecessary and itself a possible risk to the future safety of the reservoir, still had to insist on it taking place simply as the enforcement authority under the Reservoirs Act. Under the Act, it had to ensure that the owners, Western Power, complied with the 2008 recommendation of the inspecting engineer, Dr A. Hughes. The Under-Secretary of State for Wales promised to look into this not only in terms of Llanishen but also in terms of the wider application of the Reservoirs Act. However, we all knew this was unlikely to lead to any resolution of our immediate problem.

The Full Drain Down Begins

By this time, our problem was acute. The drain down of the first three metres of water had ended in June, and Western Power had now applied to the Environment Agency for permission to drain the rest of the water under section 85 of the Water Resources Act 1991. This gives permission to discharge water that may include sediments into surface water such as rivers and streams, in this case, the Nant Fawr. Previous studies carried out on Western Power's behalf had suggested that the amount of sediment on the bottom of Llanishen reservoir was minimal, so with the proviso that they constructed a rudimentary sediment trap using bales of straw in the scour channel, permission was granted by the Environment Agency.

The main drain down of Llanishen reservoir started on 3rd August 2010 and was completed about six weeks later in mid-September.

Figure 17.1. Photograph of Llanishen reservoir on 7th September 2010 when the drain down was almost completed.

The Draining of Llanishen Reservoir

Figure 17.2. Satellite photo of the emptied reservoir taken on 19th April 2011. Some of the key features are visible including the original filter beds for Lisvane reservoir; the inlet which received water from the reservoirs in the Brecon Beacons; a faint pale line shows the route of the buried pipeline which led to the draining of the reservoir; the scour or plug-hole; and the location of the valve tower. Image downloaded from Google Earth © 2023 Maxar Technologies.

At this stage, our strategy switched from trying to prevent drain down to trying to ensure the reservoir was refilled as soon as possible once the inspection and any repairs needed had been completed. We still suspected that Western Power had no intention of refilling the reservoir, and this suspicion turned out to be entirely justified, as Western Power never did refill it.

Postscript

In some respects, that is the end of the story about the drain down, apart from one further aspect. Andrew had been so incensed by Dr Hughes' and Mr Owen's intransigence and their refusal to consider alternative ways of inspecting the pipeline, as suggested by other qualified reservoir engineers, that he raised the issue with their professional body, the Institution of Civil Engineers (ICE). He asked them to consider whether this was 'improper conduct' under their professional code of conduct. Andrew suggested that there was a widespread perception that both engineers were acting to further their client's wishes and not sound engineering practice and that they had an obligation under ICE's code of practice to take into account their overriding responsibility to the public good. If the total drainage of the reservoir led to the embankments being compromised through cracking of their clay core, Andrew argued this would not be to the public good.

At its meetings in December 2010 and March 2011, the Professional Conduct Panel of the Institution of Civil Engineers considered the evidence that Andrew submitted, along with observations submitted by Dr Hughes and Mr Owens. It dismissed the allegations of misconduct against them both.

Chapter 18

The Nant Fawr Local Nature Reserve

During the period when we were trying to halt the draining of Llanishen reservoir, Cardiff Council led another initiative.

Early in 2009, Ted Thurgood and a few members of the RAG Planning Group met with Steven Phillips, the Corporate Manager of Cardiff Council, to discuss ways in which greater protection from development could be afforded to Cardiff's river corridors and the Nant Fawr river corridor in particular. Chris Powell, the Council's Parks Conservation Officer, was also at the meeting and raised the possibility of designating the Nant Fawr area as a local nature reserve. From RAG's point of view, any initiatives that gave the Nant Fawr corridor greater protection would make it harder for Western Power to push its access road across the meadows and, therefore, to build on the reservoirs.

Designating a Local Nature Reserve

After the meeting, I was asked by Ted Thurgood to let Chris Powell have all the information in our possession about the biodiversity of the meadows and the reservoirs and to begin putting together a case for the designation of the area as a Local Nature Reserve (LNR).

I began by investigating the steps that need to be taken to declare an area as a LNR. This is covered under Section 21 of the National Parks and Access to the Countryside Act 1949. The Act was initially described in terms of the UK-wide Nature Conservancy Council, which oversaw conservation until its short-sighted demise in 1991.

Subsequently, this agency was devolved into English Nature, The Countryside Council for Wales (CCW), and Scottish Natural Heritage. [Note that in 2009 CCW had not yet been replaced by Natural Resources Wales]. The procedure for declaring a LNR in the three devolved agencies differed slightly. In Wales, the steps were as follows:

1. The Act requires proposed sites to be of good quality and to provide special opportunities for study and research and/or preserve wildlife or natural features of *special* interest in the area. [My italics, because the word special is important here].
2. In Wales, the Local Authority seeking to designate a site first had to get the approval of the Countryside Council for Wales. This was to ensure consistency across the Principality, and applications for LNRs were regularly assessed at the quarterly meetings of the CCW Council. The National Parks and Access to the Countryside Act also clearly states that LNRs must be managed, and a comprehensive management plan is a key part of the application.
3. Having obtained the approval of the CCW, the Local Authority could proceed and, if agreed at a Council meeting, it could declare the area of land to be a local nature reserve.

The procedure was not that complicated but involved getting the approval of the CCW at an early stage. To this end, I contacted Sue Howard at the CCW to get some idea of how they would view a proposal. Sue thought the application would be welcomed by the CCW, especially if it was an initiative coming from local residents. She stressed the importance of emphasising community involvement and the educational value of the area in any application.

With this in mind, making a good case wasn't too difficult. The Nant Fawr meadows and woodland already contained three Sites of Importance for Nature Conservation and were adjacent to two Sites of Special Scientific Interest at the reservoirs. More importantly, there were excellent opportunities for study and research, as Cardiff High School, Corpus Christi High School and Rhyd-y-penau Primary

School were immediately adjacent to the site. There was also good community involvement through the Friends of Nant Fawr. I sent this information, along with the biodiversity records, to Chris Powell towards the end of April 2009.

Cardiff Council Gets it Wrong

We didn't hear much more about the Local Nature Reserve until later that summer. By then, Andrew Hill had taken over from Ted Thurgood as Chairman of RAG, and in early August, he rang Steven Phillips to see what was happening about protection for the Nant Fawr Corridor. Mr Phillips reported that the Council Executive had approved the 'River Rhymney and Nant Fawr Corridor Action Plan' in July 2009 and that this had included the intention to declare a LNR on the Council-owned land in the Nant Fawr corridor. He added that the Council intended to use their normal powers to declare a Local Nature Reserve in the September committee cycle.

At the Cardiff Council Executive meeting on the 1st October, the Nant Fawr Corridor was formally declared as a Local Nature Reserve prior to endorsement by the Countryside Council for Wales (CCW). The supporting documents making a case for the LNR were quite brief and did not mention community involvement or the potential of the site for educational study. It listed a few of the species that could be seen there, and the main justification presented for the LNR was the linking together of the three Sites of Importance for Nature Conservation. The Council had also helpfully provided a press release,

Fig. 18.1. A broad-leaved helleborine photographed in Rhyd-y-penau woods, July 2011.

Save our Reservoirs

and the story was duly picked up and published in that evening's edition of the South Wales Echo under the headline 'Land around reservoir to become nature reserve'.

Western Power Objects

If you have been paying attention, you may have spotted a problem with the Council's Local Nature Reserve declaration. Western Power was certainly paying attention, and in December 2009, it sought leave to challenge Cardiff Council's decision by way of judicial review. A preliminary hearing was held on 19th March 2010 in front of Deputy High Court Judge H.H.J. Seys-Llewellyn QC.

Western Power's objections to the Nant Fawr LNR declaration were based on four grounds:

1. That the Council had not properly consulted the CCW before it declared the LNR, as specified in section 21.6 of the National Parks and Access to the Countryside Act 1949.

2. That the document presented to the Council had not made clear the 'special' opportunities for the study and research of the flora and fauna in the area and had not specified the 'special' interest of the area as specified in section 15 of the National Parks and Access to the Countryside Act 1949.

3. That the Council had failed to consider how the land could be managed for conservation purposes before deciding to designate, i.e. it had failed to provide a management plan.

4. That the Council failed to take into account the fact that the land is held under a statutory trust for use as public walks or pleasure grounds requiring public access to be maintained at all times and the extent to which that obligation was or is compatible with designation as a local nature reserve.

After due consideration, Judge Seys-Llewellyn decided that Western Power's application for a judicial review of the Nant Fawr LNR declaration should be accepted on grounds 1 and 2 but not grounds 3 and 4. However, Western Power was not satisfied with this result and, a week later, appealed the decision, asking to be allowed to challenge the designation on all four grounds. The Court eventually granted this appeal, and the Judicial Review was scheduled for 23rd February 2011.

The Council Tries Again

In the meantime, the Council decided to have another go at declaring a Local Nature Reserve. This time, it followed the correct procedure and, well in advance, sent a comprehensive document, which included a management plan for the LNR, to the Countryside Council for Wales. This was considered at the CCW Council Meeting in Abergavenny on 13th September 2010 and finally approved.

On 7th October 2010, the Council Executive again considered the question of a Local Nature Reserve. On this occasion, the Council officials detailed the special interest and the opportunities for study, alongside the community involvement provided by the Friends of Nant Fawr. They also provided a detailed management plan, which showed that the area would be managed for both conservation and recreation and argued that these two activities were not incompatible. The Council Executive agreed to the proposal and decided that the land should again be declared as a Local Nature Reserve.

The Judicial Review

The following February saw the usual crowd appearing at the Royal Courts of Justice in London before Mr Justice Ouseley. Mr John Steel QC and Mr Robert Palmer appeared on behalf of Western Power; Mr Mark Lowe and Mrs Harriet Townsend represented Cardiff County Council. Although Mr Steel had been given grounds for the judicial review on four separate issues, some of these had now been addressed. The latest LNR declaration was made after obtaining approval from the CCW; it described the special interest of the area; and included a management plan. Instead, Mr Steel concentrated on just one issue, and that was his contention that there was an incompatibility between the use of the land for recreational purposes and for conservation. Mr

Save our Reservoirs

Figure 18.2. Plan showing the boundaries of the proposed Local Nature Reserve (in red). Image downloaded from Google Earth © 2023 Infoterra Ltd. & Bluesky.

The Nant Fawr LNR

Steel's argument to the Court lasted a whole morning, but I will try and summarise it in one paragraph.

The Village Green Inquiry under Vivian Chapman QC had already established that the land surrounding the reservoirs, which included the Nant Fawr LNR, had been purchased by the Council in 1948 under Section 164 of the Public Health Act 1875 for the purposes of providing 'public walks and pleasure grounds' (See Chapter 13). In other words, it had been purchased for recreation, and therefore, local people had a right to use the land for this purpose. Mr Steel argued that as Cardiff Council had declared the land as a Local Nature Reserve, its main purpose would now be for conservation. The National Parks and Access to the Countryside Act 1949, as amended by the Natural Environment and Rural Communities Act 2006 [the law is complicated], states that a nature reserve could be 'land managed not only for a conservation purpose but also for a recreational purpose if the management of the land for the recreational purpose does not compromise its management for the conservation purpose'. In other words, under the 1949 Act, management for conservation must take precedence over recreational use. Thus, the two laws conflict: the 1875 Act favours management for public access and the 1949 Act favours management for conservation. Mr Steel further argued that when the LNR was declared, the public should have been notified and allowed to object, as their original right to wander freely over the land could now be restricted by its subsequent use as a nature reserve. For example, there may have been an attempt to exclude people from a part of the meadows if some rare plant was found flowering there.

Mr Lowe, the Council's barrister, contested this view, but at the end of the day, Mr Justice Ouseley agreed with Mr Steel's assessment and concluded that the designation of the land as a Local Nature Reserve was unlawful. He, therefore, quashed both attempts by the Council to designate the land as a Local Nature Reserve, and that was that. The Council had to accept his decision and didn't pursue the idea further.

Chapter 19

The Second Planning Inquiry Resumes

In September 2009, the second planning inquiry had faltered (see Chapter 15). The planning inspector had recommended that Western Power's appeal be accepted and that the development should go ahead, but the Welsh Government Minister for Environment, Sustainability and Housing had disagreed and rejected the inspector's conclusion and the appeal. Western Power had challenged the Minister's decision in the High Court, and the Welsh Government had backed down and accepted that her decision had been flawed. So the Minister's decision was set aside, and it was decided that the second inquiry should reopen. Since the first part of the inquiry, however, there had been a significant change in circumstances. Cadw had listed Llanishen reservoir as a structure of historic importance, and this was likely to influence many of the conclusions that the inspector had reached in 2008. Effectively, we would need to start all over again.

Preliminary Steps

The resumed second inquiry was scheduled for 5th July 2011, again with Mr Richard Poppleton as the inspector. There had been a pre-inquiry meeting involving all the interested parties in mid-February 2011, at which the ground rules were established. Statements of case had to be produced by all participants and submitted to the Planning Inspectorate by 18th April, with all written representations and full statements of evidence to be received by 7th June.

Mr Steel, again representing Western Power, announced that the developers were now focusing on what they were calling 'Option D' as the access arrangement. This involved all traffic for the development entering via the Lisvane Road entrance. He added that they would be making a planning application for a mini-roundabout at the Lisvane Road entrance and applying for listed building consent for the damage that would be caused to the reservoir structure by the access roads. Mr Steel also announced that they would produce a revised Environmental Statement dealing with the new access arrangements.

Introducing lots of new material just before a major inquiry seemed to be a general strategy adopted by Western Power. We wondered if it was designed to wrong-foot us, as we had to reassess large amounts of material at short notice. It was surprising they were allowed to get away with it.

Planning applications for the mini-roundabout and listed building consent were submitted in early March 2011. A few weeks afterwards, the Welsh Government 'called in' these two applications for the Minster to decide and included them in the resumed public inquiry. Nevertheless, the Council Planning Committee considered the two applications on 11th May along with the new Environmental Statement and decided that, if it had been up to them, they would have rejected both planning applications and considered the Environmental Statement to be inadequate. This outcome was passed on to the planning inspector so that it could be taken into account when making his final decision at the end of the inquiry.

The Inquiry Opens

The inquiry opened on schedule at 10 am on 5th July 2011 in one of the Committee Rooms of County Hall in Cardiff Bay. It had a rather fractured timetable: the first part of the inquiry was due to run for seven days between 5th and 13th July. Then, there was going to be a summer break while all the lawyers took their summer holidays. It would resume on 15th August for a further five days, ending on Friday 19th August. This meant that, in total, it would last for 12 days.

Save our Reservoirs

As usual, Western Power was represented by John Steel QC and Robert Palmer, and they were instructed by Geldards solicitors. On any one day, this meant that the Western Power legal team usually consisted of six people: the two barristers, a couple of partners from Geldards, and two legal assistants whose job it was to sort through the myriad of documents they produced. The Council was again represented by Mark Lowe QC, instructed by the Council's solicitor, Ms Polly Ellis. In RAG's case, it was Anthony Dinkin QC, instructed by Harmer Planning Consultants, but RAG's Chairman, Andrew Hill, also attended the inquiry every day and provided additional briefing for Mr Dinkin. Cadw decided not to be represented in person at the inquiry and relied on a submitted written statement.

Anthony Dinkin was quite a find for RAG. Andrew Hill had first been in touch with him a couple of years earlier when he was seeking legal advice on the draining of Llanishen reservoir. He was a highly experienced planning barrister and was somewhat reminiscent of 'Rumpole of the Bailey', the fictional lawyer created by John Mortimer. He was sympathetic towards our cause and had formed a good relationship with Andrew, so he agreed to represent us for rather less than his usual fee.

Figure 19.1 Anthony Dinkin QC and Andrew Hill at the Inquiry. Photo by Richard Bosworth.

In the pre-meeting, it had been agreed that the inquiry would tackle the issues on a topic-by-topic basis rather than each participant taking turns to make their case on all issues. However, the inquiry started with each of the three counsels providing a summary of the overall case that they would be making.

Opening Statements

Cardiff Council went first, and Mark Lowe QC outlined the main issues they were contesting. These were open space issues and the proposed development's incompatibility with the Council's planning policies; the damage that would be caused to the Grade II listed structure and its setting by building houses within the reservoir bowl; and the problems that would be caused by bringing all the traffic to and from the development via the Lisvane road. Anthony Dinkin QC, on behalf of RAG, was next up and focused on the same three main points. He argued that the listing and the new access proposals tipped the planning balance even more decisively against the development and urged the inspector to dismiss the appeal.

Mr Steel's opening statement went on about twice as long as the others combined. Maybe he was just being thorough, but at times, it seemed as if he was waging a war of attrition. He stressed that the revised plan to build houses sunken down in the reservoir bowl would mean that they were barely visible from the outside and, therefore, wouldn't impinge on the 'openness' of the Nant Fawr corridor. He also made much of the fact that trespassers and vandals were currently degrading the site and damaging both its ecology and the listed building. He argued that there was no alternative other than the proposed development to stop this degradation. Finally, he pointed out that the new access arrangements would avoid the need for a new road across the Nant Fawr meadows and even suggested that the mini roundabout on Lisvane Road would improve the safety and amenity benefits of the road! However, John Steel also tried to cover his back by saying that although Western Power was going to pursue the proposal for a mini roundabout, it reserved the right to re-introduce the idea of having a T-junction on Lisvane Road.

Landscape

The first major topic for consideration was 'Landscape matters'. Brian Denny from Pegasus Environmental, representing Western Power, was the first to give evidence. His main thesis was the one Steel had

Save our Reservoirs

already made, namely that as the housing was now going to be placed in the reservoir bowl, it would be largely hidden from surrounding areas and wouldn't have a visual impact. He also argued that the outline planning permission granted in 2005 to the Carlyle Trust on the fields adjacent to the Lisvane Road would have a significant urbanising effect and change Lisvane Road from being semi-rural to suburban in nature. (This is the housing development that recently went ahead in 2021 and 2022). He suggested that this development would have a much bigger impact than the mini-roundabout proposed by Western Power. He also described recent revisions to their plans that reduced the impact of the development on the Llanishen reservoir embankments. The first day of the inquiry closed at 5.30 pm.

Wednesday started with Mr Lowe's cross-examination of Mr Denny. Really, there weren't any significant points made, but there was much discussion about what constituted a semi-rural vs a suburban road. When pressed, Denny didn't seem to know much about the reservoirs' immediate history or use over the last 30 years.

The next expert witness on Landscape matters was Mr Malcolm Hockaday, on behalf of the Council. He argued that the proposed reservoir development would destroy the character and openness of the Nant Fawr green corridor. He also stressed that the nature of Lisvane Road was completely different from that of Rhyd-y-penau Road and confirmed that, in his opinion, the inspector's previous description of Lisvane Road as being semi-rural was correct. In his cross-examination of Mr Hockaday, John Steel started by questioning his credibility as a witness by claiming he was not a qualified landscape architect. In a rather unpleasant exchange, he also claimed that Mr Hockaday was biased because he lived near the area. His attack became personal and made some people present feel uncomfortable. He went on to complain that neither the Council nor Mr Hockaday had objected to aspects of the proposed changes to the northern access onto Lisvane Road in the previous inquiry, and Mr Hockaday had to point out that it was the previous inspector himself who had raised this as an issue. The discussion then turned to the visibility of the development on either side of the reservoir basin. Denny had claimed that the housing would be hidden from the surrounding areas, and Mr Steel tried to make much of this. But Hockaday maintained that the proposed two-storey houses would project by 2m and the three-story houses by 4m. So they would be clearly visible from outside the area. This did not appear to please Mr Steel.

Ecology

On Thursday, 7th July, the topic switched to ecology. The main part of the day was taken up with Dominic Woodfield's evidence on behalf of Western Power. He claimed that the new scheme had even more ecological benefits than the previous proposal considered in 2008. Less land would be taken from the SSSI if the option D access from Lisvane Road went ahead. He also claimed that the site was now being seriously degraded by commercial dog-walking and had deteriorated ecologically since the previous inquiry. Bird life on Lisvane was being disturbed, and the fungi around Llanishen were being adversely affected. He claimed that Western Powers' proposed development was the only way of halting the damage to biodiversity. Again, he was cross-examined by Mark Lowe, but Mr Woodfield dealt reasonably well with his questions.

Next up, the Council ecologist, Matthew Harris, gave evidence to the inquiry. He was ill at ease from the start, possibly because he turned up casually dressed, and the Council legal team thought it might appear disrespectful if he was not wearing a tie. There was a quick hiatus while he was furnished with one, and then he took the stand to give his evidence. When it came to his cross-examination, Mr Steel showed no mercy. In his evidence, Mr Harris had stated that the freshwater plant community of Llanishen reservoir was dependent on high water quality. He had then criticised Western Power's plans for the proposed refilling of Llanishen reservoir from the Nant Fawr stream, which was known to have enriched levels of nutrients. Mr Steel carefully led him through this evidence but then pointed out that in the 2008 inquiry, it had been established that the key species involved were actually tolerant to a wide range of water qualities, undermining his credibility and getting him flustered. By the end of his cross-examination, Mr Steel got him to agree that the development would actually be of ecological benefit!

Planning Issues

On Friday, the inquiry turned to planning issues. The main witness was Peter Waldren from RPS Planning, who represented Western Power. The main thrust of his evidence was much the same as before: that the development would provide more public open space in the Nant Fawr green corridor whilst ignoring the fact that it was Western Power itself that had excluded the public from the reservoirs in the first place. However, much was made of the deterioration of the site since the 2008 inquiry, in that vandalism had increased, sailing had ceased, and the sailing centre and the buildings had been demolished. The reservoir was now empty and redundant. Again, it did not appear to occur to him who was responsible for all this. Mr Waldren claimed it would cost £833,319 over five years to re-establish sailing at the reservoir and suggested that the Council would struggle to find such an amount. He also had the nerve to suggest that the impact of the development on the listed building would be acceptable and welcome, with no harmful effect. He did not seem to think there would be any issue regarding its 'setting' if the interior was filled with houses instead of water!

When Mr Steel finished taking him through his evidence, Mr Mark Lowe QC led the cross-examination of Mr Waldren on behalf of the Council. He focused mainly on the cost estimates of re-establishing sailing, which in many cases seemed widely exaggerated.

Reservoir Structure

Next up was Western Power's reservoir engineer, Dr Andrew Hughes. Like most other Western Power witnesses, Dr Hughes stressed the deterioration of the reservoir structure due to neglect and vandalism. He dwelt on the point that, in his experience, reservoirs that no longer served their original purpose were often uneconomic to maintain and were usually drained and abandoned. He argued that this was the case at Llanishen, as well as providing what appeared to be exaggerated estimates for refilling the reservoir and maintaining it. He also sought to introduce the question of reservoir safety into the debate and produced inundation maps showing the areas of Cardiff that would be affected if there were ever a major breach of the reservoir dam. However, all previous inspections of the reservoir structure, including his own in 2008, had found the dam to be in good condition and safe to store water up to its 'top water level'. No other significant problems had been discovered when the reservoir was drained. Dr Hughes reported that the infamous 'Lisvane main', which led to the draining of the reservoir, had been excavated and inspected. The pipe was not enclosed in concrete where he inspected it but turned out to be in 'surprisingly good condition for its age'.

Another useful point that Hughes made was that he thought RAG's concerns about the clay core of the embankments drying out and cracking when the reservoir was drained down were entirely misplaced. He quoted several instances where reservoirs of a similar construction had been left empty over many years, in one case for nearly 60 years, and there were no problems when they were refilled. This meant that if the reservoir were ever to be reinstated, for example, if the courts upheld the Council's lease for sailing there, it would make it hard for Western Power to use this as an argument against refilling.

Heritage Matters

The last major topic before the inquiry broke up for the holidays was heritage matters and, in particular, the Grade II listing of the reservoir structure in 2009.

Dr Malcolm Hockaday was again the major witness to appear for the Council. He pointed out that the continuous encircling dam of Llanishen reservoir, which is almost a mile long, is an important feature of its structure and that dividing it by cutting two access points for the roads would be damaging to its integrity. He also stressed that the relationship between the reservoir dam and the water it contains signifies its historic structure. Replacing the water with a housing estate would destroy this relationship. Finally, he made the point that Llanishen is an integral part of the historic Taf Fawr water supply system for Cardiff and that all the other reservoirs in the scheme were now listed. Damaging Llanishen would have an adverse impact on the whole Taf Fawr system.

Neil Burton was the heritage witness appearing for RAG. He had a career in the conservation of historic buildings spanning almost 40 years and had been an Inspector of Historic Buildings for English Heritage. Many of the points he made echoed those of Malcolm Hockaday, and he quoted much legislation and planning guidance which emphasised the importance of preserving historic buildings in a way that respects their original function. He stressed that the function of Llanishen reservoir was to contain water rather than to contain a housing estate and that the enclosed basin and the water within it formed an important part of its setting.

As expected, Western Power produced a heritage witness with a rather different take on things. Dr Jonathan Edis started from the assumption, advanced by Western Power, that the dam would not be used again for its original purpose of containing water. He suggested that new uses would have to be considered to secure the building's survival. He claimed that the listing of Llanishen reservoir was purely down to its historical interest and had nothing to do with its architectural interest or its setting, and suggested that now the reservoir was empty, people would be better able to observe and appreciate the listed structure, as much of it was previously hidden underwater! He also argued that, in the past, the water in the reservoir had largely been hidden from view from the surrounding area, and therefore, the water contributed little to the setting of the listed building in its historical context. With regard to the access roads, he tried to convince the inquiry that the damage to the listed structure caused by the two proposed roads would be minimal and not significant in a structure the size of the enclosing embankments. The resulting views of the cross-section of the embankment would also give people a better appreciation of how they were constructed. He also mentioned another advantage of the proposal: that the removal of the ugly metal fence installed by Western Power around the top of the embankment surrounding Llanishen reservoir would enhance the setting of the listed building! It's creditable that he said this without any sense of irony. In summary, he concluded that the development would have many clear benefits and minimal heritage impacts. The lesson I took away from his evidence is that if you look hard enough, you will be able to find an expert witness who will agree with just about any position.

The summer break began on Thursday, 14th July, and the inquiry resumed on Monday, 15th August.

Transport

The last remaining topic was transport, and this focused on the proposed access on Lisvane Road. On Monday 15th, Mike Axon of transport consultants Savell, Bird & Axon was the first witness called by Western Power.

He outlined how the developers were now considering two options where the lane from the reservoirs and allotments met Lisvane Road. The first was a priority 'T' junction, and the second, now their favoured option, was a mini roundabout. The main details of the proposed junctions had been agreed with the Council prior to the inquiry, and both parties had agreed a Statement of Common Ground on transport issues. Therefore, the Council was not contesting the transport proposals and fielding its own expert witness at the inquiry. However, as became clear from the rebuttal evidence submitted by Simon Howell, the Council's Transport manager, there were still quite a few outstanding concerns that had not been agreed.

Some months earlier, in May, the Council's Planning Committee had met to consider the proposed junctions. They concluded that they would have refused them because of: (1) the urbanisation of Lisvane Road due to the proposed traffic calming measures; (2) the effect of traffic volume increases on the amenity of local residents and users of Lisvane Road; (3) the removal of trees around the junction and (4) the possibility of dormice using the woodland alongside the access lane.

As with Denny's earlier evidence, Axon made much of Western Power's assertion of the suburban rather than semi-rural nature of Lisvane Road, supported by the outline planning permission granted for 64 houses on either side of Lisvane Road, just east of Chartwell Drive. Mike Axon claimed that Lisvane Road was safe and stated that there had been only two accidents on the stretch of road by the reservoir entrance in the five years up to the end of December 2010. Traffic speeds had been measured on two occasions on either side of the proposed junction, and the average speed was 30 mph. The Council had required that there be three raised tables to the west of the junction to moderate traffic speed. These would have been sited by the junctions at Mill Road, Marion Court and South Rise. Increased traffic flow on Lisvane Road from the proposed reservoir development was estimated by Axon as being 60 cars per hour heading west along Lisvane Road and 25 cars heading east.

Ron Kelly was the next witness to appear. He gave evidence on behalf of RAG and the Lisvane Community Council. Ron lived in Lisvane and was a regular user of Lisvane Road. He had worked in transport planning for over 25 years. He was led through his evidence by Anthony Dinkin QC. Ron considered that a mini roundabout was inappropriate because the traffic flows along Lisvane Road were much higher than those anticipated coming in and out of the reservoir. He claimed these unbalanced flows would contravene national guidance on the use of roundabouts. He pointed out that the proposed junction would lead to more traffic signs, road markings and traffic calming measures, which would be detrimental to the semi-rural nature of Lisvane Road. He further suggested that Western Power's figures for traffic flow into and out of the development were unrealistic, as they had been too optimistic in predicting the number of people using public transport to access the development, and their estimates had not been properly justified.

When Ron Kelly had finished, another local resident gave evidence. Julia Magill lived opposite the Lisvane entrance to the reservoirs and represented herself and her immediate neighbours. It should be stressed that Julia was not an expert witness but simply a local resident who objected to the proposals. Julia and her neighbours had commis-

The Second Planning Inquiry Resumes

sioned a report on Western Power traffic proposals by the Royal Society for the Prevention of Accidents (RoSPA). This report, undertaken by TMS Consultancy, was presented to the inquiry in evidence. It concluded that:

- The approach speeds and projected traffic flows would give rise to a significant increase in the risk of accidents, both in the case of a simple priority T-junction and a mini roundabout.
- Neither design catered adequately for the safety of vulnerable road users such as cyclists or pedestrians.
- The increased traffic flows would lead to an increased risk to neighbouring residents entering or leaving their properties, and neither of the proposed designs addressed these issues.
- The safety audits carried out on behalf of Western Power missed a significant number of potential hazards, and the RoSPA report suggested that both proposed junctions should be rejected on the grounds of road safety.

Because of these omissions, which had been overlooked by Mr Axon and Mr Dawson, Julia Magill went on to suggest that both their evidence on road safety was unreliable. She then proceeded to invoke the European Convention on Human Rights, which confers a duty on public bodies to protect citizens from foreseeable harm. She suggested that the proposed junctions, whichever was chosen, would increase the risk to residents of serious accidents, whether as drivers, pedestrians or cyclists. She argued that the Planning

Figure 19.2. Julia Magill gave evidence on local traffic issues. Photo by Richard Bosworth.

183

Inspectorate and the Welsh Government had a duty to protect residents from this increased risk by refusing planning permission to access the reservoir development from Lisvane Road.

Julia Magill was cross-examined by Mr Steel. He adopted a strategy that he had used with a number of other witnesses: to try and cast doubt on their credibility. Either John Steel or Geldards had done some background research and discovered that, 30 years before, Julia had taken a law degree at Durham University. Therefore, he implied that she was disingenuous in appearing simply as an interested resident. However, Julia had never practised law professionally and protested against this being brought up, as it had no relevance to the evidence she was giving on road safety. Nevertheless, he pursued a combative line of questioning on legal matters, which Julia tried to answer. However, the inspector intervened when Mr Steel began to criticise her for not having documentation about a particular legal case. He pointed out that Julia was appearing as a local resident, not an expert witness, and that subjecting her to such aggressive questioning was unreasonable. John Steel clearly recognised he had over-stepped the mark; he back-pedalled and later apologised to Julia in person.

Other Interested Parties

On Wednesday, 17th July, the inquiry moved on to consider the evidence of other interested parties. Fred Davies again gave evidence on behalf of the Fly Fishing Club. He made the case that if Llanishen reservoir were refilled, the previous recreational activities, such as sailing and fishing, would again be able to take place. He insisted that it would be possible to run a thriving fishery there.

Written evidence was also considered from a number of other local residents, organisations and local politicians. A Section 106 agreement was presented to the inquiry. This is a document agreed between a developer and the local Council about measures the developer must take to reduce the impact of the development on the local community. In this case, it covered things like providing affordable housing; subsidised bus tickets for residents of the development; providing funds for the establishment and ongoing management of the wildlife areas; upgrading features on local roads; improving local footpaths and recreational facilities in Rhyd-y-penau Park; providing extra funding for local schools; and funding the relocation of sailing facilities. In total, it was going to cost Western Power about £12.6 million pounds.

Closing Statements

The final day of the inquiry was spent on the closing statements of the three barristers.

Mr Anthony Dinkin QC was first up on behalf of RAG. The first issue he dealt with was the incompatibility of the proposed development with the Council's policies to protect the river corridors and the loss of open space. He went on to consider the heritage listing of Llanishen reservoir and its importance in the context of the whole Taf Fawr water supply system. The proposed development would both cause significant damage to the listed building and destroy its setting. He claimed that Western Power's contention that the development would allow the listed building to be better appreciated was 'utter nonsense'. He also maintained that Western Power's estimates for refilling the reservoir with water were grossly exaggerated, and there was no good reason why it could not be refilled, and sailing and fishing resumed. Finally, Dinkin again stressed that the use of Lisvane Road as an entrance and exit for 324 dwellings would have a detrimental effect on both the character of the road and road safety. He concluded that the balance of evidence was against the development and that planning permission and listed building consent should be refused.

Mark Lowe QC, for the Council, was next. He began by pointing out the cynicism of the Western Power case. Throughout the inquiry, Western Power had presented itself as a landowner that was weighed down by the costs of maintaining a redundant reservoir and seeking some way of offsetting these costs. Mr Lowe pointed out that this was not simply a misfortune that had happened to it, but it was a multi-national utility that had bought the site looking to make a profit from a housing development and that they were well aware of the risks at the time. He went on to cover many of the points made by Dinkin: the loss of open space; the incompatibility with local planning policies to protect the Nant Fawr river corridor; the damage that would be caused to the listed building and its setting; and the harm that would be caused to the character of the Lisvane Road by using it as the sole access point. He also raised the point that the Wildlife Trust was no longer prepared to take on the long-term management of the site (see Chapter 8) and the uncertainties that this would bring to the maintenance of the site's ecology and SSSIs. In conclusion, he urged the inspector to consider the balance of issues, which he argued came down firmly against allowing Western Power's appeal.

Mr Steel's summing up can most charitably be described as comprehensive. After his introductory comments, he began by attacking RAG, saying we put undue pressure on the Council, made unfounded accusations against Western Power and gave wide publicity to our false claims. He also accused us of unduly influencing local politicians, although perhaps he had forgotten about something called democracy! He said RAG was 'peddling in myths' by claiming that there was a realistic prospect of sailing being resumed, the wildlife protected, and the site put to some other sort of community use without a housing development. He stated that there was absolutely no possibility of this happening!

Once again, Mr Steel focused on the deterioration of the site since it had been owned by Western Power, particularly the damage to the SSSI due to trespass by dog walkers and the damage to the listed building by vandalism. He also reiterated the estimated cost of refilling the reservoir and resuming sailing there, money that he claimed the Council could not afford. He concluded that the only viable solution was the proposed housing development. He further claimed that this would result in no loss of recreational or open space, as argued by the Council, but rather a gain of 25 ha of amenity open space and 7 ha of recreational space. Furthermore, the proposed development was the only way of preserving the listed embankments and allowing people to view them fully and understand their significance. As to the proposed exit from the development onto Lisvane Road, he claimed this would not affect its character and would actually improve road safety. In conclusion, he thought that when all the issues were taken into account, there was an overwhelming case for planning permission to be granted.

Inquiry Closes after a fashion

When Mr Steel finished, the formal part of the inquiry closed, although technically, the inquiry did not finish then. Although the Countryside Council for Wales had not objected to the effect of the latest plans on the SSSIs, they had requested that further surveys be undertaken of bats and dormice, which are European-protected species. Further bat surveys had been conducted in the summer, but the dormouse survey had not been carried out. It's not clear why it hadn't, but John Steel argued that the survey must be undertaken before the inquiry closed, and the inspector agreed. The survey was scheduled for the autumn, and given the need to analyse the results and write a report, a closing date for the inquiry was provisionally set as 13th January 2012.

John Steel also made the point that should there be any change in Welsh Government Planning Policy before the formal closing of the inquiry, then the inquiry would have to be resumed in the light of such policy changes. We were immediately suspicious. Was this some new ploy that Western Power was planning? Andrew Hill was particularly concerned because he knew that the current UK Government was at that time considering a change in planning law to create a 'presumption in favour of sustainable development'. If the Welsh Government were also thinking of adopting this change before the end of the year, it might mean that the inquiry would need to be reopened again.

Despite our fears, this did not happen, and the inquiry duly closed on 20th January 2012, no dormice having been found.

Chapter 20

The Minister's Decision

Throughout 2012, we waited for the Minister's Decision. It was nerve-racking, but there wasn't much else we could do. We knew that the inspector had been scheduled to submit his report to the Minister on 12th April 2012. However, Mr Poppleton's recommendations would not be made public until the Minister published his decision. We did not want to hassle the Welsh Government or ask our elected representatives to apply pressure, as we were concerned that this might give Western Power grounds for appeal. We imagined that as the previous Minister's decision in 2008 had been overturned on appeal, the Welsh Government Planning Officers would be taking extra care to make sure that Western Power would have no grounds to contest this decision, hence the delay. Given the timing of the inspector's report, we thought we might hear from the Minister in May or June. When May and June passed, the late summer or early autumn seemed a possibility, but still we heard nothing. All we could do was wait.

Changes in RAG

During this period, there were significant changes in RAG. Andrew Hill and his partner, Mary Corin, left Cardiff and moved to Cornwall. Thankfully, they both agreed to continue acting in their roles as Chairman and Secretary until the next RAG AGM in March 2013. They had both put in an enormous effort to further the RAG campaign, and it is hard to overstate Andrew's contribution. He had managed to get the reservoir structure listed by Cadw, and although the Village Green initiative had ostensibly failed, it had established the right of the local community to access the whole of the Nant Fawr meadows. We believe this is what deterred Western Power from pursuing its plans to drive an access road across the meadows from the roundabout at the top of Rhyd-y-Penau Road.

Much soul-searching followed as to who would take over as Chairman of RAG. There were no volunteers amongst the committee, and I was reluctant because I was aware of the vast amount of time Andrew had spent working on the reservoirs issue. Ultimately, with no one else in the offing, I agreed to stand. I was hoping that by the 2013 AGM, we would have heard the Minister's decision and that all I would have to do was bring RAG's successful campaign to a close!

Unfortunately, by the time the AGM came around on 21st March 2013, there was still no sign of a decision on the Second Inquiry. I took over the Chairmanship of RAG and had the pleasure of presenting Andrew with a RAG plate and a mug, specially commissioned from local potter Molly Curley. Everyone at the AGM showed their appreciation for all Andrew's efforts in an extended round of applause, and Ewart Parkinson led a rendition of 'For he's a jolly good fellow'. There was a change of other key personnel on the committee. Phil Savage took over as Secretary, and Ceri Davies became the Vice-Chair. We also welcomed Anne Gee and Chris Lewis as new committee members. Fortunately, Andrew had agreed to remain on the committee as he still often visited Cardiff, and his experience was invaluable to us.

Figure 20.1. Andrew Hill with the RAG plate commemorating his chairmanship. The author is on the right. Photo by Richard Bosworth.

Figure 20.2 A typical RAG AGM held in Rhyd-y-penau Primary School Hall. Photo by Richard Bosworth.

The Inspector's Report and the Minister's Decision

The decision of Carl Sargeant, the Minister for Housing and Regeneration, was finally announced one month later, on 24th April 2013, along with the inspector's report from a year earlier. We received both documents the following day. The inspector's report contained the following recommendations:

On the open space considerations, the inspector concluded that the visual impact of the development upon the open character of the green would be minimal and that the development would enhance connectivity between Lisvane and Cyncoed. He considered that the proposed development would provide adequate compensatory amenity space for that lost to housing. In terms of sailing, he thought the proposed sailing lake would be adequate for beginners to learn the fundamentals of sailing, whilst more advanced tuition could take place in Cardiff Bay. He was also convinced by Western Power's arguments that were the development not to take place, there would be little prospect of sailing and fishing returning to the reservoir. As far as nature conservation was concerned, he did not think that the development would have a deleterious effect on either Lisvane reservoir SSSI or the Embankments SSSI. Instead, he concluded that the development would bring significant benefits for biodiversity due to the new wetland habitats being created.

This was not looking good…

Next, he considered the proposed access from Lisvane Road. He noted that the Council's Highway department had not objected to the plan given the highway improvements agreed with the developer, although the Local Planning Authority had objected to the adverse impact on the appearance of Lisvane Road. He made a detailed analysis of the mini roundabout and the road safety issues as he saw them and rejected most of the arguments that RAG had made. However, he was concerned about the dangers that would be posed to vehicles leaving and entering the houses directly adjacent to the mini-roundabout and considered this unacceptable. He also thought the proposed changes would have a negative effect on the character and appearance of this part of the Lisvane Road.

The final topic addressed was the effect of the development on the listed building and its setting. Western Power had tried to argue that the reservoir structure was unremarkable and listed only for its historical connections, but the inspector concluded that it was a highly significant listed structure. However, he thought that the damage caused by the proposed access points, where two roads cut through the embankments, would not in themselves cause significant harm to the integrity and significance of the historic asset. He then turned to the question of 'the setting'. He considered that the main issue here was the bowl of the reservoir and that its historical setting was clearly to contain water. He considered that the proposed housing estate would destroy this setting and would seriously diminish the asset's historical significance. Therefore, he concluded that Western Power's plans were incompatible with the character and setting of the listed building.

His final overall conclusion was that Western Power's appeal should be dismissed, and the applications for planning permission, the listed building consent and the mini roundabout should all be refused!

In his covering letter, the Minister agreed with the inspector's conclusion, and his decision was also that the appeal should be refused. We had won!

That evening, there was much rejoicing amongst the members of RAG, but we had got this far before. In the first part of the inquiry, the Minister rejected Western Power's plans, but then Western Power appealed against the decision, and the Welsh Government backed down (See Chapter 15). We now had to wait another six weeks to see if Western Power would again challenge the Minister's decision. The deadline for them to appeal was 6th June 2013. Again, we had another nerve-racking few weeks, but the 6th of June came and went, and no appeal materialised. Had Western Power finally had enough?

Some Promising Signs

There were other encouraging signs, as shortly after the Minister's decision was announced, the three houses at the top of Rhyd-y-penau Road that Western Power had bought were put up for sale. If nothing

Figure 20.3. Western Power sold the three houses it had bought alongside Rhyd-y-penau roundabout in May 2013. Photo by Richard Bosworth.

else, this suggested that they had definitely abandoned the idea of putting in an access road across the Nant Fawr meadows from the roundabout. The three houses were subsequently sold by auction on 21st May 2013 for a combined total of £957,000.

Despite this, there was no indication of Western Power's future intentions, so I wrote to the Chief Executive inviting the company to join the local community in re-developing the area as a local amenity. His reply was non-committal, and he stated that Western Power was currently reviewing the options open to it. Having already faced four planning applications, we fully expected another to arrive any day. We received reports of surveyors being seen on the Lisvane side of the reservoirs, so we were concerned that they were considering another access route from that side and perhaps coming up with a development plan for Lisvane reservoir, which was not protected by a 'listed building' designation. We remained on high alert.

Trip to Allenstown

In August of that year, Phil. Bale, one of the local councillors in Llanishen, decided to take matters into his own hands. He travelled at his own expense to Allentown in Pennsylvania to lobby the Pennsylvania Power and Light Corporation (PPL), the American company that owned Western Power. When he got there, he contacted the local newspaper to explain the reason for his visit and got extensive coverage in the following morning's edition. He then rang the company to ask for a meeting with PPL's Chief Executive. As he was not available, PPL offered an appointment with Rick Klingensmith, the President of PPL Global. When they met, Phil put the case against further attempts to develop Llanishen reservoir and explained that the local community didn't want their development, Cardiff Council didn't want it and neither did the Welsh Government. On the web, PPL made much of its environmental commitments, and Phil explained the importance of the site in terms of its biodiversity and historical significance. Mr Klingensmith listened politely to the arguments and was clearly familiar with what was happening at Llanishen. Phil later described him as a charming guy. However, Mr Klingensmith stuck

Figure 20.4. Phil Bale outside PPL's Headquarters in Allentown Pennsylvania. Photo by Phil Bale.

to the company line and said the decision on how to proceed was down to PPL's UK subsidiary. He did not give any indication that the company was planning to change course.

Although it didn't seem that the trip made much headway, as things turned out, it is possible that Phil's visit may have been more significant than at first appeared.

Chapter 21

RAG Finances

All of the public inquiries placed a huge stress on RAG's finances as barristers and expert witnesses are very expensive. The resumed second inquiry in 2011 was the final major legal confrontation, so this seems like a good place to break off briefly from the main story and describe how RAG raised its funds.

From the outset in 2001, we knew we would have to raise a lot of money if we were to take on a powerful multinational corporation like the Pennsylvania Power and Light Corporation, which owned Western Power. However, we also realised that we couldn't set our annual membership fee too high, as this would deter people from joining RAG and that much of our political influence would come from the number of people we represented. After some discussion, the steering committee, which was formed to set up RAG, decided to recommend an annual subscription fee of just £5 per person. We reasoned that this was likely to encourage people to join and that, in any case, many members would be prepared to make a donation in addition to their membership fee. This is exactly what happened.

The initial meeting of the Reservoir Action Group was held on 4th December 2001. Just three months later, at the end of February 2002, we had over 600 paid-up members. One year later, in March 2003, the figure was about 1600 people, and by 2005, we had well over 2000 members. Many people matched their membership fee of £5 with a £5 donation. Some were even more generous. We undoubtedly benefited from the fact that two of the communities surrounding the reservoirs, Lisvane and Cyncoed, were amongst the most affluent parts of Cardiff. This meant that with over 2000 members, some years we received almost £20,000 a year from our membership alone.

This may seem like a lot of money, but we knew it would all be needed, and more, if we ever got to legal proceedings and needed to engage lawyers and other experts to represent us. (Barristers can cost in the region of £7,000 per day plus expenses, and a public inquiry might go on for a couple of weeks!). As it turns out, we effectively fought three public inquiries (in 2006, 2008 and 2011) and an inquiry into the village green application in 2007. Each required legal representation, but in some cases, we could not afford a barrister to be present during the whole inquiry, just the parts vital to making our case.

Clearly, we had to raise additional funds to cover these large outgoings, and a major role of the first two RAG Chairmen, Ted Thurgood and Andrew Hill, was to encourage people to donate to our 'fighting fund'. They were ably supported by our second Treasurer, Dulcie Wilks, who took on the role of Fund Raiser in Chief. Dulcie led by example and arranged several successful garden parties at her house, raising well over £2,500. Similarly, renowned local potter Molly Curley, helped by other family members, held open studio events that raised a significant amount. Molly also designed and made RAG plates and mugs that were sold to raise money for the 'fighting fund'. There were many other initiatives, such as coffee mornings and Fair Trade sales, as well as the production of RAG notelets, Christmas cards and calendars. Other local organisations also chipped in, and we received generous donations from the Cardiff Reservoirs Fly Fishing Club, the Friends of Nant Fawr, the Lisvane Bridge Club and the Lisvane Graig Protection Society.

Much walking was done to raise funds for RAG. Phil Bale undertook a sponsored climb of Mount Kilimanjaro in Tanzania that raised several hundred pounds. With help from various friends, Chris Lewis arranged three sponsored walks starting in Pontcanna fields in 2011, 2012 and 2013. These were well organised, and it was possible to opt for one of five distances ranging from a three-mile 'teashop' stroll around Bute Park up to a gruelling 21 miles, which involved trekking from Pontcanna, up to Roath Park, past the reservoirs, on to

*Figure 21.1. Local politicians preparing for the RAG Sponsored walk. From L to R: Cllr Phil Bale, Jenny Rathbone AM, Cllr Julia Magill, Julie Morgan AM, Eluned Parrott AM, Jonathan Evans MP, and Cllr Andrew Graham. Chris Lewis, the event organiser, is holding the RAG poster.
Photo by Richard Bosworh.*

Caerphilly mountain, then across to the Garth mountain before returning to Pontcanna. On each of the routes, there were manned checkpoints along the way. The walks were a great success, with many RAG members and their families participating. They were also popular with local politicians. One of my abiding memories was from the first walk in 2011. Jonathan Evans, the Conservative MP for Cardiff North, did one of the shorter routes with an entourage from his office and arrived back at around 4 pm just in time for tea and cake and to catch the local journalist from the South Wales Echo. The next day's paper featured photographs of Jonathan and a fulsome article about his exploits. On the same day, Julie Morgan, AM for Cardiff North and Jenny Rathbone, AM for Cardiff Central, had undertaken the 21-mile route and, at 4 pm, were nowhere to be seen. At 6 pm, there was still no sign of them, and at 7 pm, although it had been a nice sunny day earlier, the heavens opened. They still had not arrived, and we were beginning to get worried. By 8 pm, all but two of us had gone home, but eventually, Julie and Jenny arrived at the hall looking tired, soaked through and bedraggled. There was no one there from the press to photograph them, which was probably just as well, but I know who got my vote that day!

Although events such as these raised significant sums of money for RAG's fighting fund, individual members were also generous. Many gave gifts of several hundred pounds, one or two gave four-figure sums, and one benefactor, who wished to remain anonymous, gave us a five-figure sum. Paul Glossop is a good example. Paul was brought up in Cyncoed but now lives in the United States. He was a very generous donor to our fighting fund and took a great interest in the RAG campaign. Support such as this was humbling and also enormously encouraging to those of us on the RAG committee and showed how much the reservoirs meant to members of the local community, both past and present.

Over the entire campaign, RAG raised approximately £305,000 in subscriptions, donations and fundraising activities. Our average annual expenditure on administrative activities and publicity was £1,285, although this figure was higher in the early years when we were setting up the campaign and producing lots of reports. In all, we spent approximately £235,250 on legal fees, expert witnesses and other professional advice. This may seem a lot, but I'm sure our opponents, Western Power Distribution, paid many millions in legal costs alone.

Unfortunately, the RAG campaign also led to substantial legal fees for public bodies, including Cardiff Council, the Countryside Council for Wales, Cadw, and the Welsh Government itself. Perhaps that is the price that needs to be paid for democracy. At least all the lawyers must have gone home happy.

Chapter 22

Celsa Purchases the Reservoirs

On 3rd September 2013, a few weeks after Phil Bale had returned from Pennsylvania, I was at work when I got an email from Julie Morgan AM saying that she needed to speak with me urgently about the reservoirs. I was immediately worried that Western Power had submitted yet another planning application and that we would have to start all over again.

When I 'phoned Julie, she explained that she had been due to meet with Robert Symonds, Western Power's Chief Executive, later that month to discuss Western Power's intentions regarding the reservoirs. However, that morning, she had received a letter from him cancelling the meeting because Western Power no longer owned the reservoirs! Symonds said they had been sold to Celsa (Wales) Limited, and neither Western Power Distribution nor the Pennsylvania Power and Light Corporation had any continuing involvement with the site.

It took a little while for this to sink in. After all these years, Western Power had thrown in the towel and walked away. We had finally beaten them off! I didn't get much work done that afternoon, as I spent most of my time 'phoning colleagues on the RAG Committee and passing on the good news. That evening, we also emailed the entire RAG membership to let everyone know.

So, who were Celsa, and why had they bought the reservoirs?

Grupo Celsa

Grupo Celsa is a privately owned Catalan steel company started in 1967 by Francesc Rubiralta Vilaseca and his brother. It began with a rolling mill in Barcelona, later expanding internationally to the UK, Poland, France and several Nordic countries. It specialises in making steel products for the construction industry, such as concrete reinforcing bars, wire rods, and flat bars. It had established a presence in Cardiff in January 2003 when it took over the plant belonging to Allied Steel and Wire, which had gone into receivership the year before. The rolling mill is situated in the Castle Works, the blue building clad in corrugated iron that runs alongside the central link road by Bute East Dock. As well as the rod and bar mill inherited from Allied Steel and Wire, in 2006, Celsa opened a new melt shop fitted with an electric arc furnace. Here, all sorts of scrap steel are melted down and recycled into new bars and rods.

Although Allied Steel and Wire was founded in 1981, the Castle Works rod and bar mill had an even longer history as it was originally built by the steel company GKB between 1936 and 1938 (See Chapter 2). Ever since then, the Castle Works had been provided with cooling water directly from Lisvane reservoir, with water being piped from the reservoir directly to the steelworks. The water is used to cool the steel after it comes out of the furnace and travels through the works.

We were later to learn that in 2013, when Western Power was looking to dispose of the reservoirs, Celsa's current contract with them to obtain water from Lisvane reservoir was about to end. Celsa was keen to continue with the supply from Lisvane as the water from the reservoir had been used in the works for nearly 80 years and was a known quantity. The company was concerned that water from a new source might have pollutants or impurities that would affect the health of their employees when the water is sprayed onto the hot steel in the works. Instead of negotiating a new contract, Western Power offered Celsa the opportunity to buy the reservoirs for a nominal sum, which we later discovered was £1. It must have seemed like a bargain, as it would secure Celsa's essential water supply for the foreseeable future.

Making Contact with Celsa

RAG first tried to contact Celsa two days later, on 5th September. I emailed James Ellis, who was the Human Resources Manager dealing with the media following news of their purchase. I didn't get a reply, so a couple of weeks later, I rang him, and we spoke briefly. James explained that they were completely taken aback by the amount of publicity surrounding their purchase of the reservoirs and the number of people wanting to talk to them about it. That they were not anticipating this reaction was itself surprising, as the local press had published regular articles about the reservoirs over the last decade, and a quick search on the internet would have revealed the degree of local interest and involvement in the ongoing saga. He reiterated that Celsa's aim in purchasing the reservoirs was to secure its water supply from Lisvane and that staff were currently assessing the entire site before deciding what to do with it. He also mentioned that the steel industry as a whole was experiencing difficult times and that the attention of Celsa's management was focused on trying to keep the company afloat. He promised to get back to us as soon as he had any further information about their plans for the reservoirs.

We didn't hear anything further from Celsa over the next couple of months, although Cllr. Heather Joyce, the leader of Cardiff Council, met with them in mid-October and afterwards made the following statement to the Council:

> *"Celsa confirmed its acquisition of the two reservoirs in North Cardiff for strategic purposes in order to protect the water supply for the company's plant in Cardiff, which currently comes from the Lisvane reservoir. Llanishen reservoir was also acquired in order to meet the long-term expansion plans of the company and future needs for additional water supplies. Until such time as trading conditions in the U.K. improve considerably, Celsa will not, in the short-term, be able to give commercial consideration to undertaking any non-operational work such as refilling Llanishen reservoir, as their limited financial resources are focused on supporting day-to-day business operations."*

This was consistent with what we had heard directly from James Ellis. Most importantly, it suggested that Celsa did not intend to develop Llanishen reservoir for housing or anything similar and that its ultimate aim was to refill it!

Alternative plans for the reservoirs

As Celsa was clearly preoccupied with other issues, the RAG Committee decided to focus on putting together our own vision for the site as a public amenity, which could, in due course, be presented to Celsa.

In October 2014, I met with two senior representatives of RSPB Cymru: Lewis James (Head of Reserves) and Cellan Michael (South Wales Area Manager). We discussed the possibility of turning Llanishen reservoir into a wetland bird reserve, but I think the RSPB was experiencing financial difficulties at that time, and they did not seem interested in getting involved directly.

Another option was returning Llanishen reservoir to its original uses: sailing and fishing. We were still in touch with Anne Barrett (formerly Anne Curtis), who used to run the sailing centre there, as well as Fred Davies and Jim Winterbottom from the Cardiff Reservoirs Fly Fishing Club. Both these activities could generate income, and RAG began to think about setting up a Community Interest Company that could run the reservoirs to benefit the local community while still providing Celsa with the water they needed for their works.

In early January 2014, we met with our local politicians in Lisvane Memorial Hall to discuss the situation. Julie Morgan AM reported that she had met with James Ellis in December, during which he said Celsa would be amenable, in due course, to consider a presentation proposing alternative uses for the site. We agreed at the end of the meeting that RAG would start to put together a business plan for the redevelopment of the reservoir, which could ultimately be presented to Celsa. However, we didn't have much experience writing business plans, so Julia Magill, who was now one of the Labour Councillors for

Llanishen, agreed to arrange a meeting with the Council's Economic Development Unit to see if they could help us out.

Ceri Davies, Bernard Adshead, and I met with Robert Jackson from the Economic Development Unit in February 2014. We explained what help we needed, and he offered to find some organisations to help us draw up a business plan. He didn't get back to us until April, and then it was to recommend the services of the Wildfowl and Wetlands Trust, which, as described in Chapter 8, had been one of the main cheerleaders for Western Power's scheme. It seemed ironic and somewhat inappropriate that they now wanted to advise us. They had drafted a proposal, but it did not deal at all with what we hoped would be our main income stream: fishing and sailing. They seemed to have little expertise in these areas, and besides, wanted to charge us £11,000 for their advice. We politely declined their offer and decided to look elsewhere ourselves.

The RAG Annual General Meeting in March 2014 was a tricky one. It was my first as RAG Chairman, and there were one or two vocal members who were upset that we had not yet arranged a meeting with Celsa. There were suggestions that a delegation from the RAG committee should turn up at Castle Works and demand to see the Chief Executive of Celsa UK. Failing that, we should fly out to Barcelona and speak to the CEO of the overall Celsa Group. However, the RAG Committee was reluctant to be confrontational with the Celsa Management and thought that a more conciliatory approach would yield better results in the long term.

Visit to Downing Street

Shortly after the AGM, another opportunity to promote our cause presented itself. Jonathan Evans had decided to step down as the MP for Cardiff North at the 2015 general election, and Craig Williams was standing as the prospective Conservative parliamentary candidate. I had a call from Craig to see if I would like to go to Downing Street to meet with the Prime Minister, David Cameron, and discuss the situation at the reservoirs. I was unsure what to do, as RAG had always avoided linking itself to any political party and had always fostered cross-party support. I rather suspected that this had a lot to do with bolstering Craig's election prospects, but at the same time, the chance to talk to the Prime Minister about our campaign to get Llanishen reservoir refilled seemed too good to miss. In the end, I decided to go, but not without some misgivings.

The visit to Downing Street was due to take place on 23rd April 2014. A few days beforehand, Craig let on that it wouldn't be the private face-to-face meeting that I had been expecting but more of a reception. I still wasn't sure exactly what to expect. On the 23rd, we met beforehand in the Red Lion pub on Parliament Street and then walked across the road to Downing Street. As we approached, it became clear that many people were going to this event, and we were ushered through the front door, stripped of our mobile 'phones, and then led up the iconic staircase past the portraits of previous Prime Ministers to a couple of large reception rooms on the first floor. We ended up standing with a group of Welsh Conservative MPs and their respective guests in the middle of the room.

When David Cameron arrived, he began 'working' the room, spending about two minutes speaking to each of the guests and their attendant parliamentary candidates in turn, with the inevitable photographer recording each encounter. When he reached us, I had prepared a quick spiel to explain the situation at Llanishen reservoir and what we hoped to achieve by getting it refilled. He was attentive and pleasant but then offered some platitude and moved on to the next group. Once he had done the rounds, he delivered a brief speech about the importance of volunteers to 'The Big Society' and left. I'm sure that given the other 30 or 40 local campaigners he spoke to, he had not registered much about the reservoirs and our campaign. It was not the meeting I had envisaged, but it still proved useful. A photograph was taken of Craig and myself with the Prime Minister, which I put on the RAG blog. (see Figure 22.1). I found out later that the Celsa management had seen this photograph, and it may have persuaded them to take RAG more seriously.

Figure 22.1. The visit to Downing Street with Craig Williams and the Rt. Hon. David Cameron. Photograph provided by Craig Williams MP.

Council Changes

Another significant development in March 2014 was that Heather Joyce stood down as the leader of Cardiff Council, and Llanishen Councillor Phil Bale was elected leader in her place. Phil had been a staunch supporter of RAG since the early days, and as well as doing a sponsored climb of Mount Kilimanjaro on behalf of RAG, he had also visited Allentown, Pennsylvania, in August 2013 to lobby the Directors of Western Power's parent company. Since the Second Public Inquiry in 2011, Julia Magill had also been elected as a Llanishen Councillor. She was also appointed to the Council Cabinet in March 2014. Both of them were committed to seeing Llanishen reservoir refilled and re-opened to the public and were now in positions where they could call on Council officials to help resolve the issue.

The Blue Heart Document

After our unproductive involvement with the Council's Economic Development Unit, we continued our search for help devising a business plan. Eventually, we were put in touch with Professor Calvin Jones from the Cardiff University Business School. Calvin was much more accessible and actually listened to what we wanted. As someone whose research specialised in tourism, he was able to give us good advice on the potential impact of redeveloping the reservoirs. Ceri, Bernard and I met with him to discuss various scenarios. We agreed that he would produce a short report, which we could use to sell our vision for the reservoirs to Celsa and other key stakeholders, emphasising the social, economic and environmental benefits. We aimed to have this ready by the end of September.

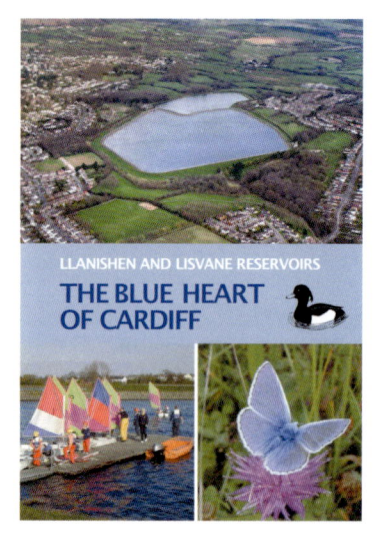

Figure 22.2. The 'Blue Heart' Document.

During this period, Phil Savage (RAG Secretary) and I also held periodic meetings with representatives of the Cardiff Reservoirs Fly Fishing Club, as well as Anne Barrett, who used to run the sailing centre. We were trying to persuade them to develop their own business plans so that we could estimate the income these two activities would generate. However, they both seemed reluctant to commit anything to paper. Anne was working on her own ideas for redeveloping the reservoirs and had persuaded an architect friend to mock up some drawings of what a new visitor centre might look like. These looked promising, and Anne kindly agreed to let us use a couple of the drawings as illustrations in the report that Calvin Jones was preparing.

Calvin delivered his report on time towards the end of September, and we were pleased with the content, although not its visual impact. I passed the text, along with some photos, to my daughter Liz, a graphic designer, and she came up with an attractive layout. The report entitled 'The Blue Heart of Cardiff' was printed in early October, and we started sending copies to all the key stakeholders.

A Visit to the Reservoirs

We had learned that on 6th August 2012, Western Power had arranged for Llanishen Reservoir to be officially registered as 'abandoned' under Section 14 of the Reservoirs Act. By 2014, it had also been empty for four years, and we wanted to check that it was still in a serviceable condition and capable of holding water safely. RAG engaged Chris Hoskins, an experienced reservoir engineer, to come and inspect it, but first, we had to get permission from Celsa. Somewhat to our surprise, they agreed to the visit, but only on the condition that we were accompanied by James Ellis.

The visit was arranged for 6th October 2014. Ceri Davies, Bernard Adshead and I went along from RAG, and it was the first time any of us had been there for a number of years. The reservoir was still empty, and there was much vegetation growing in the reservoir basin, but surprisingly, there was also quite a lot of standing water in the lower parts of the basin (See Figure 22.3 overleaf). It was difficult to understand why this should be, as the scour valve (the plug hole) was in the lowest part of the reservoir, and this should have been left locked open by Western Power after the reservoir was drained. Chris thought that debris and silt had probably blocked the scour valve. Apart from that, he didn't see anything else that caused him too much concern. However, he wanted to see the reports from the inspecting reservoir engineer when the reservoir was officially recorded as abandoned and any other recent reports from the supervising engineer. James said he could provide these, as Western Power had passed them on to Celsa. He also assured us that Celsa was keen to consider the local community's wishes when finally deciding what to do with Llanishen reservoir.

Figure 22.3. The view across Llanishen reservoir in October 2014. Note the standing water and vegetation growing in the reservoir basin.

Meeting with Dŵr Cymru / Welsh Water

Our next meeting also turned out to be important, although we didn't realise its full significance at the time. We were still working on our business plan for a Community Interest Company to take over the reservoirs, but we had begun to worry about the financial implications of this approach. Although we thought we could make enough income from sailing and fishing to cover day-to-day running expenses, the implications of a major problem with the reservoir structure were daunting. I started to investigate the possibility of taking out insurance on the reservoir against such problems, but after contacting several commercial insurance brokers, I discovered that there were no insurers that seemed prepared to offer cover on a reservoir. This made me wonder how other reservoir owners dealt with this issue, and the obvious people to ask were Dŵr Cymru / Welsh Water (DCWW), the previous owners of Llanishen and Lisvane. I sent a tentative email to Peter Perry, the Chief Operating Officer of DCWW, asking if he would meet with us. He responded promptly in a helpful and friendly way, and we arranged a meeting for 17th November 2014.

The meeting was held in the Welsh Water Offices in St. Mellons. Ceri Davies, Bernard Adshead, and I represented RAG, and we met with Peter Perry and Mike Davies (The Regulation Director of DCWW). We gave them copies of our 'Blue Heart' document and explained what we hoped to achieve in setting up a Community Interest Company. On their part, Peter told us that DCWW had just signed a contract with Celsa to carry out regular maintenance at the reservoirs but that Celsa remained the owners and were the sole undertakers under the Reservoirs Act with responsibility for reservoir safety.

Peter thought that reservoir safety was one of the major factors we would need to consider. He explained that if we managed to negotiate a long lease with Celsa and were involved with controlling water levels and maintenance, we could be deemed joint undertakers and, therefore, jointly responsible for safety under the Reservoirs Act. When we asked about insurance, he doubted that we could obtain this through an insurance company, and even if we did, he thought it would be prohibitively expensive. DCWW are a big enough company to cover these potential risks themselves. We then discussed annual maintenance costs. Peter suggested that these were likely to be in the region of tens of thousands of pounds, but more significant were unexpected repairs that may crop up occasionally. Works that had to be carried out on a short time scale, in the interests of safety, were often very costly. We discussed the possible involvement of DCWW in the Community Interest Company that we hoped to set up, but Peter explained that while they would be happy to engage with us and provide advice, they would not provide funding or services for an enterprise that they did not own. Finally, when we asked if DCWW might be interested in buying Llanishen reservoir from Celsa, he said they had no plans to do so. We did not think to ask about leasing!

We were grateful that Peter and Mike had been so open with us, and the meeting gave us much to think about. The insurance issue was clearly an important one, as well as unexpected high maintenance costs. The idea of setting up a Community Interest Company to refill and manage the reservoirs was looking less and less attractive.

Chapter 23

Celsa Engages with RAG

First Meeting with Celsa

Two thousand and fourteen finished with a significant breakthrough: RAG finally met with the Chief Executive of Celsa UK. On 15th December, Ceri Davies, Bernard Adshead, and I went to the Castle Works, where we met with James Ellis and Luis Sanz Villares. Luis was younger than I expected, dapper, and absolutely charming.

Luis began by outlining the problems that Celsa was facing. In the UK, it had six sites, which together employed over 1000 staff. The most extensive operation was in Cardiff, with about 750 personnel. Celsa is only involved in steel production, and all its steel is produced by recycling scrap metal. Therefore, it scores well in terms of sustainability. However, in the UK, the company must pay both direct and indirect emission taxes to offset CO_2 production. As the UK is highly reliant on fossil fuels, electricity here is expensive compared to other countries. For example, in Norway, which has more hydro-electric generation, Celsa's energy costs are roughly half those in the UK. Celsa's electric arc furnace uses vast amounts of energy, accounting for 40% of Cardiff's total electricity consumption, and that cost the company over £50m in 2014. Another issue that Celsa faced was cheap imports from countries like China, which rely on blast furnaces rather than electric arc furnaces. Blast furnaces are much more polluting in terms of emissions but are cheaper to run.

As a result of these factors, Celsa UK had been running at a loss for the last few years, although Grupo Celsa remained committed to its UK operation. Luis stressed that their primary focus was returning

Figure 23.1. The meeting with Celsa. L-R: Ceri Davies, Richard Cowie, Luis Sanz & Bernard Adshead

the company to profitability and that they did not have the financial or human resources to do much at the reservoirs in the immediate future. He also provided some background to the purchase of the reservoirs. He confirmed that when Western Power bought the reservoirs in 2004, a 10-year contract to supply the steelworks with water had been put in place, which expired in October 2014. Celsa approached Western Power in August 2013 about renewing the contract to provide water, and it suggested that Celsa buy the site. The negotiation to purchase the reservoirs took place over just two weeks as Western Power was keen to offload them as quickly as possible.

For our part, we briefly described how RAG's primary aim had been to stop Western Power's plans for a housing development and then to protect the area so that future generations of Cardiff residents could enjoy it. We handed over our 'Blue Heart' document and described our plans to set up a Community Interest Company that could re-introduce sailing and fishing, and re-establish some form of public access to the site. We also showed them pictures of Lisvane reservoir in the summers of 1995 and 2003 when it almost dried out. In both cases, the steelwork's water supply was only saved by pumping water from Llanishen reservoir into Lisvane. With Llanishen reservoir empty, this option no longer existed. So, to secure their water supply, we argued that it was in both our interests to see Llanishen reservoir filled as soon as possible.

After that, the discussion ranged more widely. Luis stressed that Celsa had no plans to develop the reservoirs and did not want to antagonise the local community. He asked for more time to consider the 'Blue Heart' document, along with the legal and technical issues. He stressed that they were steelmakers and had little knowledge of the issues involved in operating reservoirs. Luis asked about our timescale and when our business plan would be ready, and we replied that we hoped to have something to present to him in about six months. However, we did not mention our growing concerns about insurance and possible large maintenance costs. We agreed to meet again in about six months and on the importance of maintaining a dialogue between us.

After the formal meeting, James Ellis took us on a tour of the steelworks, from the electric arc furnace through to where the molten steel was coming out in bars and then being shaped into other products. It was awe-inspiring, particularly the giant furnace, which was like an erupting volcano whenever a new load of scrap steel was added. The whole building shuddered when this happened. The other noticeable thing was how few staff were involved. There were only a handful of workers in each building, and all seemed busy. It was certainly a lean operation.

Figure 23.2. Celsa's electric-arc furnace.

We came away from the meeting feeling encouraged. Although nothing had been promised, Luis Sanz listened to us and did not dismiss any of our proposals. He came over as someone who was straightforward to deal with. His main plea was to have more time so that they could familiarise themselves with the issues. All-in-all, it was a positive end to the year.

Sad News

The New Year got off to a sombre start. Ewart Parkinson had been awarded an OBE in the New Year's Honours list for his voluntary work and community service. I wrote to him with congratulations on behalf of the RAG committee and received a reply from his family saying he was very ill. Ewart died on 9th March 2015, and RAG lost a great mentor and friend. Although Ewart never wanted to be on the committee, he was always there in the background, offering advice and encouragement. Given his experience as a former Director of Planning and his far-reaching vision on planning matters and their impact on people, he would be sorely missed. Ewart and his wife Pat lived in South Rise, backing onto the reservoir, and I was sorry that Ewart would not now be around to find out if we managed to get his beloved Llanishen reservoir refilled.

RAG AGM 2015

In the spring of 2015, we also got the welcome news that Andrew Gregory, the Council's current Director of Strategic Planning, was prepared to come to the RAG AGM to update us on the Council's discussions with Celsa. I think this was mainly thanks to continued pressure from the Leader of the Council, Phil Bale, and Councillor Julia Magill. On the grapevine, we had gathered that significant progress had been made in discussions between the Council and Celsa. Hopefully, Andrew would come to the AGM with some good news.
We had good attendance at the AGM, and fortunately, there was enough positive news to silence our critics. Andrew Gregory's presentation had a great impact, especially when he hinted strongly

that a 'public utility' was in advanced negotiations with Celsa to purchase the reservoirs, but he would not be drawn any further. He suggested we could expect an announcement imminently. After he left the meeting, there was a fairly intense discussion about which public utility company he could mean. The obvious candidate was Welsh Water, but Peter Perry, Welsh Water's Chief Operating Officer, had also told us that it was not interested in buying the reservoirs. But if it wasn't Welsh Water, who could it be, and what designs might another company have on the reservoirs?

The Rising Water Level

Another issue raised by RAG members around this time was the increasing amount of water in Llanishen reservoir. As we had noticed when we visited the previous October with reservoir engineer Chris Hosking, there was more water in Llanishen reservoir than expected, given that the reservoir was abandoned and the scour valve should have been left locked in the open position. Over the winter, there had been a lot more rain, and by the spring, the reservoir was more than a third full. Several people had begun to express concerns that the reservoir might be becoming unsafe, especially as the embankments had been allowed to dry out for a number of years, which could have compromised their clay cores.

By this time, we knew that Welsh Water was managing the site on behalf of Celsa, so we got in touch to ask what was going on. We received the following explanation from Ian Christie, their Director of Water Safety. Early in 2014, Celsa's Supervising Engineer noted that there was a significant amount of silt behind the scour intake, and there was concern that this could move in a storm event and send a large volume of water and silt through the scour main into the Nant Fawr with a risk of pollution and flooding. Celsa was advised that the scour should be closed, the silt cleared, and then the scour reopened. Celsa arranged for the scour to be closed and requested that Welsh Water arrange the silt clearance and reopening of the scour valve as their agent. Ian Christie said that DCWW contractors would carry out this work under the supervision of Celsa's Supervising Engineer,

Figure 23.3. Llanishen reservoir inadvertently refilling because of the blocked scour valve.

hopefully before the end of June. Celsa was aware that the reservoir volume was now well above 25,000m³ and was increasing with each rainfall event, meaning that it was no longer technically 'abandoned' under the Reservoir Act.

No Announcement

Andrew Gregory had told us at the end of March that an announcement about the reservoirs was imminent, but April came and went, then May, then June, and still, we hadn't heard anything. We pressed our local politicians to find out what was happening, but all we were told was that negotiations were still continuing and some issues needed ironing out.

On 10th July, the RAG Committee visited Welsh Water's recently opened visitor centre at Llandegfedd reservoir near Pontypool. This was an opportunity that Peter Perry had offered when we met with him back in November, as the centre there provided a similar range of activities to the ones we hoped to offer at Llanishen, namely sailing and fishing. We were shown around by Siân Robinson, the Director of Estates for Welsh Water. We took the opportunity to ask Siân if there was any truth in the rumour that Welsh Water was negotiating to buy Llanishen reservoir, but she denied this was the case.

A few days later, we put the same question to Celsa. Ceri, Bernard and I had arranged a meeting with Luis Sanz and James Ellis as a follow-up to our meeting six months earlier. There was not much change to report on either side, but of course, we mentioned what Andrew Gregory had told us at the AGM and asked whether Celsa was, in fact, negotiating with Welsh Water. Luis replied that as Welsh Water was now managing the day-to-day maintenance of the reservoirs on behalf of Celsa, they spoke to them regularly on a whole range of subjects. He politely refused to be drawn on the matter any further.

As 2015 carried on into the autumn with no further news, we grew increasingly despondent because it was beginning to look as though the deal, whatever it was, had fallen through. None of the politicians we contacted seemed able or willing to tell us what was happening. Also, there had been no attempt to unblock the main scour on Llanishen reservoir, and it was still filling up with water. Whenever I contacted Tracey Williamson, who was now in charge of dam safety at Welsh Water, there seemed to be another reason why the work had been delayed for a further few weeks. It seemed ironic that we were hassling them to drain down the reservoir when what we actually wanted was to see it refilled, but it was clear that the reservoir would have to be emptied and the scour unblocked before it could be re-commissioned.

During the autumn of 2015, we tried to keep up the pressure by getting RAG members to write to Andrew Gregory to ask what was happening. Julie Morgan and Julia Magill arranged for the Welsh Government Minister for the Environment, Carl Sargent AM, to visit the reservoirs, and he subsequently had a meeting with Celsa to encourage them to refill Llanishen. We also organised a survey, which went to all households in Cyncoed, Lisvane and parts of Llanishen, asking people what activities and facilities they would like to see at the reservoirs in the future.

Celsa Engages with RAG

Sadly, 2015 ended tragically for Celsa and its employees. On the morning of Wednesday, 18th November, there was an explosion at Celsa's Castle works, in which two people were killed and five were injured. We were sorry to learn that one of those killed was Peter O'Brien, who was a popular member of the local community in Llanishen and a former member of RAG. It must have been a difficult time for everyone impacted by this terrible event.

The Celsa era effectively ended two weeks into 2016 when, on Friday, 15th January, I received a 'phone call from Peter Perry. He told me that Welsh Water had just negotiated a lease with Celsa whereby it would effectively take over control of the reservoirs, although Celsa would still own them. There was going to be a big announcement on the following Monday at 12 noon at the reservoirs, and he wondered whether I could be there to represent RAG? You bet!

Chapter 24

Welsh Water Returns

The Welsh Water Announcement

On Monday, 18th January, a small group congregated at the reservoirs on a cold, overcast and blustery day. Chris Jones, its Chief Executive, represented Dŵr Cymru / Welsh Water; there was a small congregation of politicians, including Carl Sargeant AM, the Minister for the Environment; several members of the RAG committee; and a

Figure 24.1. Chris Jones of Welsh Water explains the plans for the reservoir to the late Carl Sargeant AM, Welsh Government Minister for the Environment.

group of journalists. Chris Jones told us that Welsh Water had negotiated a lease on the reservoirs and that it was taking over the site to improve the resilience of its water supply but also to provide the opportunity for the public to enjoy various water-based recreational activities, as well as protecting the site's important biodiversity. It appeared that Welsh Water intended this to be a long-term commitment as the lease was for 999 years. Chris mentioned that he had never signed such a long lease before, which led him to wonder, had he signed it 999 years ago, who would have been the reigning monarch then? The answer was King Canute, which somehow seemed appropriate! Afterwards, some of the politicians and I were asked to provide comments by the press, which allowed us to express our delight at such a positive result. It sounded almost too good to be true and was exactly the outcome we had campaigned for so vigorously over the years.

The next day, the RAG negotiating team had a previously scheduled meeting with Luis Sanz at Celsa. Now, it was not really necessary, but we went along anyway to thank Luis for arriving at a solution that met all our aspirations: Celsa had secured its water supply; Welsh Water could expand its portfolio of visitor attractions; and RAG had achieved its aim in that the public would have access to a much-loved local beauty-spot for the foreseeable future.

The Reception at City Hall

On 5th February 2016, Phil Bale, as leader of Cardiff Council, organised a reception at City Hall to celebrate the successful conclusion of the long-running reservoir campaign. This was funded by Alastair Milburn, the former editor of the South Wales Echo; the South Wales Echo itself; and local businessman Raj Aggarwal. To all three, we are very grateful. Unfortunately, we could not invite all RAG members to the event, as there were over 800 at the time, so it was limited to people who had made a significant contribution to the campaign, such as past and present committee members, newsletter deliverers, and major donors. Local politicians from Cyncoed, Llanishen and Lisvane were also invited, along with representatives of Welsh Water and Celsa. About 120 guests ended up attending.

Save our Reservoirs

Figure 24.2. The reception at City Hall. From L-R. Chris Jones, the CEO of Dŵr Cymru / Welsh Water; Phil Bale, Leader of Cardiff Council; the author representing RAG; and Luis Sanz, CEO of Celsa Steel UK.

The reception was held at 2 pm in the ground floor foyer of City Hall, which provided elegant surroundings for an enjoyable and relaxed event. Phil Bale spoke on behalf of the Council, Luis Sanz for Celsa, Chris Jones for Welsh Water, and I represented RAG. It was nice to have a public opportunity to thank both Luis and Chris for negotiating such a successful outcome to our campaign. It was the last time that we had any formal contact with Celsa, and we now focused on establishing a good working relationship with Welsh Water.

Welsh Water Takes Over

From the outset, Welsh Water kept the local community informed of developments. At the next RAG AGM, which took place in late March 2016, Peter Perry, the Chief Operating Officer and Siân Robinson, the Director of Procurement and Estates, came and talked about their plans. They confirmed that their reservoir engineer had declared the structure of Llanishen reservoir to be sound. However, they added that before it was refilled, Welsh Water would take the opportunity to repair the damage to the stonework caused by vandals and upgrade some of the valves and other pipework. They warned that this remedial work would take over 12 months to complete and that the reservoirs would have to remain closed during this period. They confirmed that Welsh Water's goal was to use the water supply for industrial purposes but also to open the site to the public for recreational activities. They said that the company wanted to involve the local community in developing the plans for the reservoirs and hoped to keep in close contact with RAG. This was all very encouraging.

The next few months were spent in detailed surveys and assessments of the reservoir structure and surrounding land. On 1st July 2016, work started. A compound was set up in the small car park at the end of Keeper's Cottage lane, and the first major job involved the removal of the large laurel hedge that ran from the entrance down the side of the main southern dam. The rubble of the Keeper's Cottage was also cleared away, which was complicated because it was found to contain asbestos. The surrounding topsoil had to be removed and replaced with uncontaminated soil. A temporary fence was installed around the site's outer perimeter in September, and access was restricted.

October 2016 saw the first of what was to become a series of regular meetings between RAG and Welsh Water. The RAG team, consisting of Ceri Davies, Bernard Adshead and myself, met with Siân Robinson and Gwyn Thomas in the 'Old Cottage' pub in Lisvane. This became our regular meeting venue. Gwyn was the Head of Regional Communications for Welsh Water and was responsible for the interaction between Welsh Water and the local community. By our second meeting in February 2017, it had become clear to Welsh Water that the repairs needed to the reservoir were more significant than initially anticipated and that a complete drain down was required. The work was, therefore, going to take much longer than the 12 months initially forecast. Siân mentioned that they were looking at the possibility of using water from the Nant Fawr stream to refill Llanishen reservoir, but we warned that this had a high nutrient content, which might lead to problems with blue-green algae blooms, similar to those that had occurred in Lisvane reservoir in the past.

In March 2017, planning permission for a new permanent perimeter fence was obtained, and shortly afterwards, work installing the new fence began. Despite this, incidents of vandalism increased, and in early April, there were several occasions when people accessed the site overnight. One involved serious damage to the contractor's machinery, and several sections of the temporary fence were knocked down. In fact, it wasn't only the temporary fence that suffered; in some places, the new permanent fence was damaged by people loosening the posts before the concrete had fully set. It was frustrating that Welsh Water was doing its best to develop what the local community wanted, but there were anti-social elements who were disrupting the work and causing delays to the long-awaited outcome. The new perimeter fence was finally finished in August 2017.

Reservoir Repairs

Once the site was relatively secure and closed to the public, Welsh Water used the opportunity to conduct a whole series of repairs. The drain down of Llanishen reservoir began in June 2017. In some ways, this was frustrating, as we wanted the reservoir refilled, and it was already two-thirds full of water because of the blocked scour valve. However, essential repairs were needed that required the reservoir to be empty, and Welsh Water took the opportunity to carry out additional works that would keep the reservoir operational for at least another 100 years. The scour was first cleared by specialist divers before the drain down could start. Water was released slowly to prevent a sudden surge going into the Nant Fawr stream and sweeping away the fish and invertebrates that lived there. It was also filtered first to remove any sediment. The drain down was completed by the end of 2017, and early in the new year, work started on clearing vegetation from the basin. While the reservoir was empty, repairs were carried out to the scour valve and the stone pitching on the embankments. The main valve tower was also upgraded, and all the valves and pipework replaced. The refill of Llanishen reservoir didn't begin until June

2019 and was scheduled to take two years, although it wasn't completed until late spring 2023.

In October 2017, work began on some chambers located close to the fence on the eastern side of Lisvane reservoir. This meant the footpath running behind Rhyd-y-Blewin farm and 117 Black Oak Road was closed. It was anticipated that the work would be completed by mid-November, but inevitably, it overran and wasn't completed until the end of the year.

This was followed by repairs to the water main running along the east side of Llanishen reservoir, which again was initially scheduled to last six weeks but ended up taking almost two years. The main was in such poor condition that Welsh Water eventually decided to replace it, which was particularly inconvenient for the many people who enjoy walking in the Nant Fawr meadows as the lower parts were closed to the public during this period. The water main had nothing to do with the reservoirs but just happened to run alongside them, and Welsh Water took the opportunity to do this work while they had contractors

Figure 24.3. Construction of the new pumping chamber on the western side of Llanishen reservoir.

in the vicinity. The main is a backup, which can provide drinking water to Cardiff from Pontsticill reservoir and improve the resilience of the city's water supply in times of drought.

The other major infrastructure work that was undertaken in 2019 was to install a new pumping station on the western side of Llanishen reservoir (see Figure 24.3), close to what had been the old sailing compound. This enabled water from the Nant Fawr to be pumped into Llanishen reservoir. Pipework was also installed that would enable water from Llanishen reservoir to be supplied directly to Celsa in addition to the supply from Lisvane.

In August 2019, Welsh Water started removing the ugly palisade fence that Western Power had installed around the edge of Llanishen reservoir. This seemed like a significant step, as many people had viewed the fence as a symbol of Western Power's attempt to thwart the aspirations of the local people and ruin a much-loved beauty spot. I'm not sure what happened to it, but I always thought it would be an appropriate outcome if Celsa had melted it down in their arc furnace and turned it into something useful. The fence was gone entirely by the end of 2019.

Figure 24.4. Removal of the fence around Llanishen reservoir.

The ENRaW Grant

At the beginning of 2018, during one of the regular meetings between representatives of RAG and Welsh Water, Siân Robinson mentioned that there were two new members of the DCWW Estates team: Vicky Martin (Head of Visitor Attraction Strategy) and Mark Davies (Head of Visitor Attraction Operations). Shortly afterwards, Vicky began attending our meetings regularly and took over from Siân as our main contact with Welsh Water.

Later that year, in early November, Vicky 'phoned me to see if RAG would be interested in becoming a partner with Welsh Water in applying for funding from the Welsh Government to develop the facilities for visitors to the reservoirs. This was under the government's Enabling Natural Resources and Well-Being (ENRaW) scheme, which was designed to promote facilities for broadening access to the natural environment and improving the quality of urban areas. In particular, there was an emphasis on the beneficial effect on people's health by engaging in outdoor activities and interacting with nature. The reservoir scheme seemed to tick all the boxes as it was within the capital city, it was an area rich in biodiversity, and it also offered the opportunity for people to get involved with both land and water-based exercise. Another factor was that the Welsh Government was encouraging applications from collaborations between businesses, public bodies and local community groups, so Welsh Water was hoping to involve Cardiff Council and the local Health Board in the application, as well as RAG.

It sounded like a good opportunity, but I needed to get the committee's approval before RAG could sign up for any such collaboration. We had spent the last 17 years holding the owners of the reservoirs to account, and we still saw ourselves as a campaigning organisation. Were we to get directly involved with Welsh Water, this could limit our ability to object to anything they planned to do. On the other hand, being part of the ENRaW scheme would give us an input into the future of the reservoirs that we might not have otherwise. In the end, we agreed to become one of the partners and the bid was duly submitted jointly with the other three applicants in December 2018.

During the summer of 2019, we heard that the joint bid for an ENRaW grant had been successful and that we had been awarded £930,000. This would pay for a network of new paths around the reservoirs, an outdoor education centre, bird hides, facilities for re-establishing sailing, and a community engagement manager. This post was advertised almost immediately, and interviews were held on 29th October in the Council's Park Department offices in Forest Farm. Representatives from Welsh Water, Cardiff Council and RAG formed the interviewing panel, and of the six candidates considered, the unanimous decision was to appoint Annie Smith, who started work on 6th January 2020.

In early February 2020, we had the first ENRaW Project Board meeting. RAG was represented by Bernard Adshead (RAG Treasurer) and myself. There were also representatives from Cardiff Council, the Health Board and Welsh Water. Vicky Martin and Annie Smith represented Welsh Water, accompanied by the project manager who was overseeing the project and who could update us on the technical issues. Items that the RAG representatives brought up several times at the Project Board included the possibility of reinstating fly fishing at the reservoirs, the issue of water quality and subsequent blue-green algae problems if water from the Nant Fawr were used to refill Llanishen reservoir, the recurring issue of unauthorised entry and vandalism, and finally, the advisability of allowing dog-walking around the reservoirs. Being able to walk dogs was a popular request in a public consultation that Welsh Water carried out, but we were worried about the impact on the waxcap fungi growing on the embankments. As mentioned in Chapter 7, waxcaps are intolerant of nitrogenous fertilisers, and even if visitors are good about using bags for their dogs' faeces, the problem is that the dogs will inevitably be urinating on the grass, and their urine is high in nitrogen and phosphorus. This is likely to have a negative effect on the fungi. Despite our protestations, Welsh Water wanted to allow dog walking. However, although Natural Resources Wales had originally agreed to allow dogs on short leads to be walked on the paths of the Embankments SSSI, a few weeks before the reservoirs were due to open, it changed its mind and concluded that no dogs should be allowed on the embankments. Recent research in Belgium had shown that nutrient enrichment of the soil from dog urine is even more significant than previously thought, and the risk to the waxcap fungi was judged to be too high.

Fishing was another sensitive issue, as the fishermen had been very supportive of the RAG campaign over the years, and we knew that

Welsh Water did not plan to allow fishing at the reservoirs in future. The reason for this was that it anticipated that many more people would be walking around the reservoir than previously, and it was concerned about the dangers of back-casting. This technique, used in fly fishing, involves flicking the fishing line backwards and forwards several times before casting it into the water. The line can travel behind the fisherman for up to 20m, and with a sharp hook on the end, it can be a hazard to anyone walking behind. We suggested that one solution would be to allow fishing from boats, but Welsh Water did not seem keen on this idea, possibly because it might interfere with sailing and other water sports.

I wouldn't want to give the impression, however, that the meetings were contentious. Overall, they were constructive as we all had a common aim to make sure that the reservoirs could be reopened to the public as a recreational resource where people could both engage in water-based activities and enjoy visiting tranquil surroundings close to nature. Besides which, both Vicky Martin and Annie Smith from Welsh Water were nice people with whom it was a pleasure to interact, as were the other members of the Board: Nic Hutchinson from Cardiff Council and Cheryl Williams from Cardiff and Vale University Health Board. Inevitably, things became more complicated in March 2020 when the Covid pandemic and lockdown began. However, we continued to hold project meetings online every two months, although the involvement of Cheryl from the Health Board was reduced as she had other Covid-related issues with which to deal. The Welsh Government extended the ENRaW project by six months because of delays caused by the pandemic, and we held our last Board meeting in March 2023.

Application for Planning Permission

In July 2020, Welsh Water released its plans for the reservoirs. Initially, there was a four-week consultation period during which the public was asked to provide feedback, revisions were made to the plans in the light of these comments, and an application for planning permission was submitted to Cardiff Council on 23rd October 2020.

Figure 24.5. An artist's impression of the new visitor centre overlooking Lisvane reservoir. Photo courtesy of Dŵr Cymru Welsh Water and Feilden, Clegg, Bradley Studios.

The plans included a new visitor centre, paths around the reservoirs, a traditional Welsh roundhouse that would act as an education centre, parking, bird hides, picnic areas and facilities for water sports. The design of the visitor centre was distinctive and quite controversial (Figure 24.5). Some people liked it; others weren't so keen. I think the main issue was the three 'boxes' stuck on top of the building, the function of which was not obvious. Without these, the building would have a lower profile, and many thought it would be more attractive.

As well as the network of paths, two new entrances were planned. The main entrance and car parking would be accessed from Lisvane Road, but also included were new pedestrian entrances at the top of Rhyd-y-penau Park, from Keeper's Cottage lane off Rhyd-y-penau Road, and a third close to where the two reservoirs meet behind Black Oak Road. Some residents living near these proposed entrances were concerned that visitor parking would become an issue. Although these were primarily viewed as pedestrian entrances, many people were likely to drive to the reservoirs, park their car near one of the entrances and then walk onto the site. In particular, those on the Cyncoed side would save people who visited by car from areas south of the reservoir (most of Cardiff) from having to drive around through Llanishen to Lisvane. Welsh Water regarded the parking problems as an issue for Cardiff Council, and the Council seemed reluctant to act until a problem actually arose. It looks like we will have to wait and see how things develop once the site is reopened.

Apart from a few concerns such as these, most responses to the planning application were positive. However, due to the extent of the application and the significance of the site for biodiversity, the Planning Committee asked for further information and some additional surveys to be carried out. It took quite a while for Welsh Water to collect and provide all the requested information, and it wasn't until 16th June 2021 that the Planning Committee passed the application. Even then, it wasn't until 7th September 2021 that both parties signed a S106 agreement and planning approval was finally awarded, although the approval included 41 conditions specifying aspects of the construction and operation of the visitor attraction. In the autumn of 2021, the contract for the construction was advertised and awarded to BECT Building Contractors of Rumney in Cardiff. Work started on the visitor centre on 24th January 2022 and was scheduled to finish in April 2023, although there were delays in the supply of materials resulting from the invasion of Ukraine. The site will now reopen to the public on 28th July 2023.

Setting up the Friends Group

Since the Welsh Water announcement, the RAG committee had been discussing the future of the Reservoir Action Group. We had been set up as a campaigning organisation to prevent the proposed housing development on Llanishen reservoir, and, against all the odds, we had achieved our goal. However, over the last 22 years, the campaign has received massive interest and support from the local community, and many people are now engaged with the future of the reservoirs. It seemed a shame to close RAG down and let all this local involvement go to waste. The obvious answer was to morph RAG into a 'Friends' group that could continue to involve local people with the reservoirs in various volunteering roles, much as the successful 'Friends of Nant Fawr' do with the neighbouring meadows and woods. Nevertheless, it was difficult to see how RAG itself could become a 'Friends' group, as its constitution was framed in terms of it being a campaigning group, and it would have to be completely rewritten. The committee decided that the best course was to propose setting up a separate 'Friends' group and that once the reservoirs were reopened, RAG could follow the steps laid out in its constitution for its dissolution.

We assumed that Welsh Water would have experience of volunteering at its other sites, but it turned out that it didn't, although Vicky Martin was enthusiastic about setting up a volunteering group at Llanishen and Lisvane. If successful, it could become a model for some of Welsh Water's other sites with public access. We, therefore, offered to draft a constitution for a new group at the reservoirs and help set it up. Bernard Adshead, the RAG Treasurer, played a key role in this. However, it turned out to be a lengthy process as every step had to be examined in detail by Welsh Water's legal department and discussed in various company committees, but eventually, we got there. A competition was held at Rhyd-y-penau Primary School to design a logo for the Friends group, which was won by 8-year-old Arushi de Silva. On 20th July 2021, the inaugural meeting of the Friends of Cardiff Reservoirs was held outdoors at the reservoirs, and a committee was elected.

RAG also supported the 'Friends' with a donation of £500 to get the group up and running. During the construction phase of the new visitor centre and grounds, public access to the reservoirs has been restricted, as the whole area has been closed on safety grounds. Therefore, the volunteering opportunities have been limited, but once the reservoirs are reopened, the 'Friends' group hope to be engaged in a whole range of activities, including conservation work, assisting the rangers and helping with site interpretation.

The Friends Group suffered a setback in December 2022 when their first elected Chairman, Paul Davies, died unexpectedly. Paul was involved in groups such as the Conservation Volunteers, the Wildlife

Trust, and the Friends of Bute Park, so he brought much relevant experience to the role. He will be sadly missed.

Concluding remarks

Before I finish, I would like to express RAG's thanks to both Celsa and Dŵr Cymru / Welsh Water. When Western Power departed in 2013, it left behind an empty, degraded and abandoned reservoir. Celsa Steel bought the site to secure its water supply but also wanted to meet the aspirations of local people. The arrangement with Welsh Water was ideal, and the latter has invested significantly to restore the reservoirs and open them as a public recreational resource. It has taken seven years, but DCWW kept the local community well-informed of progress throughout. The end result is well worth the wait, with a spectacular new visitor centre, great recreational facilities and a plan to protect the important heritage and biodiversity of the site. Thanks to both companies, RAG has now achieved its second goal of seeing the reservoirs protected for the enjoyment of future generations.

After 22 years, it's strange to think the Reservoir Action Group will soon be disbanded. In the autumn of 2023, we plan to hold the final meeting of RAG, at which we will invoke the group's dissolution procedures. So many people devoted so much time to 'Save Our Reservoirs', and if you were a member of RAG or supported the group in other ways, thank you. We couldn't have achieved what we did without the steadfast support of the local community. Hopefully, this account has given you a better understanding of all that happened.

Six months ago, I discovered that RAG had outlasted its arch-nemesis, Western Power Distribution. In June 2021, the Pennsylvania Power and Light Corporation sold Western Power to National Grid plc and in September 2022, the company was rebranded as National Grid Electricity Distribution. So Western Power is no more. Perhaps we played a small part in its demise?

Appendices

1. Sources of Information — A-1
2. Scientific Names of Species — A-9
3. Grassland Fungi List — A-14
4. Members of the RAG Committee — A-19
5. Timeline of Key Events — A-21
   Index — A-29

Appendix 1

Sources of Information

Much of the information in this book is based on personal recollections, internal minutes of RAG meetings, emails, and other non-published sources. However, some sections rely on information gleaned from external sources such as Cardiff Corporation minutes, newspaper articles, government reports and academic journals. Only these external sources are included in this Appendix.

Chapter 1: 19th Century History

Cardiff Corporation Minutes 1881-1887. Accessed at Cathays Heritage Library, Cardiff.

City of Cardiff (1930). Record of the Cardiff Waterworks Undertaking 1879-1929. Western Mail & Echo Ltd., Cardiff.

Hill, A. (2008). Evidence submitted to Cadw in support of listing Llanishen Reservoir as a structure of Architectural and Historical Interest. Unpublished.

James, D.C. (1982). The genesis of sanitary reform in Cardiff, 1774-1850. The Welsh History Review, 11, 50-66.

Priestley, C.H. (1906). Cardiff Corporation Water Works. From: 1906 Institution of Mechanical Engineers: Visits to works. (www.gracesguide.co.uk).

Priestley, C.H. (1923). Cardiff Corporation Waterworks. Western Mail Ltd., Cardiff

Rammell, T.W. (1850). Report to the General Board of Health on a Preliminary Inquiry into the Sewerage, Drainage and Supply of Water and the Sanitary Condition of the Inhabitants of the Town of Cardiff. Her Majesty's Stationery Office, London.

South Wales Daily News (1884). Llanishen: the new reservoir. 4th December 1884.
Wheatley, J.L. (1905). History of the Cardiff Corporation Waterworks Undertaking. Cardiff Records, Vol 5., 457-469.
Williams, J.A.B. (1881). Report on the Water Supply of the Borough and District. Report submitted to Cardiff Corporation on 30th May 1881.
Williams, J.A.B. (1884). Specification and Tender of and for the new Storage Reservoir and other Works at Llanishen. Cardiff Corporation Waterworks.

Chapter 2: 20th Century History

Bowtell, H.D. and Hill, G. (2006). Reservoir Builders of South Wales. (Book Six of Dam Builders in the Age of Steam). The Industrial Locomotive Society.
Cardiff Corporation Waterworks Committee Minutes 1901-1974. Accessed at Cathays Heritage Library, Cardiff.
Thomas, D. (2000). Hyder: the rise and fall of a multi-utility. Utilities Policy, 9, 181-192.

Chapter 3: Recreational Use

Barrett, Anne. (Unpublished). History of the Llanishen Sailing Centre.
Cardiff Corporation Waterworks Committee Minutes 1880-1974. Accessed at Cathays Heritage Library, Cardiff.
Davies, F. (2015). Cardiff Reservoirs Fly Fishing Club: a brief history. Published by the author.
Pettigrew, W.W. (1902) Notes on the Hatchery and Fish Hatching at Roath Park. Cardiff Naturalists Society: Report and Transactions, 34, 53-62.
South Wales Daily News (1892). Angling in Llanishen Reservoir. Letter to the Editor from 'Bittern' on 28/11/1892.
Waterworks Engineer's Annual Reports 1960-1972. Accessed at Cathays Heritage Library.
Western Mail (1899). Trout for Llanishen Reservoir. Article on 02/05/1899.

Chapter 4: Wildlife

Buisson (2017). Lisvane Reservoir SSSI Wintering Waterfowl Condition Assessment. APEM Scientific Report P00001231/02 to Dwr Cymru / Welsh Water, April 2017.

Ingram, G. C. S. and Salmon, H.M. (1929). The birds of the Llanishen reservoirs. Transactions of the Cardiff Naturalists' Society, 62, 45-56.

Odin, N. (1984). Llanishen and Lisvane Reservoirs' Ornithological Report. Published by Cardiff Naturalist's Society, Ornithological Section.

Young, S.F. (1972). The Birds of Llanishen / Lisvane Reservoirs. Published by Cardiff Naturalist's Society, Ornithological Section.

Chapter 5: The Formation of RAG

Western Mail Business News, Wednesday 18/07/2001. '£1m-a-mansion housing estate for reservoir site' by Siôn Barry.

Chapter 6: The First Planning Application

Hyder Industrial Group Ltd. (2002). Planning application 02/2570N submitted to Cardiff Council on 17/12/2002 for residential, sailing lake and clubhouse, wetlands habitat and educational/community centre through re-profiling of existing reservoir and surrounding bund all with structural landscaping, roads, footpaths, cycleways and associated highway works .

Chapter 7: Waxcap Fungi (Part 1)

Boertmann, D. (1995). The genus Hygrocybe, Fungi of Northern Europe, 1 (3rd printing), Danish Mycological Society.

Griffith, G.W., Bratton, J.H. & Easton, G. (2004). Charismatic megafungi: the conservation of waxcap grasslands. British Wildlife 16, 31-43.

McHugh, R., Mitchel, D. Wright, M. Anderson, R. (2001). The Fungi of Irish Grasslands and their value for nature conservation. Proc. Roy. Irish Acad. 101B: 225-242.

Rald, E. (1985). Vokshatte som indikatorarter for mykologisk værdifulde overdrevslokaliteter. Svampe 11: 1-9. [With English summary]

Vesterholt, J., Boertmann, D. & Tranberg, H. (1999). Et usaedvanlig godt år for overdrevssvampe. Svampe, 40, 36-44. [With English summary]

Chapter 9: The Campaign Ramps Up

Hill, A. (2005). The historical importance of the Lisvane and Llanishen Reservoirs in the rapid expansion of Cardiff in the Nineteenth Century: a case for Listing. An application to Cadw for listed building status.

Land Registry Title No. CYM205691 detailing the transfer of land at Llanishen and Lisvane reservoirs Cardiff from Dŵr Cymru Cyfyngedig to Western Power Distribution Investments Limited, dated 11/10/2004.

Western Power Distribution Investments Ltd. (2003). Planning application 03/2662N submitted to Cardiff Council on 05/11/2003 for residential, sailing lake and clubhouse, wetlands habitat and educational/community centre through re-profiling of existing reservoir and surrounding bund all with structural landscaping, roads, footpaths, cycleways and associated highway works .

Chapter 10: Waxcap Fungi (Part 2)

Countryside Council for Wales (2005). Notification of Llanishen and Lisvane Reservoir Embankments as a Site of Special Scientific Interest. (26th September 2005).

Countryside Council for Wales (2006). Transcript of the CCW Council Meeting in Cardiff on 6th February 2006.

Royal Courts of Justice (2007). Judgment of Mr Justice Collins in the High Court case between Western Power Distribution Investments Ltd. and the Countryside Council for Wales. Case No: CO/10183/2005. 26 January 2007.

Sources of Information

Chapter 11: The Third and Fourth Planning Applications

Western Power Distribution Investments Ltd. (2006). Planning application 06/00934E submitted to Cardiff Council on 13/04/2006 for residential, sailing lake and clubhouse, wetlands habitat and educational/community centre, re-profiling of existing reservoir all with structural landscaping, roads, footpaths, cycleways and associated highway works.

Western Power Distribution Investments Ltd. (2006). Planning application 06/01101E submitted to Cardiff Council on 12/05/2006 for residential, sailing lake and clubhouse, wetlands habitat and educational/community centre, re-profiling of existing reservoir all with structural landscaping, roads, footpaths, cycleways and associated highway works .

Chapter 12: The First Planning Inquiry

Planning Inspectorate Wales (2007). Report of the Inquiry carried out by Mr Alwyn Nixon in November 2006 as a result of the Appeal by Western Power Distribution Investments Ltd. against the failure of Cardiff County Council to determine its planning application (03/02662/N). [The second application]. Ref: APP/Z6815/A/05/1184945.

Chapter 13: The Village Green Application

Chapman, V. (2008). A report on the Application to Register the Land Known as The Meadows, Llanishen Reservoir, Cardiff as a New town Green. (Report to Cardiff County Council on the Village Green Inquiry led by Mr Vivian Chapman Q.C., published on 9th July 2008).

Chapter 14: The Run Up to the Second Public Inquiry

Land Registry Title No. CYM347739 detailing the transfer of Gwern-y-Bendy woodland from Stuart Wyndham Murray Threipland and Rupert Sanders to Western Power Property Developments Limited, dated 10/10/2007.

Chapter 15: The Second Planning Inquiry

Planning Inspectorate Wales (2008). Report of the Inquiry carried out by Mr R. M. Poppleton in May – Aug 2008 as a result of the Appeal by Western Power Distribution Investments Ltd. against the failure of Cardiff County Council to determine its planning application (06/1101/E). [The fourth application]. Ref: APP/Z6815/A/07/2042394 published on 13th November 2008.

Western Power Distribution Investments Ltd. (2008) Report on an Inspection of Llanishen Reservoir under the Reservoir Act 1975 (Section 10(2)) conducted by Dr A. K. Hughes. Published May 2008.

Chapter 16: The Second Listing Application to Cadw

Cadw (2009). Listing Statement for Llanishen reservoir dam under the Planning (Listed Buildings and Conservation areas) Act 1990. Listed 24th July 2009.

High Court of Justice, Cardiff Court. (2010). Judgment of His Honour Judge Milwyn Jarman QC in the case between Western Power Distribution Investments Ltd. and the Welsh Ministers. Case No: CO/12451/2009. 22 February 2010.

Hill, A. (2008). An application to the Welsh Assembly Government for the protection by listing of the entire Taff Fawr to Llanishen Water Supply Scheme, including the Beacons and Llanishen reservoirs. (Submitted July 2008).

Chapter 17: The Draining of Llanishen Reservoir

Binnie, C. (2010). Llanishen Reservoir, Cardiff. A review by Chris Binnie on behalf of the Reservoir Action Group. February 2010.

Hansard HC Deb. vol. 506, col. 514-517, 25th February 2010. The threat to Llanishen Reservoir: contribution by Julie Morgan MP.

Hansard HC Deb. vol. 513, col. 344-346, 6th July 2010. Llanishen Reservoir: contribution by Jonathan Morgan MP.

Reservoirs Act 1975. Elizabeth II. Chapter 23. Her Majesty's Stationery Office, London, UK.

Warren, A. (2010). Reservoir Act 1975: Llanishen reservoir. A review of The 2008 Inspection Report and its recommendations carried out by Dr A. K. Hughes. Commissioned by the Environment Agency. April 2010.

Chapter 18: The Nant Fawr Local Nature Reserve

Barker, G.M.A. and Box, J.D. (1998). Statutory Local Nature Reserves in the United Kingdom. Journal of Environmental Planning and Management 41(5), 629-642.

Cardiff Council (2009). Minutes of the Cardiff Council Executive Meeting held on 1st October 2009.

Cardiff Council (2010). Minutes of the Cardiff Council Executive Meeting held on 7th October 2010.

Royal Courts of Justice (2011). Judgment of Mr Justice Ouseley in the High Court case between Western Power Distribution Investments Ltd. and Cardiff County Council. Case No: CO/15591/2009. 23 February 2011.

Chapter 19: The Second Planning Inquiry Resumes

Cardiff County Council (2011). Minutes of the Planning Committee meeting on 11th May 2011 at which applications 11/383/DCO and 11/384/DCO were considered along with Western Power's revised Environmental Statement for the proposed development.

Planning Inspectorate Wales (2012). Report of the Resumed Inquiry carried out by Mr R. M. Poppleton in July 2011 – Jan 2012 as a result of the Appeal by Western Power Distribution Investments Ltd. against the failure of Cardiff County Council to determine its planning application (06/1101/E). Ref: APP/Z6815/A/07/2042394; APP/Z6815/V/11/2152650; & APP/Z6815/V/11/2152661; published on 12th April 2012.

Western Power Distribution Investments Ltd. (2011). Planning application 11/00384/DCO submitted to Cardiff Council on 04/03/2011 for listed building consent to make alterations to

Llanishen Reservoir embankments to facilitate development in accordance with application APP/26815/A/07/2042394/WF for residential development, water sports lake, wetland area, sailing centre, wildlife centre, and associated infrastructure.

Western Power Distribution Investments Ltd. (2011). Planning application 11/00383/DCO submitted to Cardiff Council on 07/03/2011 for a mini-roundabout on Lisvane road and lighting/re-surfacing of access track between Rhyd-y-penau road and Llanishen reservoir, and all associated works.

Chapter 20: The Minister's Decision

Welsh Government (2013). Letter from Carl Sargeant AM, the Minister for Housing and Regeneration giving his decision on the Appeal by Western Power Distribution on the non-determination of their planning application No. 06/1101/E, as well as their applications for Listed Building Consent (11/00384/DCO) and a Mini-roundabout on Lisvane Road (11/00383/DCO). Published on 24th April 2013.

Chapter 22: Celsa Purchases the Reservoirs

Land Registry Title No. CYM205691, CYM347739 and CYM397128 detailing the transfer of land at Llanishen and Lisvane reservoirs Cardiff from Western Power Distribution Investments Limited to Celsa Wales Limited, dated 30/08/2013.

Chapter 24: Welsh Water Returns

Land Registry Title No. CYM708419 detailing the lease of land at Llanishen and Lisvane reservoirs Cardiff from Celsa Wales Limited by Dŵr Cymru / Welsh Water, dated 14/01/2016.

Appendix 2

Scientific Names of Species

Organised alphabetically by common name.

Birds

Arctic tern	*Sterna paradisaea*
Black tern	*Chlidonias niger*
Black-headed gull	*Chroicocephalus ridibundus*
Blackbird	*Turdus merula*
Blackcap	*Sylvia atricapilla*
Blue tit	*Cyanistes caeruleus*
Buzzard	*Buteo buteo*
Canada goose	*Branta canadensis*
Carrion crow	*Corvus corone*
Chaffinch	*Fringilla coelebs*
Chiff-chaff	*Phylloscopus collybita*
Coal tit	*Periparus ater*
Common gull	*Larus canus*
Common sandpiper	*Actitis hypoleucos*
Common scoter	*Melanitta nigra*
Common tern	*Sterna hirundo*
Coot	*Fulica atra*
Cormorant	*Phalacrocorax carbo*
Dunlin	*Calidris alpina*
Dunnock	*Prunella modularis*
Gadwall	*Mareca strepera*
Goldcrest	*Regulus regulus*
Goldeneye	*Bucephala clangula*
Goldfinch	*Carduelis carduelis*
Goosander	*Mergus merganser*

Grasshopper warbler	*Locustella naevia*
Great black-backed gull	*Larus marinus*
Great crested grebe	*Podiceps cristatus*
Great tit	*Parus major*
Greater spotted woodpecker	*Dendrocopos major*
Green sandpiper	*Tringa ochropus*
Green woodpecker	*Picus viridis*
Greenfinch	*Chloris chloris*
Grey heron	*Ardea cinerea*
Grey wagtail	*Motacilla cinerea*
Herring gull	*Larus argentatus*
House martin	*Delichon urbicum*
Jackdaw	*Coloeus monedula*
Jay	*Garrulus glandarius*
Lapwing	*Vanellus vanellus*
Lesser black-backed gull	*Larus fuscus*
Little grebe	*Tachybaptus ruficollis*
Little ringed plover	*Charadrius dubius*
Long-tailed duck	*Clangula hyemalis*
Long-tailed tit	*Aegithalos caudatus*
Magpie	*Pica pica*
Mallard	*Anas platyrhynchos*
Moorhen	*Fulica chloropus*
Mute swan	*Cygnus olor*
Nightingale	*Luscinia megarhynchos*
Nuthatch	*Sitta europaea*
Osprey	*Pandion haliaetus*
Pied wagtail	*Motacilla alba*
Pintail	*Anas acuta*
Pochard	*Aythya ferina*
Raven	*Corvus corax*
Red-backed shrike	*Lanius collurio*
Redshank	*Tringa totanus*
Robin	*Erithacus rubecula*
Sand martin	*Riparia riparia*
Scaup	*Aythya marila*
Shoveler	*Spatula clypeata*
Siskin	*Spinus spinus*

Scientific Names

Skylark	*Alauda arvensis*
Sparrowhawk	*Accipiter nisus*
Spotted sandpiper	*Actitis macularius*
Stonechat	*Saxicola rubicola*
Swallow	*Hirundo rustica*
Swift	*Apus apus*
Teal	*Anas crecca*
Tufted duck	*Aythya fuligula*
Wheatear	*Oenanthe oenanthe*
Whitethroat	*Sylvia communis*
Wigeon	*Mareca penelope*
Willow warbler	*Phylloscopus trochilus*
Wren	*Troglodytes troglodytes*
Yellow wagtail	*Motacilla flava*
Yellowhammer	*Emberiza citrinella*

Mammals

Badger	*Meles meles*
Bank vole	*Myodes glareolus*
Brown long-eared bat	*Plecotus auritus*
Brown rat	*Rattus norvegicus*
Common pipistrelle	*Pipistrellus pipistrellus*
Common shrew	*Sorex araneus*
Daubenton's bat	*Myotis daubentonii*
European rabbit	*Oryctolagus cuniculus*
Field vole	*Microtus agrestis*
Grey squirrel	*Sciurus carolinensis*
Harvest mouse	*Micromys minutus*
Hazel dormice	*Muscardinus avellanarius*
Hedgehog	*Erinaceus europaeus*
Mink	*Neovison vison*
Mole	*Talpa europaea*
Nathusius' pipistrelle	*Pipistrellus nathusii*
Noctule	*Nyctalus noctula*
Otter	*Lutra lutra*
Red fox	*Vulpes vulpes*
Soprano pipistrelle	*Pipistrellus pygmaeus*
Weasel	*Mustela nivalis*

Whiskered bat *Myotis mystacinus*
Wood mouse *Apodemus sylvaticus*

Reptiles and Amphibians

Adder *Vipera berus*
Common frog *Rana temporaria*
Common lizard *Zootoca vivipara*
Common toad *Bufo bufo*
Grass snake *Natrix natrix*
Great crested newt *Triturus cristatus*
Palmate newt *Lissotriton helveticus*
Slow worm *Anguis fragilis*

Insects

Azure damselfly *Coenagrion puella*
Banded demoiselle *Calopteryx splendens*
Beautiful demoiselle *Calopteryx virgo*
Black-tailed skimmer *Orthetrum cancellatum*
Blue-tailed damselfly *Ischnura elegans*
Brimstone *Gonepteryx rhamni*
Cinnabar moth *Tyria jacobaeae*
Comma *Polygonia c-album*
Common blue butterfly *Polyommatus icarus*
Common blue damselfly *Enallagma cyathigerum*
Common darter *Sympetrum striolatum*
Emperor dragonfly *Anax imperator*
Gatekeeper *Pyronia tithonus*
Glow-worm *Lampyris noctiluca*
Green-veined white *Pieris napi*
Holly blue *Celastrina argiolus*
Large red damselfly *Pyrrhosoma nymphula*
Large white *Pieris brassicae*
Meadow brown *Maniola jurtina*
Orange tip *Anthocharis cardamines*
Painted lady *Vanessa cardui*
Peacock *Aglais io*
Purple hairstreak *Favonius quercus*

Red admiral — *Vanessa atalanta*
Red-veined darter — *Sympetrum fonscolombii*
Ruddy darter — *Sympetrum sanguineum*
Six-spot burnet moth — *Zygaena filipendulae*
Small copper — *Lycaena phlaeas*
Small skipper — *Thymelicus sylvestris*
Small tortoiseshell — *Aglais urticae*
Small white — *Pieris rapae*
Southern hawker — *Aeshna cyanea*
Speckled wood — *Pararge aegeria*

Plants

Adder's-tongue fern — *Ophioglossum vulgatum*
Bee orchid — *Ophrys apifera*
Betony — *Stachys officinalis*
Birds-foot trefoil — *Lotus corniculatus*
Bluebell — *Hyacinthoides non-scripta*
Bristle clubrush — *Isolepis setacea*
Broad-leaved helleborine — *Epipactis helleborine*
Bugle — *Ajuga reptans*
Burnet saxifrage — *Pimpinella saxifraga*
Common spotted orchid — *Dactylorhiza fuchsii*
Devil's bit scabious — *Succisa pratensis*
Early purple orchid — *Orchis mascula*
Green-winged orchid — *Anacamptis morio*
Heath woodrush — *Luzula multiflora*
Meadow thistle — *Cirsium dissectum*
Primrose — *Primula vulgaris*
Quaking grass — *Briza media*
Rest-harrow — *Ononis repens*
Sneezewort — *Achillea ptarmica*
Twayblade orchid — *Neottia ovata*
Water figwort — *Scrophularia auriculata*
Wood anemone — *Anemone nemorosa*
Yellow flag iris — *Iris pseudacorus*
Yellow rattle — *Rhinanthus minor*

Appendix 3

Grassland Fungi List for Llanishen and Lisvane Reservoirs (CHEGD Species)

Names are from the United Kingdom Species Inventory: https://www.nhm.ac.uk/our-science/data/uk-species.html.

CHEGD represents species from five groups of grassland fungi: *Clavariaceae*, *Hygrophoraceae*, *Entoloma*, *Geoglossaceae* and *Dermoloma*. These are often used together as a measure of the fungal importance of an area of grassland.

The year shown is when each species was last recorded. (My thanks to Peter Sturgess for providing much of these data).

ced*Clavariaceae* - **Spindles, Corals and Clubs (14 species)**

Clavaria acuta Sowerby	Pointed club	2022
Clavaria fragilis Holmsk.	White spindles	2022
Clavaria fumosa Pers.	Smoky spindles	2022
Clavaria incarnata Weinm.	Skinny club	2022
Clavaria straminea Cotton (= C. flavipes)	Straw club	2022
Clavulina cinerea (Bull.) J. Schröt.	Grey coral	2022
Clavulina coralloides (L.) J. Schröt.	Crested coral	2022
Clavulina rugosa (Bull.) J. Schröt.	Wrinkled club	2022
Clavulinopsis corniculata (Schaeff.) Corner	Meadow coral	2022
Clavulinopsis helvola (Pers.) Corner	Yellow club	2022

Clavariaceae - Spindles, Corals and Clubs (continued)

Clavulinopsis laeticolor (Berk. & M.A. Curtis) R.H. Petersen	Handsome club	2022
Clavulinopsis luteoalba (Rea) Corner	Apricot club	2022
Clavulinopsis umbrinella (Sacc.) Corner	Beige coral	2021
Ramariopsis kunzei (Fr.) Corner	Ivory coral	2020

Hygrophoraceae - Waxcaps (28 species)

Gliophorus irrigata (Pers.) A.M. Ainsw. & P.M. Kirk	Slimy waxcap	2022
Gliophorus laetus (Pers.) Herink	Heath waxcap	2022
Gliophorus psittacinus (Schaeff.) Herink	Parrot waxcap	2022
Hygrocybe acutoconica (Clem.) Singer	Persistent waxcap	2022
Hygrocybe aurantiosplendens R. Haller Aar.	Orange waxcap	2022
Hygrocybe calciphila Arnolds	Limestone waxcap	2022
Hygrocybe calyptriformis var. *calyptriformis* (Berk.) Fayod	Pink waxcap[*2]	2022
Hygrocybe calyptriformis f. *nivea* (Cooke) Bon	Pink waxcap (white variety)	2016
Hygrocybe cantharellus (Fr.) Murrill	Goblet waxcap	2021
Hygrocybe ceracea (Sowerby) P. Kumm.	Butter waxcap	2022
Hygrocybe chlorophana (Fr.) Wünsche	Golden waxcap	2022
Hygrocybe citrinovirens (J.E. Lange) Jul. Schäff.	Citrine waxcap[*2]	2022
Hygrocybe coccinea (Schaeff.) P. Kumm.	Scarlet waxcap	2022
Hygrocybe colemanniana (A. Bloxam) P.D. Orton & Watling	Toasted waxcap[*2]	2022
Hygrocybe conica (Schaeff.) P. Kumm.	Blackening waxcap	2022

Hygrophoraceae - Waxcaps (continued).

Hygrocybe flavipes (Britzelm.) Bon	Yellow-foot waxcap*²	2022
Hygrocybe fornicata var. *fornicata* (Fr.) Singer	Earthy waxcap	2022
Hygrocybe glutinipes var. *glutinipes* (J.E. Lange) R. Haller Aar.	Glutinous waxcap	2022
Hygrocybe ingrata J.P. Jensen & F.H. Møller	Dingy waxcap*²	2022
Hygrocybe insipida (J.E. Lange) M.M. Moser 1967	Spangle waxcap	2022
Hygrocybe intermedia (Pass.) Fayod	Fibrous waxcap*²	2022
Hygrocybe mucronella (Fr.) P. Karst.	Bitter waxcap	2022
Hygrocybe pratensis var. *pratensis* (Fr.) Murrill	Meadow waxcap	2022
Hygrocybe punicea (Fr.) P. Kumm.	Crimson waxcap*²	2022
Hygrocybe quieta (Kühner) Singer	Oily waxcap	2022
Hygrocybe reidii Kühner	Honey waxcap	2022
Hygrocybe russocoriacea (Berk. & T.K. Mill.) P.D. Orton & Watling	Cedarwood waxcap	2022
Hygrocybe splendidissima (P.D. Orton) M.M. Moser	Splendid waxcap*²	2022
Hygrocybe virginea (Wulfen) P.D. Orton & Watling	Snowy waxcap	2022
Hygrocybe virginea var. *fuscescens* (Bres.) Arnolds.	Variety of snowy waxcap.	

Entoloma - Pinkgills (13 species)

Entoloma atrocoeruleum Noordel.	Navy pinkgill	2021
Entoloma bloxamii (Berk. & Broome) Sacc.	Big blue pinkgill*²	2022
Entoloma conferendum (Britzelm.) Noordel.		2021

Entoloma -Pinkgills (continued)

Entoloma corvinum (Kühner) Noordel.	Crow pinkgill	2007
Entoloma griseocyaneum (Fr.) P. Kumm.	Felted pinkgill*2	2007
Entoloma incanum (Fr.) Hesler	Mousepee pinkgill	2022
Entoloma infula var. *infula* (Fr.) Noordel.		2007
Entoloma poliopus var. poliopus (Romagn.) Noordel.		2007
Entoloma porphyrophaeum (Fr.) P. Karst.	Lilac pinkgill*2	2021
Entoloma prunuloides (Fr.) Quél.	Mealy pinkgill*2	2007
Entoloma sericellum (Fr.) P. Kumm.	Cream pinkgill	2020
Entoloma serrulatum (Fr.) Hesler	Blue edge pinkgill	2022
Entoloma sodale Kühner & Romagn. ex Noordel.		2007

Geoglossaceae – Earthtongues (7 species)

Geoglossum fallax E.J. Durand	Deceptive earthtongue	2022
Geoglossum umbratile Sacc.	Plain earthtongue	2022
Geoglossum cookeanum Nannf. ex Minter & P.F. Cannon		2022
Glutinoglossum glutinosum (Pers.) Hustad, A.N. Mill., Dentinger & P.F. Cannon	Gultinous earthtongue	2022
Trichoglossum hirsutum (Pers.) Boud.	Hairy earthtongue	2022
Microglossum nudipes Boud.	Olive earthtongue	2022
Microglossum truncatum V. Kučera, Lizoň & Tomšovský	Olive earthtongue	2021

Dermoloma (4 species)

Dermoloma cuneifolium (Fr.) Singer ex Bon	Crazed cap	2022
Dermoloma magicum Arnolds	Black magic*2	2021
Dermoloma pseudocuneifolium Herink ex Bon	Dark crazed cap	2007
Dermoloma cf pseudocuneifolium	See note below *1	2021

Note *1
The last Dermoloma species listed was similar to *D.pseudocuneifolium*. However, DNA barcoding confirmed this is actually an undescribed, currently un-named species, that has only been recorded once before in Turkey. It is therefore the first UK record for this species.

Note *2
An *2 after the English name in the List of Fungi indicates that the species is on the International Union for the Conservation of Nature (IUCN) Red List. These are species that are considered to be threatened globally with extinction. The list can be accessed at: http://iucn.ekoo.se/iucn/species_list/.

Not all species of fungi found at the reservoirs have yet been assessed for inclusion on the red list. However, already there are 12 species that have been classified as being at global risk of extinction. The embankments SSSI has an area of just 6.2 ha or 15.3 acres, which represents an extraordinary density of globally threatened species in such a small area. This only underlines the importance of the reservoir grasslands for the conservation of global biodiversity.

Appendix 4

Members of the RAG Committee

The RAG Committee had six 'officers' and five elected members, although the Committee also had the powers to co-opt up to three additional members. The committee was elected each year at the AGM, which was usually held in March. The following people served on the RAG Committee over the years.

Position	Name	Start	End	Years
Chair	Ted Thurgood	2002	2009	7
	Andrew Hill	2009	2013	4
	Richard Cowie	2013	2023	10
Vice Chair	Richard Cowie	2002	2013	11
	Ceri Davies	2013	2023	10
Secretary	Ruth Jenkins	2002	2005	3
	Geoff Roberts	2005	2010	5
	Mary Corin	2010	2013	3
	Phil Savage	2013	2023	10
Treasurer	Rhys Thomas	2002	2009	7
	Dulcie Wilks	2009	2012	3
	Bernard Adshead	2012	2023	11
Liaison Officer	Mike Walker	2002	2023	21

Save our Reservoirs

Position	Name	Start	End	Years
Press Officer	Geoff Roberts	2002	2010	8
	Chris Lewis	2013	2023	10
Committee Members	Ceri Davies	2002	2013	11
	Peter Gretton	2002	2011	9
	Vernon Hale	2002	2003	1
	Bert Williams	2002	2007	5
	Geraint Evans	2003	2011	8
	Mike Dean	2003	2023	20
	Ruth Jenkins	2005	2009	4
	Phil Savage	2006	2013	7
	Dulcie Wilks	2012	2015	3
	Anne Gee	2013	2023	10
	Graham Good	2011	2016	5
	Martyn Wyatt	2013	2018	5
	Shaun Whittaker	2015	2023	8
	Andrew Hill	2013	2023	10
	Stephen Howe	2016	2023	7
	Julia Magill	2011	2013	2
	Bernard Adshead	2011	2012	1
Auditor	Nick Perry	2002	2004	2
	Richard Norton	2004	2023	19

Appendix 5

Timeline of Key Events

Date	Event
1864	Construction of Lisvane reservoir begins and is completed in 1865.
24/12/1879	Cardiff Corporation purchases the Cardiff Waterworks Company's undertakings for £300,000.
06/04/1883	Cardiff Corporation Waterworks Committee agree to J.A.B. Williams' proposed Taf Fawr scheme.
18/03/1884	Official ceremony to mark start of construction of Llanishen reservoir.
Dec. 1884	Construction of Heath Filter beds at Allensbank Road starts and is completed in 1886.
1885	Work on the Taf Fawr pipeline starts.
Sept. 1886	Llanishen reservoir completed.
Mar. 1886	Work on Cantref reservoir starts and is completed in September 1892.
1892	Taf Fawr system becomes operational with water supplied from Cantref to Llanishen.
Apr. 1893	Work on Beacons reservoir starts. It is completed in September 1897, with water piped down to Cantref reservoir and onward to Llanishen.

Nov. 1910	Construction of Llwyn-on reservoir begins, but is halted during the First World War. Resumes in 1919 and is completed in June 1926.
Jun. 1926	Cantref Roughing Filter opens.
1928	Lisvane reservoir is cleaned of silt.
Aug. 1929	Llanishen reservoir is drained and silt removed. Refilled by Mar. 1930.
Jan. 1936	Lisvane reservoir begins supplying water to the Castle Works in Cardiff Bay.
Mar. 1964	Llandegfedd reservoir starts supplying water to Cardiff. Llanishen reservoir now acts mainly as a reserve supply to the city.
1968	Heath filter beds are decommissioned.
Early 1970s	Llanishen reservoir stops receiving water from the Taf Fawr system.
Apr. 1974	Reservoirs change ownership to the Welsh National Water Development Authority.
1989	UK Government privatise the ten regional water authorities by stock market flotation.
1996	Welsh Water Authority takes over SWALEC and renames itself Hyder.
1999	Hyder gets into financial difficulties.
Sept. 2000	Hyder is acquired by Western Power Distribution.
May 2001	Glas Cymru acquire water assets from Western Power Distribution and sets up current Dŵr Cymru / Welsh Water.
18/07/2001	Article published in Western Mail about housing development plans for the reservoir.
04/12/2001	Public meeting in Rhyd-y-penau primary school sets up the Reservoir Action Group to oppose the housing development.

Timeline

26/02/2002	First RAG AGM - approves RAG Committee and Constitution. Ted Thurgood is elected as Chairman.
14/11/2002	Waxcap fungi are discovered on the embankments of Llanishen reservoir.
17/12/2002	Western Power submits first planning application to Cardiff County Council. (02/2750/N)
19/12/2002	Llanishen Water and Wildlife Trust distribute promotional leaflet to residents.
28/01/2003	RAG holds public meeting in lecture theatres at the Heath Hopsital. 700 people attend.
Feb. 2003	RAG submits formal response to the first planning application to the local planning authority.
Mar. 2003	The Countryside Council for Wales (CCW) announce that the reservoir embankments have been put on a list of candidate SSSIs.
Mar 2003	Cardiff Reservoirs Country Park proposal published by RAG.
01/10/2003	Western Power appeals against non-determination of its first planning application.
05/11/2003	Western Power submits second planning application for 326 dwellings to Cardiff Council. (03/2662N)
03/12/2003	Building containing fishing club HQ burns down
21/12/2003	RAG submits response to second application to Cardiff Council.
11/10/2004	Welsh Water sells the reservoir site to Western Power Distribution for £4 million
30/12/2004	RAG holds large rally at the entrance of Llanishen reservoir.
01/01/2005	Western Power stops public access to the reservoirs and starts erecting a 6' high steel palisade fence.
01/02/2005	Lisvane reservoir re-opens to the public.

A-23

21/06/2005	Andrew Hill makes the first submission to Cadw for the listing of the reservoirs as historic buildings.
18/07/2005	Western Power appeals against non-determination of its second application.
26/09/2005	The CCW notifies the reservoir embankments as an SSSI for grassland fungi.
08/11/2005	Cadw decides not to list the reservoirs.
Nov. 2005	Western Power withdraws its first planning application.
05/01/2006	Welsh Government decides Western Power's second application should go to a public inquiry.
06/02/2006	The CCW confirms SSSI status of the reservoir embankments at its meeting in Cardiff.
13/04/2006	Third planning application for 324 dwellings (06/934E) submitted by Western Power.
12/05/2006	Fourth planning application (06/1101E) submitted by Western Power.
02/07/2006	Andrew Hill makes a submission for the Nant Fawr meadows to be registered as a Village Green.
31/10/2006	First public inquiry into Wester Power's second planning application opens and closes on 21st Nov.
13/12/2006	Western Power challenges the SSSI designation in the High Court in London. Challenge fails.
24/12/2006	Keeper's Cottage burns down.
19/03/2007	Following the first planning inquiry, the planning inspector recommends to the Welsh Ministers that planning permission be refused.
13/04/2007	WPD appeals against non-determination of its fourth planning application (the second appeal).
09/07/2007	Public inquiry regarding the Village Green starts but is subsequently adjourned.

Timeline

16/08/2007	Welsh Minister confirms the inspector's view and rejects Western Power's second planning application.
10/10/2007	Western Power buys Gwern-y-Bendy wood for £60,000.
26/02/2008	Public inquiry into Village Green resumes but the application is subsequently rejected (09/07/2008).
09/05/2008	Dr Andrew Hughes' reservoir inspection report recommends draining Llanishen reservoir.
28/05/2008	Public inquiry into Western Power's fourth planning application (second appeal) opens, and after a long break, closes on 29th August.
Jul. 2008	Andrew Hill makes a second submission to Cadw regarding the listing of the reservoirs
13/11/2008	Planning inspector reports to Welsh Ministers recommending that planning permission be granted on Welsh Water's fourth planning application.
31/03/2009	Andrew Hill takes over as RAG Chairman.
16/04/2009	Welsh Assembly Minister does not accept the Inspector's report, rejects the second appeal and refuses planning permission.
07/05/2009	Cadw lists Llanishen Reservoir as a structure of architectural or historic interest for Wales.
27/05/2009	Western Power challenges the Minister's decision on the second planning inquiry in the High Court. The Welsh Government subsequently concedes, and the Minister decides the inquiry should re-open.
01/10/2009	Cardiff Council designates the Nant Fawr as a Local Nature Reserve.
23/10/2009	Western Power lodge a claim in the High Court against the Cadw listing.
22/02/2010	Appeal Court hearing rejects Western Power's appeal against Cadw listing.

26/02/2010	Western Power starts draining Llanishen reservoir. This was completed in September 2010.
19/03/2010	Western Power challenges designation of the Nant Fawr Local Nature Reserve and gets permission to proceed to a full judicial review.
07/10/2010	Cardiff Council's Executive declares the Nant Fawr Local Nature Reserve for a second time after getting CCW approval beforehand.
23/02/2011	Judicial review of the Nant Fawr Local Nature Reserve application eventually quashes both designations by the Council.
05/07/2011	The second public inquiry into Western Power's fourth planning application reopens. It runs from 5th-13th July and then from 15th-19th August.
03/09/2011	First RAG Save Our Reservoirs Walk takes place.
12/04/2012	Inspector's report to WAG recommends dismissing appeal on the fourth planning application and, therefore, rejecting planning permission. Although this was not published until a year later.
07/07/2012	Second Save Our Cardiff Reservoirs Walk
06/08/2012	Llanishen reservoir is officially recorded as 'abandoned' under The Reservoirs Act 1975.
21/03/2013	Richard Cowie takes over from Andrew Hill as RAG Chairman.
24/04/2013	Minister issues decision on re-opened second planning inquiry. Western Power's appeal and therefore planning permission is refused.
06/07/2013	Third Save Our Reservoirs Walk.
13/08/2013	Cllr Phil Bale travels to Allentown Pennsylvania to meet with Pennsylvania Power and Light Corp. executives.

Timeline

30/08/2013	Western Power sells both reservoirs and the rest of the site to Celsa Steel for £1
13/10/2014	RAG publishes 'Blue Heart Document'.
Oct-2014	Celsa agrees with Welsh Water that the latter will undertake routine maintenance of the reservoirs.
15/12/2014	RAG's first formal meeting with Celsa management.
18/03/2015	Council Director of Strategic Planning attends RAG AGM and states that a public company is negotiating with Celsa about taking-over the site.
18/01/2016	Welsh Water announces a 999 year lease of the reservoirs from Celsa with aim of refilling Llanishen reservoir and promoting recreational use.
01/06/2016	Welsh Water begins work on site, carrying out extensive repairs to both reservoirs and surrounding infrastructure.
Oct. 2016	RAG representatives hold the first of a series of regular meetings with Welsh Water management.
Aug. 2019	RAG becomes party to ENRaW project, which obtains funding from Welsh Government to help redevelop the reservoirs.
23/10/2020	Welsh Water submits planning application to Cardiff Council to develop Llanishen and Lisvane reservoirs as a visitor attraction.
16/06/2021	Planning permission is granted, subject to a number of conditions.
24/01/2022	BECT Contractors start construction of the Visitor Centre.
28/07/2023	Llanishen and Lisvane reservoirs re-open as a public recreational resource run by Welsh Water.

Index

A

Aber Valley   6
Adshead, Bernard   206–207, 209, 210–211, 216, 221, 226, 230
Aggarwal, Raj   219
allotments   41, 44, 46, 181
Axon, Mike   181–183

B

Bale, Phil   193, 196–197, 199, 205, 213, 219–220
Barrett, Anne   33–35, 202, 206
Basten, Chris   93, 121
bat   43, 187
Bateman, John Frederick   7
Beacons reservoir   14–15, 27, 146–147
Binnie, Chris   156–157, 160–161
bird   36–41, 80, 82, 86–87, 123, 177, 202, 225, 228
Bishop, Pat   54
Blue Heart document (RAG)   206–207, 209, 211–212
blue-green algae   140, 222, 226
Burton, Neil   180

C

Cadw   100–102, 125, 146–150, 154–155, 172, 174, 188, 198
Cantref Reservoir   12, 14, 27
Cardiff Bay   34–35, 58, 117, 121, 139, 153, 173, 190
Cardiff Corporation   5, 7, 9, 12, 14–16, 18–22, 25–29

Cardiff Council   34, 45, 56, 76, 93, 100, 114, 115, 118, 122–123, 127–128, 135, 136–138, 154, 157, 165, 167–168, 171, 175, 193, 198, 201, 205, 219–220, 225–227, 229

Cardiff Harbour Authority   34–35

Cardiff Naturalists' Society   58, 82

Castle Works   19, 200, 203, 210, 217

Celsa   153, 199–203, 206–207, 209, 210–217, 219–220, 224, 231

Chapman, Vivian QC   127, 129, 171

cholera   2–4

Christie, Ian   214

clay core   10, 155–157, 161, 164, 179, 214

Collins, Justice Andrew   110

commercial water supply   19

Commons Registration Act 1965   125, 127

Community Interest Company   202, 208–209

Congreve, Wendy   59

Cooke, Nicholas QC   115–116, 120

Cooper, Justin   59, 66, 121, 141

Corin, Mary   125, 188

Countryside Council for Wales   78, 93, 95, 103, 106, 110, 111, 158, 167, 169, 187, 198

 CCW   78, 103–110, 111, 114, 118, 167–169

Curley, Molly   189, 196

Curtis, Anne. see Barrett, Anne

D

Davidson, Jane AM   124, 144

Davies, Ceri   59, 61, 64, 66–67, 92, 189, 206–207, 209, 210–211, 216, 221

Davies, Fred   121, 140, 184, 202

Davies, Mark   224

Index

Davies, Mike   209
Davies, Paul   230
Davies, Stuart   152–153, 156
Dawson, Peter   139, 183
de Silva, Arushi   230
Denny, Brian   117, 175–176
Dinkin, Anthony QC   154, 174–175, 182, 185–186
dog walking   41, 100, 125–126, 177, 186, 226
dormice   43, 181, 187
drain down   153–154, 156–162, 164, 216, 221–222
drought   12, 19–20, 224
Dŵr Cymru / Welsh Water (DCWW). see Welsh Water

E

Earp, Denis   152
Edis, Jonathan   180
Ellis, James   201–202, 210, 212, 216
Ellis, Morag QC   129, 131–132
Ellis, Polly   137, 174
Ely pumping station   4, 6
ENRaW grant   224–227
Environment Agency   42, 152, 158, 160–162
Environmental Statement   75, 97, 104, 136, 173
Essex, Sue AM   55, 57, 62, 93, 99
Evans, David   141
Evans, Geraint   56, 59, 61, 66, 121, 140
Evans, Jonathan MP   161, 197, 203
Evers, Nigel   120

F

Felgate, Charles   107, 137, 143
fence   42–43, 81–83, 99–100, 105, 181, 221–224

A-31

First World War   15, 27
fish ponds   26–27, 45, 48
fishing   17, 19, 22, 25–30, 89, 100, 120–121, 140, 184–185, 190, 202–203, 208, 211, 215, 226–227
    Cardiff Reservoirs Fly Fishing Club   28–30, 60, 121, 140, 184, 196, 202, 206
    fish Stocking   26, 28–30
Friends of Cardiff Reservoirs   229–230
fungi   42, 50, 68, 73, 74–78, 85, 87–89, 94–95, 98, 103–105, 107–110, 112, 118, 123, 142, 148, 177, 226

G

Gee, Anne   189
Geldards Solicitors   107, 115, 127–128, 130, 137, 144, 148–149, 174, 184
Gibson, Charles   107–108, 117–118
Glamorgan Bird Club   58, 82–83
Glas Cymru   23–24, 65
Glossop, Paul   198
glow-worms   48, 67
Good, Graham   121, 140
Grantham, Vaughan   75
grass snake   45, 72
Green, Robert   131
Gregory, Andrew   213, 215–216
Gretton, Peter   66
Gwern-y-Bendy wood   40, 135, 145

H

Hanson, Vernon   141
Harmer Planning Consultants   137, 174
Harris, Matthew   177
Havard, Madeleine   86, 90, 142

Health Board 3–4, 225–227
Heath filter beds 7, 11, 22
Hill Bros. 9
Hill, Andrew 66, 100–102, 125–130, 133, 146–147, 154–156, 160, 164, 167, 174, 187, 188–189, 196
Hockaday, Malcolm 119, 139, 176–177, 179–180
Hoskins, Chris 207
Howard, Sue 78, 166
Howell, Simon 139, 181
Hughes, Andrew 142, 151–158, 160–161, 164, 178–179
Human Rights 183
Hunt, Garry 55, 57
Hurley, Frances 33–34
Hutchinson, Nicola 227
Hyder 23, 29–30

I

Ingram, Geoffrey 37, 40–41
insect 38, 43, 46, 48
Institution of Civil Engineers 7, 102, 146–147, 151, 156, 164

J

Jackson, Robert 203
James, John 143
Jarman, Milwyn QC 149–150
Jenkins, Ruth 56, 58
Jones, Calvin 206
Jones, Chris 23, 218–220
Jones, Rhys 45
Jones, Roy 85–86, 88
Joyce, Heather 201, 205

K

Keeper's cottage 28, 134, 221, 228
Kelly, Ron 140, 182
Klingensmith, Rick 193

L

Lewis, Chris 189, 196–197
Lippett, Ivor 65, 93
Listed Building 100–102, 125, 146–149, 155, 172–173, 175, 178, 180–181, 185–186, 188, 191, 193
Lisvane Community Council 140, 182
Lisvane Road 70, 95, 113, 125, 136, 140–141, 173, 175–176, 181–182, 184–186, 191, 228
Llandegfedd 20–22, 215
Llwyn-on reservoir 15–16, 101
Local Development Plan 123
Local Nature Reserve (LNR) 165, 167–169, 171
London Wetland Centre 58, 72, 81–83
Lowe, Mark QC 116, 137, 139, 169, 171, 174–175, 177–178, 185

M

Magill, Julia 141, 182–184, 197, 202, 213, 216
mammals 41–44
Martin, Vicky 224–227
Milburn, Alastair 219
Millet, Matthew 82
Mills, Hannah 33
Moore, Dennis 53, 74
Moore, Derek 59, 85–87, 90, 142–143
Morgan, Denys 102
Morgan, Julie AM 86, 99, 137, 161, 197–198, 199, 202, 216

N

Nant Fawr Ecology and Education Trust   142–143
Nant Fawr meadows   44, 54, 56–59, 66, 70, 121, 125–127, 130–133, 134, 139–140, 145, 165, 171, 175, 189, 193, 223, 230
Nant Fawr river corridor   54, 59, 62, 64, 66–67, 73, 80, 83, 93, 97, 113, 119–121, 123, 139–140, 144–145, 165, 167, 175–176, 178, 185–186
National Parks and Access to the Countryside Act 1949   168, 171
Natural Environment and Rural Communities Act 2006   171
Natural Resources Wales   142, 152, 226
Nixon, Alwyn   115–116, 123
Noble, Peter   130, 137
Nott, L.P.   15–16

O

O'Brien, Peter   217
Odin, Nigel   41
Oosthuizen, Charl   105, 143
Orange, Alan   75
otter   42, 87
Ouseley, Hon. Mr. Justice   169, 171
Owen-Jones, Stuart   101
Owens, Chris   160, 164

P

Palmer, Robert   107, 110, 115, 129, 137, 169, 174
Parkinson, Ewart   57, 59, 66, 94, 120, 139, 189, 213
Parry, Clare   137, 139
Pennine Embankment   10
Pennsylvania Power and Light Corporation   23, 158, 193, 195, 199, 205

Penyrheol Quarry   10
Perry, Peter   208–209, 214–215, 217, 220
Perry, Roy   75–76, 104
Phillips, Steven   165, 167
Planning Applications
    1st Planning Application   30, 54, 56, 61, 65–67, 69, 70–73, 74, 76, 84, 87, 91, 93–95
    2nd Planning Application   95, 101, 104, 118, 135
    3rd Planning Application   111
    4th Planning Application   111, 126–127, 136–137, 139, 142, 144, 173
    Welsh Water Planning Application   229
Planning Committee   57, 94–95, 114, 137, 173, 181, 229
plant   48–50, 76, 80, 89, 171, 177
pochard   36, 39–41
Poole, Jessica   107
Poppleton, Richard   137–138, 142, 144, 172, 188
Powell, Chris   165
Preston-Mafham, Juliet   74–75
Priestley, Charles   15–16
Public Health Act 1875   131–133, 171

R

RAG subscription   61, 195, 198
Rammell, T. W.   3
Randerson, Baroness Jenny   60–61, 86, 93, 99, 130
Rathbone, Jenny AM   197
Reservoirs Act 1975   142–143, 151–154, 158, 161–162, 207, 209
Rhiwbina reservoir   7, 12, 22
Rhyd-y-Blewin farm   223
Rhyd-y-penau Park   56, 128, 130, 185, 228

Index

Rhyd-y-penau Road 54, 68, 70, 95, 121, 125, 132, 134, 136, 176, 189, 192, 228
Roberts, Geoff 64, 66
Robinson, Siân 215–216, 220–221, 224–225
Roughing Filter 16, 17
Royal Society for the Protection of Birds (RSPB) 82–84, 202
Royal Yachting Association (RYA) 32–33

S

sailing 31–35, 55–56, 60, 67, 72–73, 89, 95–96, 100, 113, 117, 120–121, 123, 139–140, 142, 144, 153–154, 178–179, 184–186, 190, 202–203, 206, 208, 211, 215, 224–225, 227
Salmon, Morrey 37, 40
Sant, Mike 116, 120
Sanz Villares, Luis 210–213, 216, 219–220
Sargeant, Carl 190, 218
Savage, Phil 189, 206
scour valve 18, 155, 159, 162–163, 207, 214–216, 222
Second World War 19, 27
Section 106 Planning Agreement 123, 184
Setting of a Listed Building 101, 148, 154, 175, 178, 180–181, 185–186, 191
Seys-Llewellyn, Judge H.H.J. 168
Shimmel, Geoff 154
silt 17–18, 207, 214
Sites of Special Scientific Interest (SSSI)
    Embankments SSSI 78, 94–95, 98, 103–105, 107–110, 111, 113–114, 117–120, 123, 135, 142, 144, 148, 158, 177, 186, 191
    Lisvane reservoir SSSI 36, 41, 56, 62, 72, 80, 94, 118–119, 123, 191
Slater, Fred 74, 104
Smith, Annie 226–227

Smith, Ben   34–35
South Rise   41, 46, 57, 135, 182, 213
South Wales Echo   42, 61, 75, 87–88, 91–92, 109, 127, 168, 197, 219
Steel, John QC   107–108, 110, 115–116, 118–119, 121, 129–130, 137, 139, 141–142, 144, 149, 154, 169, 171, 172–178, 184, 186–187
Stevens, John   20
Stevens, Terry   117
Sturgess, Peter   48, 74–75, 104
Symonds, Robert   160, 199

T

Taf Fawr pipeline   7, 12, 14, 16, 17–18, 22, 155
Taf Fawr water supply scheme   5–7, 12, 14–16, 17, 19–22, 101, 146–149, 180, 185
Thomas, Gwyn   221
Thomas, Keith   146
Thurgood, Ted   54–64, 66–68, 87–88, 92, 116, 130, 139, 154, 165, 167, 196
toads   44–45, 80
tufted duck   36, 39–41, 62, 64

U

Unitary Development Plan   54, 66, 97

V

valve tower   17, 163, 222
vandalism   175, 178, 186, 221–222, 226
Village Green   125–130, 133, 134, 171, 188
visitor centre   82, 84–85, 206, 215, 228–230

W

Waldren, Peter   107, 131, 178

Index

Walker, David   93
Walker, Mike   54, 61, 130
Walker, T.A.   9
Warren, Alan   160–161
Waterworks Committee   7, 9, 15–16, 19, 21, 25–26, 28, 31
Waterworks Company   4–5, 25
Welsh National Water Development Authority   23, 29, 31
Welsh Water   23–24, 29, 35, 43, 53, 56, 65, 97–98, 109, 117–118, 134, 208–209, 214–217, 218–231
Welsh Yachting Association   33, 93, 121
Wenallt reservoir   22
Western Mail   9, 26, 54
Western Power Distribution   23–24, 30, 35, 41, 54–55, 57–61, 65–67, 70, 72–73, 74–76, 80, 82–87, 89, 90–95, 97–101, 103–107, 109–110, 111, 113–114, 115–120, 122–124, 125–130, 133, 134–135, 136–145, 148–150, 151–154, 158–162, 164, 168–169, 172–183, 185–187, 188–193, 195, 198, 199–200, 205, 207, 211, 224, 231
Wildfowl and Wetlands Trust   55, 80–81, 84, 203
Wildlife Trust of South and West Wales   58–59, 69, 72, 82–89, 91, 106, 108, 122, 142–143, 186, 230
Wilks, Dulcie   196
Williams, Bert   56, 58, 61, 63–64
Williams, Cheryl   227
Williams, Craig MP   203–204
Williams, J.A.B.   5–7, 9–10, 12, 14–16, 101, 147, 155
Williamson, Tracey   216
Winterbottom, Jim   202
Woods, Ray   103–104, 107, 109, 118–119

Y

Young, Steve   41